My Mother Killed CHRIST:

But God Loves Me Anyway

by Katie Roberta Stevens

ISBN: 0615438091
ISBN-13: 9780615438092
LCCN: 2011900639

To my husband, Frank,
who thinks
I'm beautiful.
Thank you for seeing me.

PROLOGUE—NOVEMBER 1974

My Mother's Ninth Admission:

Admission Quote: "The voices told me I should burn myself."

My mother, Clara Murphy, chuckled as she wrote "Burn in Hell" across the two-page spread of her Bible. The gleaming, red lipstick she was using as her pen was chalky as she employed her best Catholic school cursive to damn herself on the holy book. She placed the open Bible next to her in the unmade bed. She shifted her weight a little because she had been in and out of sleep all day and her nightgown was tangled around her waist.

She glanced over to the clock radio and saw that it was almost 3:00 p.m. "Perfect, the children will be home soon." She laughed wildly, which caused her to cough and pee on her bed a little. "I am a bad girl," she said aloud. "I killed Jesus Christ and I'm not wearing panties." She reached her hand down between her legs, but it felt numb there and she became enraged with disgust. "Do you want to go blind? Do you want to grow hair on your palms?" She punched her own groin so hard that it forced her into the fetal position. "You whore!" her scream was muffled as she buried her face in the sour sheets.

Abruptly, she stood and found her balance. Her delicate baby blue nightgown straightened and reached her knees. The sheer fabric clung to her full breasts that overpowered her tiny waist and shapely hips. Although her body was firm, she appeared much older when she started to walk. She limped because her feet were bare and troubled by the bumpy, painted wooden floorboards.

She stretched to grab a book of matches from the cherry wood dresser, which was cluttered with three grimy, overflowing ash trays. She struck a match and lit a cigarette. She took a puff and let the smoke envelop her with peace and comfort. She staggered into the kitchen, which was the next room in the railroad apartment, and went straight to the gas stove. Immediately, she ignited all four gas jets. The rotten egg smell of the gas warned of danger. Still, she held the cigarette to the first jet and was startled by how quickly the burner was lit from the small flame. She lit all of the others the same way and reached down to adjust all of the dials until they were on their highest setting. She turned her back to the stove and leaned on it for a minute, put her arms behind her, and made a motion as if she were going to push herself up. She stopped herself and laughed again.

"Oopsies. I'm so silly." Her smile lit up her face, and it was clear that she was extremely attractive. She looked even younger than her thirty-four years, and one would never guess that she was the mother of five teenage children. Her ice blue eyes were wide, and her aquiline nose gave her face a classic profile. She had a long, lean neck, and every now and then, she would hold her head high. But most of the time she sulked and looked sullen and yellow and her moments of prettiness were gone. Pieces of stray ash blonde hair stuck out from both sides of her head as if even her hairspray, too, could no longer hold on. She walked to the beige princess phone hanging on the ivy wallpaper. She dialed the number for the Kearny Police Department from memory and lifted her chin to strike a secretarial pose.

The phone rang and she began doing the twist while she waited. She sang, "Twist and shout. Come on, come on, baby now, come on, baby, let us work it all out," as she listened for an answer on the other end.

"Police Department. Sergeant Dougherty speaking," a male voice stated.

She giggled and then laughed big guffaws. She was afraid he would hang up so she put her hand to her mouth to signal her brain to stop. She composed herself and made her voice deeper and said, "This is Clara Murphy of 333 Jersey Street. I killed Jesus Christ. I am burning in hell for my sins. Have a pleasant day." She slammed down the receiver, and bellowing laughs and harsh coughs jumped from her throat until she couldn't catch her breath. With deep sighs, she calmed herself.

Suddenly, she began crying hysterically. She convulsed with sadness and yelled, "You will be sorry for taking my boyfriend, Tony, from me! You bastard kids! I am a human bean! I have needs!"

The heaviness of her words and sadness dropped her head far down her chest, and she stood with tears soaking her. The flimsy nightgown stuck to her breast. She pulled it away and said abruptly, "I have to watch the time. They'll be here soon."

Then, with a sense of efficiency, she approached the old, white General Electric stove and once again checked to see if the burners were on as high as they could possibly go. She was suddenly disgusted by the Spaghetti Os sauce that was caked on the front right burner. "I can't do everything. I'm tired. I'm so fucking tired," she pleaded with the empty kitchen.

She pulled over a brown and white vinyl chair from underneath the speckled Formica table. It squeaked as the metal legs dragged across the crumb-filled floor. Yesterday's Pop-Tarts, she guessed. She put the back of the chair against the stove and then stood in front of it. She lifted her left leg up on the chair first and she couldn't believe how filthy her feet looked. "Where was I walking?" she wondered aloud. "What am I, a potato farmer? I look like I just got off the boat." Again, she cackled with laughter at her use of her mother's favorite line. She lifted her right leg, until she was standing unsteadily on the chair. Then she turned around very carefully, inch by inch, because she didn't want to fall. The nervous sweat on the bottom of her feet acted like nature's Krazy Glue, keeping her safely on the vinyl. With little care, she simply plopped her butt down and sat on the stove, directly in the middle of the four flaming burners.

"Now, I will burn in hell," she said. "I was so cold all morning anyway."

She winced, and the putrid smell of her flesh burning wrinkled her nose. Then, it didn't even hurt anymore. As she closed her eyes in hope of disappearing, a hideous Satan appeared right before her face. He was a black man with a nappy, graying beard and sharp horns standing on each side of his huge head. She released earth-shattering screams. Now, she knew for certain that neighbors could hear it all. "I'm sorry, Momma. I didn't want to embarrass you."

"Come on, Clara," Satan hissed, "let me give you a little sugar. How about kissing it? Do me right after you killed Christ!"

"No, get away!" She felt the actual fire on the back of her thighs now. She fantasized about the therapeutic heat Tony gave her between her legs. That was the only time she wasn't completely cold. That was the only time she even mattered.

"Please leave me alone," she cried to Satan as the sadness and flames consumed her. Her final thought as she heard the policemen thundering up the apartment stairs was that she wished that she would have gone to confession. She needed absolution. She was a bad girl. Why did I kill the baby, Jesus? As the police began kicking the apartment door, she shrieked, "Be gone, Satan!"

Trenton Psychiatric Hospital

SUMMARY OF HOSPITALIZATION

Disposition Summary

Patient Name: Clara Murphy

This is a 34 year old, Caucasian, separated, Roman Catholic female admitted to Trenton Psychiatric Hospital for the ninth time. History revealed previous psychiatric hospitalizations here from October 20, 1958 and she carries the diagnosis of Schizophrenia Catatonic Type. Her commitment paper states that she has been hearing voices for about one week prior to admission. She claims she has heard voices telling her that she killed Jesus Christ and she should burn in hell. She inflicted burns to her face, left arm, left thigh, by sitting on the gas range. She has suicidal tendencies and appears depressed, claiming everyone would be glad to be rid of her.

Diagnosis: Schizophrenia, Chronic Undifferentiated Type

Physical: First Degree Burn, left side of face. First and second degree burns left forearm and buttocks.

CHAPTER 1—OCTOBER 1958

MY MOTHER'S FIRST ADMISSION

Admission Quote: "I belong in a state prison. I am eighteen years old, got three kids, and I am a very bad girl."

How would you feel coming home from basketball practice to find evidence that your mother set herself on fire? Did it faze me, in my freshman year, to smell charred flesh in my kitchen, instead of a savory meatloaf? Was I shocked to see my mother's singed hair rolling like tumbleweeds atop the putrid green vinyl floor? Honestly, it wasn't that unusual. Only complacency filled me when the Kearny Police Department confirmed that my mother had first and second degree burns and was in the hospital again.

You see, most children mark the passing of their youth with birthday cakes or report cards from various elementary school grades saved in a treasure box under the bed. My brothers and sisters and I categorize the moments of our childhood by my mother's involuntary admissions to mental hospitals. She was violently escorted from our home and admitted eighteen times in my first eighteen years of life. Like a tangerine, my life is divided into segments that are both sour and sweet. Was she in or out? Therefore, I begin each new chapter with my mother's admission date and quote. These are my benchmarks.

Despite witnessing her removal year after year, it never, ever clicked in my mind that my mother was going to a hospital because she had an illness. Until I was thirty-three years old and obtained a copy of my mother's actual records from Trenton State Mental Hospital, I never knew that she was sick. Instead, my overriding belief of my childhood was that my siblings and I were so diabolically evil that we forced my poor mother to go away. After all, at age fifteen she began having children and gave birth to all five of us by the time she was twenty. Who wouldn't need a rest? I completely empathized with her. To help, I was deeply committed to being so very good every day. But I must have failed, again and again, because I always made her go away. What other conclusion could an alarmed child reach after participating in a very peculiar game of peekaboo? My mother's distorted face would twist before me in rage, until I covered my eyes to scream. Then she would be gone. I covered my eyes again and, peekaboo, police officers would arrive. Peekaboo. Mommy's here. Peekaboo, Mommy's gone. Where did Mommy go? Peekaboo, can you find Mommy? Mommy, where are you? Mommy's gone. Peekaboo.

To illustrate my life story, I don't insert birthday cards with pink flowers that were preserved in a scrapbook. There is no sepia photograph of five children engaged in a group hug. To present my personal timeline—mind you, with a huge arrow pointing towards triumph—I insert my mother's hospital admission quotes. These one-liners act as flickering candles to illuminate her state of mind at each phase of my formative years. These are the pivotal moments I remember. I also add her physician's notes that confirm the extent of her illness as the icing on my cake. I devour these creamy white pages decorated with swirly blue letters that spell "catatonic and schizophrenic." These pages are my gratifying touchstones. I lick them off my fingers. I hold them to my face and breathe in the musty paper. This saturates me with blessings.

I can acknowledge that despite what my mother said or did, it wasn't my fault. She didn't lock me in the basement because I was evil. She had an illness. Oh my God, it was that simple! She had an illness. This never, ever occurred to me. It was not my fault. It was not even her fault. I can't even be angry with her... anymore.

So, if the guiding principle of my early life is completely baseless, then why should I bother to tell my story? If all along the horrific abuses were mere symptoms of a thoroughly documented illness, who am I to think I have something to share?

Connections to our past victimize us all. So, I have to speak up. When I sit among my newest peers, thrilled that I now bathe in the halo of contentment in my beachside Florida community, I hear the questions they ask about others. The words rise up mingled with the aroma of cappuccinos and linger over my head in trendy restaurant booths. On any given day, three women behind me gather for lunch and begin to divide the bill equally using a calculator. They chatter about others in the news and around the town: "How could she have a long-term affair with a married man?" "How could those animals participate in looting?" "Why would a teacher or a priest have sex with a student?" "How could that mother sleep with her boyfriend with young children at home?"

These hows and whys can be answered in my story. The reasons rise like bile from my esophagus, but I swallow the bitterness into a polite cough and do not speak. I don't want to give myself away in my new world. But there are levelheaded answers. My aim is not to excuse or pardon the behavior, but to perhaps muster some understanding. The sticky web of victimization in childhood is hard to remove. We break through it, we claw at the individual threads to throw them aside, but some sturdy fibers cling and fluster us. In a panic, we struggle to break free, but it isn't easy. As Oprah often quotes her mentor, Maya Angelou, "Once we know better, we can do better." But the knowing can take a lifetime. How do you examine a life objectively when you have been mired in it since birth?

Even as I floated in her womb, I feared my mother. I tremble even now, at fifty, when I think of her. What was most unsettling was not the physical pain or verbal abuse, but never knowing what I did wrong. How do you work to not repeat an offense if you have no idea what it was? Each day of my childhood, I rocked forward and back to calm myself and to focus. I allowed my mind to replay every word and action, like a frenetic Charlie Chaplin clip, to see what I could do differently to make my mother love me—or at least to make her stop hurting me. Finding no answer was the open sore constantly oozing. Why did my own mother hate me? What could I do to make her love me? The simmering burn of uncertainty was never extinguished.

My sister Becky likes to mock me because, as a child, I was afraid of everything. "You were afraid of dust and the light from a flashlight, for Christ's sake." I was afraid of dust because something touched me like dust whenever my mother locked me in the basement. Fingertips barely rubbing up and down the little hairs of my tiny arm felt like tumbleweeds of dust rolling across my toes. "Get it off of me!" I screamed. But what was on me was too big for a five-year-old to remove. His ever-so-slight caressing was out of my control. And that little stream of light I saw over his shoulder from the street-level window, every other second as he moved up and down, glowed like the light of a flashlight and was what I stared at to disappear. "Turn it off!"

Birth to five years old in my life was an endless cyclone of fear. Like Dorothy, I knew that I wasn't in Kansas, but my house never landed. I wasn't anywhere with firm footing. I was spinning in a black-and-white, scary movie that never transformed to color or introduced the Lollipop Guild.

My mother's own self-loathing, shame, and confusion must have bubbled through the umbilical cord like Drano. During her pregnancy with me, she probably punched her stomach, screaming, "This is not my baby. Get it out of me. This is Satan's baby!" She threw herself on the chenille bedspread face down in hopes of eliminating me. She stuck long objects, maybe cucumbers or bananas, inside of herself when no one was home, in hopes of forcing a miscarriage. She tore off her clothes and smashed through the dilapidated, green screen door to the backyard. She hopped on our swing set completely naked hoping to fly away into the clouds. If she went higher and higher, maybe she could let go and soar into the bosom of our Lord, Jesus Christ, to be forgiven for her sins.

The sun warmed her breasts and swollen belly as she pumped her shapely legs, yelling "Whee, Whee," trying to swing above the top bar. Her chin-length blonde hair glistened as she leaned her head way back and pointed her toes high. The poles lifted off the ground and then thumped back down into shallow holes as her weight and the height of her swinging both far exceeded the limits of the swing set. My two sisters, just one and two years old at the time, sat on the ground and watched her as their legs got coated with dirt like breaded chicken. Renee, the older of the two, shouted, "Look at Mommy." Becky, whose head was already filled with bright orange ringlets, just laughed as her freckled skin became more speckled by the rust-colored dirt. Neither sister was wearing any clothing or a diaper. What if a worm crawled inside them? This was the level of my anxiety, even before birth. Becky reached out her plump one-year-old hand to capture a crimson and orange October leaf because she was hungry. She would have eaten a beetle if she could have found one.

My mother soared higher, bending her nude legs to pump while she was downward, and opening them to reveal bushy, ash blonde pubic hair when she was at the height of her swing. Just then, my father arrived in the yard, dragging a sage-colored, fuzzy blanket from the bedroom. A neighbor must have called him at work...again. He weaved right and left, like a boxer, trying to avoid being hit by my mother's feet as she swung. He said nothing, but breathed hard as he worked to get hold of the chains. His six-foot-two, thin frame was agile, but he still struggled to capture her. The auburn wave in the front of his hair, that was always slicked back drooped down and covered his eyes. His face was getting redder as he struggled to throw the blanket over any part of my mother.

"Don't you tickle me! I'm very ticklish," my mother warned. He ignored every word and focused his attention as if he were trying to capture a dove in a pillow case. He finally got both hands on the swing chains and caused it to stop suddenly. "Son of a bitch," he shouted, as he shook his right hand to release the pain caused by the chain ripping his skin. As he did, my mother hopped off and used the yellow hard plastic swing seat as a shield to push him back. His feet got tangled in the blanket and he stumbled. He went down on all fours, and then popped back up on one knee. As he did, my mother raised the seat of the swing up and came down across his temple. Blood instantly splashed the yellow hard plastic. "You fucking bitch!" he shouted. She laughed wildly and darted left, getting past him, and running towards the rusty gate that led to the street. She was giddy as her heavy breasts flopped left and right. He leaped, catching her legs just below the knees from behind, finally bringing her down.

He straddled her buttocks and leaned way back beyond him to grab the blanket that was now caked with mud. He covered her with the blanket and then allowed her to slowly turn face up. She grit her teeth and struggled under his weight. His shoulders shook as he sobbed realizing that he had just tackled his pregnant wife. "God, help me, please," he pleaded. Just then, she popped up from the waist and grabbed him by the back of the neck with both hands and pulled his face into a passionate kiss. Her tongue plunged into his mouth and her right hand worked in a panic to undo his pants zipper. "Let me blow you right now!"

"No!" He screamed a guttural scream. "What the fuck is wrong with you?" Now, he was sobbing uncontrollably, and a long string of mucus spewed from his nose. He wiped it on his blue uniform sleeve and then slammed her back to the ground with great intensity.

"What are you, a fucking sissy?" She squirmed again to try to get up. He held her to the ground until she stopped struggling. Soon, she turned sullen and limp. He had seen this before and knew it was over for today. He reached down to help her up and wrapped her in the blanket and secured it with his arms. He led her inside to the bedroom and told her to rest. He locked the door with a latch from the outside.

He came back to the yard to gather my two sisters. He stood over them and his shoulders shook as he cried uncontrollably when he saw how filthy they were. He dropped to his knees to get them and pleaded, "God, help me, please. I can't do it." He was nineteen years old at the time. Soon, Mrs. Jamison came in the gate from next door and said, "I'll take them, Billy. You attend to Clara." My father went that afternoon to see his priest, Father Flannery, to beg for help. He was given a laminated card that contained this prayer to the saint for the hopeless.

St. Jude, relative of Jesus and Mary, glorious apostle and martyr, renowned for your virtues and miracles, faithful and prompt intercessor for all who honor you and trust in you! Powerful patron and helper in grievous affliction, come to my aid, for you have received from God the privilege of assisting with manifest help those who almost despair. Look down upon me; my life is a life of crosses, and my paths are strewn with thorns. My soul is enveloped in darkness, discouragement, and sometimes even a kind of despair. Divine Providence seems lost to my sight, and faith seems to falter in my heart. You cannot forsake me in this sad plight! I will not depart from you until you have heard me. Hasten to my aid. I will thank God for the graces bestowed upon you, and will propagate your honor in whatever way I can. Amen.

I tried to stay inside my mother and not be born, to avoid the path strewn with thorns, but there was nothing solid to hold onto in there. The supposedly nurturing cord delivered only anguish. When I finally did appear on September 11, 1958, I was placed in a white wicker bassinet, covered by a yellow checkered blanket, and left to starve. I screamed my hunger incessantly but I couldn't compel my mother to move. She sat cold, like marble, in an oak rocking chair, staring. She never ate, drank, or slept. She had left for another world where babies don't have to be fed or changed and where a woman can swing naked in peace.

You may look through a white satin baby book, with attached pink ribbons, that was lovingly compiled to discover your first photo, first footprint, first word, or first blonde curl from your first haircut. I page through volumes of records from Trenton State Mental Hospital to uncover the story of my first years.

Trenton Psychiatric Hospital

SUMMARY OF HOSPITALIZATION

Disposition Summary

Patient Name: Clara Murphy

This is an 18 year old married, Catholic white female admitted October 30, 1958. She carries the diagnosis Schizophrenic Reaction, Catatonic type. Three weeks after the birth of her third child, the patient became incoherent, mute and without provocation dumped a bowl of farina on her mother. She was unable to care for her children or herself. Patient was depressed, rather mute and withdrawn. On admission patient was hostile, negativistic and belligerent and had episodes of acute confusion which alternated with episodes when patient seemed to be in good contact. She admitted to suicidal ideas in the past but denied them at present. She admits great hostility towards her husband and her mother and used profane language. She added that they gave her a baby to care for that wasn't hers. Her affect was inappropriate and silly at times. She was placed on a course of electro convulsive treatments and tranquilizers.

FAMILY HISTORY: The patient has never gotten along with her mother and has tried to run away since she was twelve or thirteen. At this time, the mother placed her in a county shelter. The informant was told by an officer of the Kearny Police Department that the patient and her mother had been before him almost once a month when the patient was a child because of her constant arguments with her mother.

Diagnosis: Schizophrenic Reaction, Catatonic State.

While my mother was in the hospital, my father went to his priest again to see if my mother's tubes could be tied. The Catholic Church refused to grant permission. Over the next two years, my father and mother had two more children. In all, when she was between the ages of fifteen and twenty, my mother had five children—all one year apart.

My father could not take it anymore and he left us in a prayer to St. Jude, which was a life of crosses and a path strewn with thorns and no one to hasten to our aid. He was afraid of her violence, so he left his five children alone with her.

Memories of anyone's childhood before attending school are fuzzy, like ghosts that come and go in the night. There are things that I do remember...if I allow my mind to focus and overcome the fear. I remember all five children being lined up each night at bedtime. At the time, we were ages five, four, three, two, and one. I was the middle child at age three. My sister Renee, at five, stood first in line, with her dark brown hair cut into a bowl by my grandmother's talented hand. My sister Becky, four, was next, with her long, curly, bright red hair that reached the middle of her back and her cute little freckled face. And then, three little platinum blonds were next. First there was me, at three, and then my brothers, who resembled the cherubs in the church mural. They had round bellies, pudgy thighs, and Billy loved to run by the bedroom door showing his butt to the girls after he took a bath.

My mother smiled and kissed each child good night.

"Good night, Renee, I love you. Good night, Becky, I love you."

I got ready for my turn by closing my eyes and leaning my face up gently in sweet anticipation to receive that loving affection that could confirm my worthiness. But as my mother reached me in the line, there was a pause. I opened my eyes just enough to catch the wrinkled revulsion in her mouth as she heaved as if about to vomit. Her face assaulted me and I shrunk to protect myself from the blows.

"You are so ugly," her words punched me in the stomach. "I will never kiss you! Get away. You're not my child. I could never have a kid like you. Get upstairs to bed and pray that you don't wake up. Your middle name is Shithead. Don't you forget it!"

Tears burned and blinded me as I walked away. "Do you want something to cry about?" she called after me. As I began climbing the steps all alone, her lilting voice returned.

"Good night, Billy, I love you. Good night, George, I love you. You are my little angels." Why wasn't I an angel? Why was I born so ugly? Why does she hate me? I cried into my pillow, and tried to swallow my emptiness. There was never a warm hand to rub my shoulders to soothe the pain or to push my hair from my face so it wouldn't get glued by my tears. My own arms were too little to wrap about myself to provide some comfort. I went to sleep in a black hole of rejection and woke up to another nightmare.

Another memory is of being in the back of a taxi, reclining across the torn brown leather seat that was taped with black plastic tape. I was twirling the escaping seat stuffing in my hand. Next to me was a doll that I loved because she had removable red leotards. My mother was in the front seat, talking and laughing with a young driver. She was taking me to West Hudson Hospital Emergency Room.

I remember the ethereal glow of the white lights streaming from a bowl-shaped ceiling fixture as I lay on a gurney and felt a doctor packing my small nose with wads of dry cotton. Blood gurgled in my throat, and I felt as if I was suffocating as he worked to push a long white roll of fluffy cotton inside of me. I felt as if I were being stuffed like the taxi cab seat. How could something so soft feel so hard inside my face?

The doctor spoke as he would to a small child, but he was speaking to my mother, not to me. "Clara, sweetheart, you have to stop hitting her in the head. Do you understand?"

My mother giggled and said, "Do you want to play doctor with me?" Frustrated, the doctor just pushed harder and harder on the cotton.

When I was four years old, my younger brother Billy and I were playing in the backyard. We were sweating in the relentless summer sun, trying to build a club house out of some old pieces of wood that were decaying in our backyard for years. The wood was moldy and cracked and had beetles crawling on the underside. We decided to add color to it to make a more appealing clubhouse.

We didn't have any paint, so we used really fat crayons to color the wood. This was a time-consuming project. Just before lunch, I was finishing up a red section. My fat crayon was getting stubbier and stubbier. Before I knew what happened, a huge splinter of wood lodged itself deeply under the fingernail of my pointer finger. It hurt so bad and looked hideous as the dark blood began to seep around the wood trapped beneath the fingernail. I grabbed it tightly and tried not to cry. Billy said, "You better show Mommy."

I went into the kitchen and showed my mother, who was sitting at the kitchen table sipping coffee and smoking her cigarette. In the warmest, kindest voice, she said, "I'll take care of that for you, sweetheart." I was so pleasantly surprised. Billy looked at me as if to say, "See, I told you."

My mother said, "You just sit at the table and rest for a few minutes."

She went over to the white metal cabinet, trimmed with rust, and grabbed a copper-bottom soup pot. She filled it with water and turned it on to boil. She said, "Once it is sterilized, then we can get it out." It felt so good to be taken care of. If I knew it was so easy to get attention, I would have suffered a million rotten wood splinters.

As smoke began to puff from the rolling boiling water, she said, "OK, sweetheart, come here to me, now. " I walked over and started to worry about the pain I would feel from the sterilized needle being placed under my nail. I had seen this operation before on my older sister when my mother took a splinter from the bottom of her foot from the boardwalk at the Jersey Shore. Becky really screamed. I was sure that a splinter under a finger nail would be worse.

As I got closer to my mother next to the stove, she turned and abruptly grabbed me by the hand that contained the splinter and lifted me off the ground. She almost jerked my arm right out of its socket. She pulled my hand and bent it back as if it were a detached object. I was trapped in her flowered house dress as I struggled against her. She moved quickly as she attempted to immerse my entire hand into the boiling water on the stove. "You have to sterilize it," she groaned. She pulled harder and harder, twisting my little wrist beyond its limits. Suddenly, I forgot the pain from her twisting because I could feel droplets of boiling water jumping up and burning my palm. "Sterilize the needle, not the finger," I wanted to scream, but there was no time. After seconds, it was too hot to bear. The heat awakened every nerve in my body and I swung at her with my free arm, landing blows on her side and back. "Stop!" The primal screams shocked her.

"Stop it, Shithead!" she said through a tight mouth as she struggled to lift me higher and into the pot. "The Goddamn neighbors will hear you!"

Her spittle hit my face as her dentures slid in and out of her mouth. (She had dentures in her twenties because the mental hospital said her teeth were making her crazy.) I continued screaming as loudly as I could. From the intermittent squeak of a clothesline wheel outside in the background, I thought that I could hear that Mrs. Dunn, who shared a yard with us, was hanging her wash.

Billy started running towards Mrs. Dunn. My mother gave up on putting my hand in the boiling water and began stinging my cheek with slaps. Fortunately, she was already exhausted from the struggle and missed with most blows. Soon Mrs. Dunn ran up to the fence from the adjoining yard and said with a bit of a brogue, "Clara, is everything okay?"

Quickly, my mother unleashed my hand, and I sprinted out the front door while she went to the back porch. I could hear my mother explain that I was a big baby because I was afraid of the needle that she sterilized to remove a splinter. My mother added, "Don't worry, Eileen, this is not the first time this one has embarrassed me in front of the neighbors. You know, she is my problem child."

"We all have one of those," added Mrs. Dunn cheerfully. She was referring to her fat son, Gerry, who tried to hang himself in the bathroom shower after seeing an episode of the *Three Stooges*.

By invoking the times I had embarrassed my family, my mother was referring to the garbage men incidents. Although I was of Polish descent and was the spitting image of my mother, with wavy blonde hair and the lightest blue eyes, she told me that I was not her daughter. I came from the garbage man and my father was a "Negro." So many mornings, I heard the whining of the garbage truck outside my window and the sound filled me with the hope that my true family would find me. In my flannel pajamas, with bare feet, I ran as fast as I could, down the steps from the bedroom, out the front hallway, and down the broken concrete porch steps, to chase the garbage truck as it pulled away.

"Take me back, take me back!" I yelled. The black garbage men pointed at me and laughed. The truck seemed to be mocking me as well as it churned the ugly garbage in its belly. My grandmother yelled at my mother, "Get her, quick. The neighbors will see her. She is such an embarrassment."

Whenever my brothers and sisters and I were walking to the park or the library with my mother, and we came upon some neighbors, my mother pointed to me and told people, "My Katie is a deaf mute." I stood and tried to look silent and still, but on the inside I was screaming, "Hey, Mom, I can hear you right now!" But I smiled politely as the neighbors looked upon me with sorrow. She also told people at the butcher store or the shoemaker that I was retarded, or as she would say, "My Katie is a Mongoloid."

Most neighbors gave me a knowing look and quickly went on their way, but some strangers actually engaged my noble mother in a long conversation about the sacrifices and obstacles involved in raising a retarded child. My mother elaborated by saying how I was so slow to develop that I didn't speak until I was five years old. She added that she took me to specialists around the globe. I reasoned that if they knew what was going on in our house, they would understand why it was better if I never uttered a word.

Our family often served as entertainment for our neighbors. My mother sometimes woke us up in the middle of the night in a panic, screaming something like, "Let's go butter the knees!" She'd rip off our blankets and force us to run down the hallway steps, out to the front porch, stampeding our little feet as fast as we could. We stood as close as we could to each other with cold wind stinging our legs as we danced around in our underwear to keep warm. Up and down the street, we could see neighbors' heads appearing in their front windows. Finally, they shook their heads, and I imagined them whispering, "Those poor kids," before they went back to sleep. Sooner or later, the knees must have been buttered because my mother yelled at us to get back to bed. "What are you doing out at this time of night? You think I'm running a whorehouse? Get to bed, all of you!"

Other times, the neighbors, too, felt forced to come out of the safety of their homes after my mother woke us up and rushed us into the middle of the street because of the big inferno. There was a fire under her feet and she was burning in hell. Fire trucks filled the street and red strobe lights danced on neighboring apartment houses like it was a block party. The fire chief towered over my mother and shouted down into her face, "Jesus fucking Christ, Clara, one day we're not going to show up! Fucking crazy bitch!" He practically spit on my mother and looked down on us like roaches as the neighbors formed a circle as if preparing for a stoning.

Trenton Psychiatric Hospital

PROGRESS NOTES

Patient Name: Clara Murphy

Progress Notes: The patient is angry and unwilling to cooperate. She expresses hostility towards her mother and husband. She said that they lock her up while her husband goes free. She would like to leave this place and go home to wash diapers. She now has five children. The patient is Roman Catholic, but never attended church regularly. However, when she got sick last year, she ran to the church and the priest found her baptizing herself with holy water stating that she killed Jesus Christ.

The patient is rather childish. She looks happy and when asked what she does in the house she states, "Washes diapers." She tells the examiner that she gets fearful when she sees people. She further stated that nothing bothers her, except her mother. She definitely said that she hates her mother. She told the examiner that she usually gets sick after she has a baby.

CHAPTER 2—OCTOBER 1963

MY MOTHER'S SECOND ADMISSION

Admission Quote: "My father is the King of Poland."

Going to school started the best and worst part of my life. At five years old, I attended Immaculate Mary School, where my two older sisters were in first and second grades. The best part about Catholic school was that every day we learned about the power of a magical God who saw everything and could save anyone. Certainly, he saw what was happening to me and was on his way to save me. Each day, right after lunch, I sat enthralled as Mrs. Mckenna read, in her soothing voice, the story of a different saint who overcame terrible circumstances to give her life to God. She would raise her penciled-on eyebrows and purse her red lips as she really exaggerated the words. I was in a trance because it seemed we had so much in common, the saints and me. They were being tormented in life, and once they gave themselves to God, they lived in glory. I would simply give myself to God. Although fear remained the overriding theme in my life, my spirit was elevated by the hope that God would save me if only I was as good as I could be.

On the first Thursday of every month in Catholic school, my class was led into the church by Sister Rose, who was shorter than our tallest first grader. Before allowing me to participate in any religious exercise, Sister Rose forced bobby pins into my scalp to attach a Kleenex to my head. "I cannot, for the life of me, believe that Miss Murphy here forgot her uniform beanie once again," she said to the class. Then she turned back to me to ask, "What is wrong with your mother? Do you have an answer?" If you only knew, Sister Rose.

"No," I whispered.

"No, Sister," she corrected. If her words didn't reach everyone, the white Kleenex waving on top of my blonde head became a sort of badge of neglect that told all passers-by that I had a mother who didn't care enough to send me to school in my complete uniform. This, to Sister Rose, was a mortal sin in and of itself.

The twenty-four students in my class would file into the polished wooden pews—eight to a bench, sitting right outside the confessional. The golden oak confessional looked like a miniature version of our Immaculate Mary Church. It, too, had three beautiful steeples. The priest would be nestled under the middle steeple and two confessors could enter on either side.

As my first-grade class anxiously awaited our turn to enter the confessional, the smell of incense and burning candles filled our nostrils and made us breathe rapidly like animals caught in a trap. Our Fruit Loops churned in our stomachs as we anticipated entering the darkened private vestibules that were draped with purple curtains. Before my turn to confess, I tried to ignore Father O'Malley's bellowing voice echoing throughout the church, making even the candles flicker in fear. "You did what?" he shouted at his current victim. This led so many of us to drop on our knees to clutch our "glow in the dark" rosary beads to our chest. "Please, God, forgive me for being a horrible daughter," I whispered rapidly into the crucifix.

As my turn for confession approached, my body transitioned to autopilot and I simply put one clean saddle shoe in front of the other across the marble floor until I reached the velvet drape. This musty fabric was the only barrier preventing my shame from seeping out like the angel of darkness to encompass the church community at large.

Inside, the confessional box was so dark that I couldn't even see my own hands trembling in front of me as I made the sign of the cross. Once my knees touched the red leather kneeler, which seemed to screech in fear, another noise startled me. A miniature magic sliding window door slid open, revealing a large shadow. The shadow could have been God's or Father O'Malley's. It was hard to discern myth from reality in first grade.

On my first visit to the confessional, the sliding screen reminded me of a window that appeared on the television show *Captain Kangaroo*. I pictured a big, friendly man in blue jean overalls saying, "Good morning, boys and girls." But that pleasant vision was erased as quickly as an Etch A Sketch when Father O'Malley demanded "Speak up, girl, what have you done?"

The words stuck to my tongue as I just tried to please the impatient priest. I came up with enough sins to sound contrite, but not enough to seem like a major sinner. "I don't know what I do, but my mother says I am evil. Please help me be good. Please tell me what to do to make her love me. Help me to be good in word and deed." I didn't really know what a deed was, but Sister. Rose used this terminology when instructing us on the protocol of confession.

After a deep silence that caused me to wonder if Father O'Malley had fallen asleep, he sniffled and mumbled something that ended with "I absolve you of your sins. Say three Hail Marys and three Our Fathers and an Act of Contrition." As I stood up to get out, thinking I had gotten away pretty easily, he added, "Find it in your heart to forgive your poor mother and please pray for her. I promise that God will watch over you and will deliver you from your suffering. Amen."

"Amen," I replied.

A contrite child left the confessional with her head down, so that Sister Rose would think that her charge had learned her lesson and would never sin again. So I tilted my chin to my chest and proceeded to the altar, right in front of a glowing and golden elevated rack of candles. Parishioners dropped coins in the deposit box in front of the candles, grabbed something that looked like a really long match stick, and lit a candle to say a prayer for a loved one.

As I knelt in front of the magnificent riser of glowing light, I shook with grief that I never had a coin to light a candle for my mother. How could I get her to like me if I couldn't afford this special prayer? Why didn't my family even have one quarter to spare? Instead of whispering the Our Fathers and Hail Marys I was assigned by Father O'Malley, my thoughts got lost in the dancing lights.

I accessed a profound and mysterious place in my chest and left all sensory input behind. I struggled to really connect with my God, the miracle man. I pictured him as a handsome God that allowed me to rest my head on his shoulder as I sat on his lap. He was really the only father I had ever known since ours left. "My holy Father, please make my mother love me. Help me to know what I'm doing wrong. I'll try every single day to be a good daughter. I don't even know what makes her so mad, but whatever it is, I promise I will never do it. Please, please, dear God, help me to be an instrument of your peace for my family." I was sobbing in front of the candles and had to stay there for a few more minutes so that my class didn't see. Sister Rose must have thought that I was doing a really good confession

I had heard the words "instrument of peace" somewhere before, and they seemed to be precise for what I needed. All of the Gospels I heard in church seemed to offer me some advice that could help me overcome my circumstances. I wanted to know how to sow kindness and love as the sower went to sow some seeds. I wanted to be caring and forgiving like the Good Samaritan, who stopped to help his enemy on the road. I wanted to be brave like Noah, who took his family away from the storm. If only I could be as devout as St. Catherine, who Sister Rose said was amazing. St. Catherine received the stigmata, or marks of Christ, on her hands and feet while she lived. Did I have the physical signs on my body? Could others see what was happening to me?

In this deep place of piety and desperation, I made my required act of contrition.

O my God,
I am heartily sorry for
having offended Thee,
and I detest all my sins,
because I dread the loss of heaven,
and the pains of hell;
but most of all because
they offend Thee, my God,
Who are all good and
deserving of all my love.
I firmly resolve,
with the help of Thy grace,
to confess my sins,
to do penance,
and to amend my life.

The first confession in Catholic school is followed by your first Holy Communion. The girls look like miniature brides, with lacy white dresses puffed up by crinoline slips. They wear matching veils decorated with eyelet. The boys wear little white suits and satiny bow ties and polished white oxford shoes. Each child kneels at the altar awaiting the priest and his two altar boys as they make their way down from one chubby cherub face to the next. As he approached, the priest said as quickly as an auctioneer, "Body of Christ," and if you could speak without vomiting from nerves, you replied, "I receive you, oh Lord. Amen."

You accepted your wafer from the priest's fingers that were still wet and warm from the previous tongue of one of your class-mates. This modest round circle, or host, that the priest put in your mouth was no bigger than a flavored Nabisco candy. Yet it was somehow the same as the most powerful, all-knowing, all-seeing being in the universe. And we were swallowing him. I feared that if I drank too much water, God could swell inside me and pop out of my chest like an alien.

After the whole class received the first Communion, the processional of mini brides and grooms of God marched down the center aisle of Immaculate Mary Church onto Kearny Avenue in Kearny, New Jersey. As I walked down the aisle alongside William Steinmetz (we were of equal height), there were so many flashbulbs blinking in our eyes that William started to cry. With all of the excitement of trying to calm poor William, I thought that I must have missed my family in the pews.

Outside the church, several girls received beautiful pink and white carnation bouquets from their parents. They paused to stand in front of the statue of Mary to have their photos taken with their new Polaroid cameras. The statue of Mary looked particularly beautiful for the pictures because the May Crowning Ceremony was held just a week or two before the First Communion Ceremony. The entire school, from kindergarten through eighth grade, gathered in the church courtyard and sang:

"Oh Mary, we crown thee with blossoms today. Queen of the Angels, Queen of the May."

Then the prettiest girl in the school, Mary Francis Blake, who had long, blonde, spiraling, wavy curls past the middle of her back, walked up and placed a crown of baby pink roses onto stone white Mary's head. Mary looked so loving and peaceful throughout the event. She looked worried that day as I waited in front of the shiny, holy Mother of God statue, a six-year-old girl with skinned knees, dressed as a bride. I couldn't see any signs of my family. One by one, the other girls and boys drifted away with their families, carrying their carnation bouquets or ripping off their boutonnieres.

Some walked over to Pete's Ice Cream Shop, probably for a wet walnut sundae with hot fudge. "Oops, be careful of getting chocolate on that pretty white dress," I cautioned as I watched them go. Others walked across to the other corner to Texiera's Bakery to get crumb buns and fresh, warm poppy seed rolls with butter. Others got into cars, probably to drive to Top's Diner for a hearty breakfast, maybe sausages wrapped in pancakes.

Soon, I was standing alone. Just me and Mary. I tried not to cry in front of Mary because I wanted to be like her. She was not even afraid when an angel appeared right in her house to tell her that she was chosen to be the Mother of Jesus through an Immaculate Conception. She just hopped right up on that donkey and took a quick trip to Bethlehem. These thoughts of Mary's sense of adventure almost kept the tears from streaming down my face. But then I saw Sister Rose walking towards me. This was never a good thing. Usually, when she walked towards you, she carried a yardstick. She never hit students with it. Instead she used it to tap on your desk as you repeated prayers or poems that you were supposed to memorize. We had to do this once a week—even in first grade. She tapped out the rhythm of the poem, and when it was your turn, she also tapped your desk. The tapping seemed to imply that if she tapped your desk and you missed your cue, your face or hands would be tapped with the ruler instead. I admit I have never seen this happen, but I have heard the cries of boys in the cloakroom. Their faces were always red when they emerged.

But Sister Rose and I had a secret. Every once in a while, with a stern face, she would command me to meet her in the cloakroom. My classmates would straighten their backs in their desks and make sure their feet were touching the floor. There was perfect silence as my saddle shoes and Sister Rose's black oxfords squeaked the twenty or so steps to enter the cloakroom. When we both entered, Sister Rose would put her finger up to her mouth as if to say, "Shush, this is our little secret." She would call out,

"What did I tell you?" for the sake of my classmates, and then she would smile sweetly because we were playing a joke on the rest of the class.

While we were in the cloakroom, Sister Rose walked over to a special cubby that she kept locked. She opened it up with a key on a rubber band that she kept in her deep pocket and handed me a pink handheld Barbie mirror. Then she went behind me and combed my shoulder-length blonde hair with her right hand and used her left hand to smooth it. "You have beautiful hair," she whispered. "It's like a halo." Then she reached in and pulled out a baggie that contained a white washcloth that was already wet. "Close your eyes now." She rubbed it roughly all across my face and said, "Now, you look beautiful." She stood face to face with me, and we were of equal height and equal weight. I wondered if she had trouble keeping food down because of her nerves, too. She reached her fabric-draped arms across to straighten my uniform blouse collar. "That's my pretty girl," she said. "Now, off with you."

When I exited the cloak room, my face was red from the washcloth. My classmates turned their heads ever so slightly to see what happened to me. Sister Rose emerged with her yardstick and said, "Let that be a lesson to the rest of you." She gave me a quick wink and went on with the lesson.

In these special moments, my heart filled with love for Sister Rose until it overflowed into my nervous stomach. "Why couldn't Sister Rose be my mother?" While she was speaking in front of the class reviewing a story, I would fantasize about her taking me away and loving me. It was refreshing to be treated kindly. The warmth of her hand on my head was as strong as the sun on the first day of summer vacation. Yet my fantasy bubble burst each time the strict Sister Rose appeared and forced a boy to kneel in front of the class with his arms straight out balancing three voluminous dictionaries for an entire class period.

The truth was that I never had to worry about Sister Rose punishing me because I made sure I would never misbehave or miss my cue during poetry reciting. Other kids in the class recited a poem of just a few lines, and I couldn't wait for Sister Rose to call on me. When she did, I stood up and said:

Vespers
Little Boy kneels at the foot of the bed,
Droops on the little hands little gold head.
Hush! Hush! Whisper who dares!
Christopher Robin is saying his prayers.

God bless Mummy. I know that's right.
Wasn't it fun in the bath to-night?
The cold's so cold, and the hot's so hot.
Oh! God bless Daddy—I quite forgot.

If I open my fingers a little bit more,
I can see Nanny's dressing-gown on the door.
It's a beautiful blue, but it hasn't a hood.
Oh! God bless Nanny and make her good.

Mine has a hood, and I lie in bed,
And pull the hood right over my head,
And I shut my eyes, and I curl up small,
And nobody knows that I'm there at all.

Oh! Thank you, God, for a lovely day.
And what was the other I had to say?
I said "Bless Daddy," so what can it be?
Oh! Now I remember it. God bless Me.

Little Boy kneels at the foot of the bed,
Droops on the little hands little gold head.
Hush! Hush! Whisper who dares!
Christopher Robin is saying his prayers.

I loved Christopher Robin's family. Sister Rose tried to hide how pleased she was with my poem recital by squeezing her wrinkled face as if there were a bad smell under her nose. But I could tell she was happy because she nodded her wrinkled head, framed by her the white cardboard habit, with approval and then said, "Why can't you other slackers memorize such a wonderful poem?" Then she turned to me and said, "You said it so fast, you almost lost all of the meaning. Where's the fire?" But I had to say it fast just to remember every word.

As she approached me, there on the main street on the day of my Holy Communion, as I stood all alone in front of the statue of the Virgin Mary, I tried to pretend that I was having a conversation with Mary. I was devastated that nobody came for me, but was filled with shame to again be the needy kid in the class. I just wanted to be like everyone else.

When she got close, Sister Rose said nothing. She reached her black habit-draped arm around my shoulders and gently guided me. Without even realizing I was walking, I was floating down Church Street, across Fourth Street, two blocks more, until we were standing before the front porch of my house.

Sister Rose spun me around until we were face to face. I couldn't look into her face, but could only look down. She put her cold, diminutive hand under by burning hot chin and carefully lifted my face towards hers. Her tone was very stern as she shushed me. It wasn't a motherly shush, like Christopher Robin might have heard. It was more of a cut-the-crap shush.

Sister Rose said, "Enough now with the crocodile tears."

She waited for me to wipe the drops from my face with a crumpled tissue I pulled from my scratched little white Communion pocketbook that held my older sister's prayer book.

"Are you listening to me?" she asked. "Look at me now. Eyes forward." (She said this in class all the time. "Eyes on me, boys and girls. Let's put on our thinking caps!")

"You are a very brave girl," she said. "God loves you no matter what. Do you understand me?"

I nodded my head. As I turned to go up the four crumbling concrete stairs to my house, my mother's head appeared in the window like Vincent Price rising from a coffin in one of those scary movies we weren't allowed to watch. Her head was perfectly still, framed by the drab olive green curtains in the living room window. I looked back to see if Sister Rose saw her. She did, and the intense look in Sister Rose's eyes was like a powerful ray gun that forced my mother back from the curtain and out of the light.

When I entered the house, it was the same as if it were a school day. There was just one foot of floor space between the front door and my mother, so that as I flung the door open and bolted in, I smacked right into the wall that was her. The dark hallway was lit by one old fixture that was basically a light bulb hanging from a twisted wire. It cast an eerie *Twilight Zone* lighting effect over both of us as she towered over me. Within this space, I dropped to the floor, lifted my hands to protect my head, and cowered as she began the daily process of interrogating me. In the background, I could hear Bobby Vinton, the Polish Prince, singing the same song that was on the record player when I left for school in the morning.

Night after lonely night, we meet in dreams
As I run to your side
You wait with open arms, open arms
That now are closed to me
Through a veil of tears
Your vision disappears
And I'm as blue as I can be.

The melancholy song was interrupted by my mother's questions, "Did you cross the street on a red light today?"

"No," I'd answer meekly.

"What did you say? Speak up!"

"No."

When I dropped my guard for just a second so that my answers were audible, her hand stung my face, and I could feel heat flushing my cheek and blood sliding between my throat and my nose. I lowered my head in shame as her words stung even more.

"You filthy liar! Let's try this again. Did you cross the street on a red light today?"

"No, I promise."

"You think you are so smart. Do you think you are going to get away it? I have the report from my secret agent right here."

As I sunk deeper and deeper into the floor, she flipped through a black and white composition notebook, scanning the white space with great interest.

"You shithead! I had you followed. You think I'm stupid. You think I'm the crazy one. I'm not the crazy one. You're sick. You need to talk to Father O'Malley. You sneaky little monster!"

"No, no, please," I begged with little conviction because I already had the sinking feeling that nothing I said was going to work. It was as if we were just two actors reading our scripted lines in a play. It was a dress rehearsal I endured again and again.

Then, she added an ad lib: "You gave a blow job, didn't you?"

I had no idea what this meant, but I could hear in her voice that this phrase made her even more agitated, so I just screamed, "No!"

"You filthy pig! You're a little whore aren't you? Now, you'll have to make your confession and do a novena. Until you can see Father O'Malley, I will lock you in the basement. It is for your own good. That will stop you from having sex."

> *Blue on blue, heartache on heartache*
> *Blue on blue now that we are through*
> *Blue on blue, heartache on heartache*
> *And I find I can't get over losing you.*

She dragged me through the living room to a hallway, where she already had the basement door open and waiting. Then she lifted me up and began descending the stairs. The stairway was extremely dark, even at noon, and the familiar musty odor began to overwhelm me on the first step. Each stair creaked sympathy for me as we went lower and lower into hell. Suddenly, I'd find my courage and began kicking her or biting at her hands as she carried me down the steps. But she had the strength of ten men when that dark mood controlled her.

If I quiet myself and focus on what happened in the basement, fear shakes every fiber of me. The basement was limbo. Sister Rose told us this was an intermediate place somewhere between heaven and hell. Unbaptized babies or people who ate meat on Friday were sent there after they died. It was outside of the presence of God, but free of the torment associated with hell. But there was a presence and there was torment in the basement.

Now as I struggle to picture the faded memories, I can see filtered light from one street-level window that was there in the basement. I can recall some sights and sounds and touches. There was some type of antique sub kitchen on a wooden floor that gave when you stepped on to it. There was a deep sink or wash basin. There was a yellowed porcelain stove that had a bread box and an oven. Next to that was a dirty ringer washing machine with a big round tub. I can remember pulling back my arm to protect it from someone trying to run it through that ringer.

I remember being dropped quickly onto the concrete basement landing and then hearing my mother giggle as she ran back up the stairs, taking two at a time. She slammed and locked the door behind her with a little latch. I remember her coughing over and over as she struggled to catch her breath. When she did, she sang, "You're getting nothing for Christmas. Na, na, na, na na! Mommy and Nanny are mad. You're getting nothing for Christmas 'cause you ain't been nothin' but bad."

Poor thing. Why was she singing about Christmas? I could hear her light the match above me in the new kitchen and cough as she struggled to calm herself with a cigarette. Then I heard her slide out the kitchen chair as it whined across the floor. I imagined her pouring her coffee and sitting to enjoy it with a cigarette after completing a job well done.

I see myself sitting on the basement steps and just viewing light and shadows from my perch on the landing. Then, someone would approach me from behind the furnace, and it became much more like Dante's second circle of hell in the basement. My body recalls only shadows and light touches, disgust and depravity all swirling around in endless circles of shame. "Why would my mother do this to me?"

From all of the religion during the school day getting muddled and confused with my home life, I thought that God was with me in the basement. Yet I recall whispers, like soft prayers, about money for cigarettes being exchanged. God or a man from the tavern next door rocked me and soothed me and stroked my arm over and over like a soft blanket to get me prepared. Whatever or whoever it was that touched me in the basement, I hate to admit that it was much better than being hit. It was the only time in my life that someone touched me in a loving way. The pain was not physical, but came from the shame in knowing that I was involved in mortal sin.

In the basement, it was communicated to me in some way that everything was going to be all right. It was whispered into my mind that I was someone special and that my mother didn't mean any of what she did. I would be OK because I had a special friend. Like my mother on the swing, I left the basement. I was not really there because the real me was able to escape using a special trick. If I said the rote Our Fathers and Hail Marys of the rosary over and over very quickly, I left the musty basement and my spirit soared into the arms of Mother Mary, where I sat in her lap on the left side, while Baby Jesus sat on the right.

Angel of God,
my Guardian dear,
to whom His love
commits me here,
ever this day (or night)
be at my side,
to light and guard,
to rule and guide.
Amen.

Trenton Psychiatric Hospital

SUMMARY OF HOSPITALIZATION

Disposition Summary

Patient Name: Clara Murphy

Interval history indicates that prior to the admission patient was depressed slept all day and neglected her children. She frequently recited poetry dancing around the room stating that she was the Queen of England. The patient stated that her Uncle Pete came into her bedroom with a snake that crawled up her leg and then he turned around and left. Committing physician described her as depressed, agitated, confused, and exhibiting bizarre behavior, delusional with underlying grandiose ideas. She claimed her real father is the King of Poland and her mother died when she was born. For some reason she was given to the people who raised her as their own. She appears frustrated and silly. She stated that her troubles started when she was very young and stuck a bobby pin in her ear. She is extremely delusional. She admits to hallucinatory experiences. She is grandiose, circumstantial, and irrelevant in her replies.

CHAPTER 3—FEBRUARY 1965

MY MOTHER'S THIRD ADMISSION

Admission Quote: "My mother can kiss my ass."

When my mother's mother, our Nanny, thundered down the street, coming from work, in her size 24, flowered Lane Bryant dress, kids from the block whispered throughout the neighborhood like a secret communications system, "Nanny is coming, Nanny is coming." Eventually, the message passed from kid to kid, from block to block. It reached one of us at just around 5:00 p.m. at "the courts" where we were playing box ball, baseball, stickball, or football. The minute the message reached us, the bat was dropped, the ball was rolled to the ground, and we sprinted home from the park as fast as we could. We passed our siblings along the way. We raced up the steps to the bathroom and all washed our hands and faces before dinner. Nanny inspected them before we sat down. There was never an incidence where they didn't pass inspection.

Nanny was the closest thing we had to a loving parent. My mother and we five children lived with Nanny, who was a rare type of woman for the 1960s. First, she weighed over three hundred pounds. She was the biggest person in our neighborhood in body and spirit. She adhered to the "It takes a village philosophy" long before Hillary Clinton came on the scene. All of the kids were afraid of her, because she had no problem dragging one home by the ear to his mother if he was doing something inappropriate. As Nanny passed Gerry Mclintock sitting on his stoop, she barked, "You get a broom and get these leaves and debris off this sidewalk before your father gets home from work." Gerry jumped up and ran to the house to get a broom.

Kids moved out of her path as she took the same route each day wearing her tweed coat and swinging her black leather pocketbook at her side. You could always smell Nanny coming, too, because she liberally applied Jean Nate perfume or Avon Cream Sachets, which she smeared all over her meaty arms, under her jowls and behind her wrinkled knees.

I say she was rare because she was a divorced, working woman. She was the only one in this circumstance in our whole neighborhood. She had no use for man and one never lived in our home. To her, that would be like having a rat in your house. She worked full time as a bookkeeper during the day. At night, every night, she went to bingo. There was bingo on Monday and Wednesdays at Immaculate Mary, on Tuesdays and Thursdays at Our Lady of Lourdes, and on Fridays at Mother of Peace. She played twenty bingo cards at a time and could keep track of all of her numbers without even using bingo chips.

She was an aggressive bingo player and yelled, "Shake 'em up!" at the caller if the same numbers were being pulled over and over. When another player yelled "bingo" for the jackpot prize, she shouted, "You got to be kidding me, for Christ's sake," and then she packed up her supplies in old cookie tin and headed to the door.

The best part about visiting Nanny at bingo was that she'd smile and say, "Sit down, have a snack." Nanny was so big that she sat on two folding chairs while she played, one under each cheek. She'd signal you to pull up a chair, and as you sat down, she introduced you to her bingo table neighbors. When Nanny did this, the other women barely looked up to acknowledge you because they were keeping track of their many bingo cards. Nanny lifted her big, jiggling arm and waved for a bingo girl to come over to her table. They usually ran to her side because Nanny was a big tipper. Nanny would say, "Bring us three hot dogs with kraut, two bags of chips, and a Coke and a coffee." As you enjoyed the juicy Sabrett hot dog that was boiled in sauerkraut juice, you had to be amazed about how Nanny used her hand and her eyes to scan the numbers and to keep track of a full table and work the boards without missing a beat while she ate her snacks.

When she won, she leaned over and said, "See, you were my lucky charm." One positive compliment from Nanny erased a year of my mother's insults. She didn't really need her seven-year-old granddaughter for luck, because it seemed she won quite often. Nanny loved all forms of gambling. We never owned a car throughout our childhood, so we always took taxis with Nanny. She loved to gamble so much that she would sometimes sway her swollen body forward from the back seat of the taxi, closer to the driver, and say, "Hey, Cabbie, I bet you fifty bucks that this light is not functioning and is longer than one minute, thirty seconds."

"You're on," the taxi driver would reply, and the two of them would sit staring at the second hands of their watches. Whenever Nanny lost, she simply shrugged and said, "Double or nothing at the next light."

Nanny also ran for-profit bimonthly chartered bus trips to Seaside Heights, New Jersey, for a group of local woman to play bingo. She filled every seat on the bus to bring the ladies to Surf Skill Bingo on the boardwalk. Throughout the two-hour ride from Penn Station in Newark to Seaside Heights, one group of six ladies would participate in an intense poker game. Four of the ladies sat across the back seat. Nanny and another lady sat in the last two seats before the back seat, facing the aisle, so that they could see the back seat.

The ladies all wore dresses, and each opened her legs wide so that the fabric of her dress made a little table. Here, they kept all of their nickels, dimes and quarters for poker and exchanged money all the way down the Garden State Parkway. Mrs. Choffo turned her cards over in her blue-veined hand and said, "Diamond flush to the ace," with a big smile on her face. Nanny paused for a minute and then flipped her cards over and said, "Full house, jacks over eights." There was moaning and complaining, and then whichever lady stored the pot in her lap transferred it to Nanny's lap and the game continued.

The trips to the shore were fun for us, too, except for when our mother joined us. We all travelled by taxi from Kearny to Penn Station in Newark, New Jersey, where we would board the chartered bus. We kids piled onto each other's laps or sat on little booster seats that popped out of the floor in the taxi. Before getting on the bus, my mother made sure all five children used the bathroom. I remember her squeezing into the bathroom stall with me, yanking down my pants, sitting me on the toilet bowl seat, and standing above me, screeching, "Go!" By the time I was in third grade, most of my classmates did not have to endure their mothers going to the bathroom with them. It was so humiliating and invasive.

My body froze the instant she entered. I tried so hard to contract my pelvis to give her just one drop of urine so she would be happy, but my body would seize up and nothing would come out. She would grab my short hair and use it to jiggle my head back and forth. "I said go! We are going to miss the bus because of you and the whole day will be ruined!"

"I'm trying. I'm really trying," I answered. Her frustration rose in her hands and she slapped me, causing my head to crash into the grey metal stall covered with graffiti. *For a good time, call Clara,* I should have written.

I couldn't go to the bathroom no matter what she did to me. Eventually, she would give up and walk away, leaving me on the floor of the stall. I would pull myself together and run so that she wouldn't leave me there in Penn Station. She'd say, "You wash your filthy face and don't say a word to your grandmother." Today, no matter how desperately I have to use the bathroom while in a public place, I cannot urinate if someone else enters the bathroom, even with multiple stalls, in a restaurant, movie theater, or sports stadium. Even if I am midflow, my body simply turns off if the main door is opened and I hear another woman's voice seep through the cracks in the stall.

Once we got to the bus, no matter how much Dramamine they gave us, my sister Becky and I always suffered from motion sickness due to the smell of the diesel fuel that seemed to permeate the back of the bus. My grandmother packed sandwich-size brown paper bags lined with baggies just in case we needed to vomit. But my mother started each trip by warning us that we better not get sick. This caused so much anxiety that it made matters much worse.

As soon as the bus started rolling, I tried to just look forward so that I didn't get sick. My brothers and sisters talked to me, but I tried not to turn my head, so that I could prevent the motion sickness. Inevitably, saliva started filling my mouth. I swallowed over and over in a panic to keep it from happening. I could feel the gag start in my chest and begged myself, "Don't do it. Don't do it. Don't get sick." Before I knew it, I was throwing up on the seat and on my clothes. Of course, I didn't have the bag ready because I thought that I could control it.

When my grandmother was our chaperone, she would simply say, "Go get cleaned up." But when my mother was on the trip, she would drag me into the bathroom and rip sheet after sheet of heavy-duty brown paper towels out of the dispenser, squirt them with pink industrial soap, and rub them all over my face and chest. The paper towels tore my skin like sandpaper. When she was done rubbing wildly, she would say, "This is your fault. You ruined the trip for everybody. You got me in trouble with Nanny again!" She would stop jostling me for a minute, compose herself, take out a lipstick from her purse, put on a fresh face, and walk out. Never once would she look back to see if I was following her.

Nanny would go directly from the bus and walked up a ramp right into Surf Skill Bingo and never went to the boardwalk with us. She sat on her two folding chairs and played Bingo for six hours. Sometimes we sat by her side and played pretend Bingo and enjoyed the hot dogs, soda, and donuts that she bought.

Other times, we played games using paper bingo boards from the already finished bingo special games. They were made of pastel-colored papers of pink, yellow, and mint green. Some were all dotted with red circles from the bingo stampers.

We kids loved to go off to a corner of the bingo hall and play school. My sisters and I kept our cardigan sweaters buttoned but took our arms out of our sleeves and pulled the sweaters over our heads to cover all of our hair. The blue sweaters made perfect habits so that we could pretend to be nuns teaching our classes.

We created rows of make-believe students from our paper specials so that they could represent our students sitting in their assigned seats with their already corrected red-inked test papers. The paper student who got the most red marks on the bingo papers had to stay after school and be punished. Punishments ranged from being spanked with a paddle to going to the principal's office.

Our little brothers served as errand boys between our classrooms. Renee would say "Billy, come here to me." My brother Billy would jump up from the corner and run over to her. Renee would say, "Take this note to Sister Becky and don't lollygag in the hallways."

Billy would bring the fake note to my sister, who was two steps away, and ask her class to excuse her for a moment. "Your guardian angel is sitting on your shoulder watching everything you do." Then she would turn and give her class the evil eye as if they were making too much noise. She would pretend to write a note back and say, "Please take this back to Sister Renee immediately."

When we got bored playing inside, Nanny gave us a dollar each to get a slice of pizza at Maruca's Pizza, and then we could go to the beach. Since we were all under the age of ten and were unsupervised on the beach, she wanted us to be very careful in the ocean. We were often there with her during the off season, so there were no lifeguards on duty on the beach. So Nanny would have us stand before her as she looked over her cat-eye glasses. In the most deadly and serious tone, which stopped all talking or pushing and shoving, she said, "Go into the water up to your knees. If you go any further, the undertow will get you!" She repeated the warning, "The undertow will get you. It will pull you under and wash you away forever."

This struck such fear in me that even today, as I live on the beach in Florida, I never go into the ocean past my knees. Every time my husband asks me to go in, I reply, "No way, the undertow will get me!"

Besides her work and gambling activities, Nanny also made money when items from her warehouse "fell off the truck." She brought home dolls, electronics, household goods, and knick-knacks. Billy and I took these items up and down the streets in our small town to all of the local bars to sell them for her. We brought home the money, and Nanny would tip us fifty cents for doing a good job.

Aside from her paycheck, her gambling winnings, and her side deals, Nanny made a good buck from the U.S. government. She received Aid to Dependent Children for us five children and disability payments for my mother. So, financially, things were okay when Nanny was alive.

Nanny ran a tight ship in the household. We kids went to morning mass every day at 7:00 a.m. Our school uniforms, with all of their many pleats, were dry cleaned and pressed on a weekly basis. Our white uniform blouses were all washed in a bleach dishwasher detergent, like Cascade, to be sure they were a crisp white. Each day after school, we had to complete all of our homework before going out to play with our friends, and we had to polish our shoes before we went to bed.

At the dinner table, there was no real conversation because Nanny stated that children should be seen and not heard. Our elbows never touched the table. We never chewed with our mouths open and we always cleaned our plates. We didn't use napkins, but instead passed a single dish towel from person to person around the table. We couldn't leave the table until we had cleaned our plates and drunk our full glass of milk. This caused me some strife, because I was never hungry and I was probably lactose intolerant. I say this because I frequently vomited at church after having cereal. There were many, many nights where I was forced to stay at the dinner table for hours by myself because I couldn't eat my food or drink my milk. That meant no TV and to bed without supper the next night.

There were many other things that Nanny would never tolerate. The first and most important was saying any negative words about a sibling. If someone called a brother or sister a brat or a jerk or any other name, she lined us up and shouted, "You kids better stick together like glue. You are all youse got. If I ever hear of one of you not sticking up for the other, I will crack your ass in fourths. You hear me?"

Her round face turned crimson and her fat cheeks puffed like a blowfish as she grit her teeth and seethed, "If anyone ever touches your brother or sister, you kick them in the shins! If that doesn't help, you kick 'em where it hurts."

The second thing Nanny couldn't tolerate was poor performance in school. "Education is the ticket to success," she said daily. You didn't even want to come home from school without an E (Excellent) on your report card in every subject. Once Renee got a G (Good) on her report card and she could not go out and play for a month. She was so scared that at first she hid her report card under the bathroom scale and pretended that it didn't come. Of course, Nanny knew it came because the rest of us had our report cards. When Nanny asked Renee where the report card was, Renee denied ever getting one. When Nanny asked Renee if she wanted her to call the principal, the almighty Sister Mary Catherine, to find out the truth, Renee broke down and told Nanny that it was under the scale in the bathroom. Renee, our hero, added as a side bar, "I knew that the scale was one place you would never look." That didn't bode well for Renee, and she was in the house, doing the dishes, ironing, cleaning floors, and had to see Father O'Malley after school every day for a month. Because Renee was our rock and we never saw her in a position of weakness before, the rest of us *never* brought home a bad report card. That was that.

When Nanny did feel the need to punish us, she hit us on the backside with the back of a hairbrush. The biggest recipients of this treatment were my brother Billy and my sister Becky. She didn't hit Renee because she was Nanny's right-hand girl. She didn't hit Steve because he was the youngest and was her "Butterball." She didn't hit me because she was upset when I was not treated fairly by my mother. So, every now and then, you heard Nanny say, "Get him, girls," and just like the flying monkeys in the *Wizard of Oz*, my sisters would grab Billy and bring him back for punishment, and Nanny would crack his ass in fourths with a hairbrush.

Nanny made us do ten push-ups every night before we went to bed. This was unusual considering her love of food and lack of exercise, but it was never questioned. Nanny's love of food was perhaps the best part of our childhood. Because she worked full time, Nanny had to depend on restaurants to feed us. So Monday night's menu was takeout from the Greek diner, Tuesday's was delivery from Chicken Galore, Wednesday's was pizza night, Thursday's was submarine sandwiches, and Friday's was fish and chips. This was good eating!

On the weekends, Nanny thought that she was giving us a big treat by cooking. She made homemade soup every Saturday.

We all hated it. Renee once pulled a hair from her head and threw it in the soup and said, "I'm not eating it. There's a hair in it."

Nanny said, "OK, you're excused," and Renee gave us all a little smirk while she was walking away.

Breakfast and lunch were a little harder for Nanny, but she streamlined the process a bit. We had oatmeal for breakfast almost every morning. When we protested, Nanny said, "It'll stick to your ribs."

We were within walking distance of our school, so we came home for lunch every day. When we walked in, even when our mother was in the mental hospital, there was lunch waiting for us every day. Before leaving for work in the morning, Nanny made us all Taylor ham and egg sandwiches on poppy seed kaiser rolls and left them on the table wrapped in foil. It was cold by the time we ate it, but it was wonderful to have lunch waiting for us when we arrived.

Because of Nanny's weight, though, she never came to any school events. Whenever we were in a school play, a little league game, or a Catholic Youth Organization basketball game, there was never anyone in the audience for us.

When you made your first basket and the crowd cheered, your eyes scanned the stands for a familiar face that belonged only to you, and there was none. When you had a solo in the choir, danced "Tea for Two" on stage, received a citizenship award, won the state championship track meet, no one was there. It seemed only St. Thomas Aquinas, highlighted by dusty light streaming in from the skylights in the gym, stared down at us where he dwelled in the golden mural above the school gym bleachers. He seemed to be saying, "Nice shot," when I made my first basket on the basketball team.

Despite all of the food and structure Nanny showered upon us, she had a very noticeable mean streak. She treated my mother like a slave. My mother spent every single day of her life at home, cooking, cleaning, ironing, scrubbing floors, and keeping house according to Nanny's standards. Unfortunately, my mother and Nanny fought constantly, and the fights always ended with the police coming to our house and taking my mother away.

The fight always started in a typical manner. Once my mother, who was twenty-five years old at the time, waited until after dinner, when the table was cleared and the dishes were done, then asked my grandmother for a few dollars to go out to bingo. My grandmother sat cleaning her teeth with a toothpick, paused, and then said that there was no reason for my mother to go "whoring around."

My mother said that bingo was not whoring around. She always pleaded, "Please, Momma, I am a human being. I have to leave the house sometimes."

My grandmother said, "You have five children. You're going anywhere. You made your bed, now you lie in it."

The discussion escalated as my mother became more and more hopeless and frustrated. Soon, there was cursing and name calling and sometimes slapping. Then, as if out of nowhere, my grandmother got a calm look over her face and told one of us to bring her the phone. My mother begged, "Please, Momma, don't do it. I'll stay home." My grandmother rolled her eyes in her pie-faced head and said, "Too late."

Within fifteen minutes, there was a knock on the door. Two policemen with blue uniforms, shiny badges, guns, and dangling knight sticks grabbed my mother and wrestled her to the ground as she screamed, "No, Mamma, no." She cried in front of the young police officers, who she knew from school or the neighborhood, "Please, Sonny, please, Hank, I am not crazy."

They just looked so sad and said, "Yeah, we know Clara, we know," as they physically dragged her from the house. As she reached the squad car, she settled down and went peacefully. We kids huddled together crying on the front porch, where we'd hear her ask, "Do either of you have a cigarette?" before they slammed the car door. Sometimes, the police officers could be heard mumbling to each other, "What a shame. Such a beautiful girl." From the porch, I whispered, "Oh, blessed St. Thomas, patron of schools, pray for us."

Trenton Psychiatric Hospital

SUMMARY OF HOSPITALIZATION

Disposition Summary

Patient Name: Clara Murphy

The patient is a 25 year old Catholic separated, Female. Patient was sent to this hospital for her third admission because of her agitated, excited, disturbed behavior at home. Patient has neglected her five children, slept all day, played one record constantly all night and danced by herself. She states that she hates her mother and that there is constant friction between them and she used considerable foul language. The patient states that her mother weighs over 300 pounds and is addicted to Bingo. She goes to Bingo every night and charters a bus to the Jersey Shore to play every other weekend. She says her mother is never home to cook and leaves all the work to the patient. The patient stated that her mother worked her like a slave and the minute she sat down to rest, her mother called her stupid. She was observed engaged in bizarre behavior such as pouring water over her head stating that she was baptizing herself. On admission patient was loud and profane. During her stay, patient was on Thorazine 100 mgs. She has abated somewhat to her intensely irritated and highly excited state. A program of 10 ERTs are planned for her. She wishes to return to her mother and five children to go school to study a few courses. Her mother is an accountant and seems to be able to provide for the children with the help of aid to dependent children.

CHAPTER 4—MAY 1969

MY MOTHER'S FOURTH ADMISSION

Admission Quote: "I want to stay away from my mother."

I was actually relieved each time my mother was taken from our lives. Even though there was no legitimate parental love in our home, there was far less fear and anxiety with Nanny. She was tough, but she was consistent. You knew the rules and what she expected and what she wouldn't tolerate. You didn't have to come home from school each day and guess what you were coming home to and how you were going to survive. She was not home much because of her work and her bingo, but when she was home, we felt safe.

My sisters and brothers and I made up for the lack of attention at home by excelling at school. By my mother's fourth hospital admission, I was in the sixth grade and my two sisters were already in seventh and eighth grades. At this time, I started going to mass twice on Sunday. Not because I was more religious and prayed more. All students in our school were required to attend the 9:00 a.m. children's mass, and I went to the second one to watch my sisters perform at the 11:00 a.m. hootenanny mass.

Renee stood on the altar, tilting her shoulder-length brunette hair from side to side as she played the guitar and sang directly next to her teacher, Mr. Capezio. He was full of respect for Renee and often let her select the songs for the mass and plan the harmonies. Renee would gaze into his hazel eyes and laugh at his jokes and do anything to please him. He wasn't exactly good looking because his face was scarred with deep pits from acne. Still, he was over six feet tall, had olive skin, brown curly hair, and a mustache that he smoothed all day with two fingers whenever he was nervous. Renee's crush went unnoticed because he was not interested in females.

Becky always looked sharp on the altar as she danced, sang, and played tambourine wearing a plaid mini skirt and white go-go boots. Many boys watched her during the whole mass instead of watching the priest turning bread into Jesus's body. Even though it was church, it felt like I had a front row seat to the *Ed Sullivan Show* because they sang songs from the radio. It was so joyous to hear prayers that were once only mumbled in Latin now sung with guitars. When we went to church on a daily basis in primary grades and the mass was in Latin, I used to think "Et cum spiritu tuo" was God's phone number. Now, mass was more meaningful.

They sang songs by top musicians of the day and rewrote them slightly for church. Favorite songs included John Denver's "Follow Me" and "You Fill up My Senses" ("Annie's Song") and Simon and Garfunkel's "Sounds of Silence." Meanwhile, all of the parishioner responses were sung with the guitar as well. Even the final words, "The mass is ended, now go in peace," were strummed on three acoustic guitars. It was magical. Their songs literally did fill up my senses and allowed me to think that God really did love us after all. Although the singing group comprised eight to ten people each week, I would tell people on the way out, "They are my sisters."

My brother Billy was a talented dancer. Each year, our school put on a musical production, and inevitably he was given a solo dance performance. One year he was dressed as a hobo and danced around a lamppost prop to the song, "Wouldn't It Be Lovely" from *My Fair Lady*. Even though he was in fifth grade, he was already taller than me at five foot seven. His height gave him such elegance on the stage. He seemed so much older than the other children in our school. His dance was beautiful and rivaled Gene Kelly in *Singing in the Rain*. Yet, somehow I was more enthralled with the lyrics of the song, as they seemed to allow me to put actual words to the aching feeling inside of me.

> *Oll I want is a room somewhere*
> *Far away from the cold night air*
> *With one enormous chair*
> *Oh wouldn't it be loverly?*
>
> *Lots of chocolates for me to eat*
> *Lots of coal making lots of 'eat*
> *Warm face, warm 'ands, warm feet*
> *Oh wouldn't it be loverly?*

My brother George was called "Whitie" because his hair was so light that teenagers on the basketball court and at street hockey games started calling him "White Owl." This name was taken from the White Owl cigar boxes that many of us used as pencil boxes in school. At home, we shortened it to Whitie. He excelled in all sports and eventually became an All-State runner. When we all ran to the courts, a large park in the center of our town, after school, we stood in a group waiting to be selected for pick-up baseball, basketball, or football games by the older kids. Whitie was always selected first because he was good at every sport, and he was a mascot for the older kids.

At home, Whitie was called "My Butterball" by Nanny. He was without a doubt Nanny's favorite. His ringlets of platinum blonde hair, his wide blue eyes, and his full lips and freckles across his nose allowed him to be cute way beyond his toddler years. Nanny showed that she could not resist his charms by showering him with special gifts. When she bought a box of Yodels for all of us kids to share, Whitie got his own separate box of Yodels. We other four kids would sit together with Whitie and peel off the dark hard chocolate layer of the Yodel first, trying to keep the pieces of chocolate as big as possible. Then, we would unroll the Yodel and eat the cream inside, and finally finish the dry dark cake. When we did finish and wished we had more, Whitie would go to his special box and say, "Oh, look, I have nine more Yodels here. I guess I'll have another." We would call him a brownnoser and walk away.

While we all gathered around one living room television and took turns manually changing the television dial, which made a machine gun sound, and shouted "I'm watching this" and "Oh no you're not, we're watching this," Whitie was in Nanny's bedroom watching his own TV that he got from Nanny as a Christmas gift. While we took turns adjusting a wire hanger to use as our antenna, Whitie had perfectly good rabbit ears in Nanny's room.

This set up some sibling rivalry and caused Billy and Whitie to always compete with each other. They both would go to the corner deli and put cases of cupcakes on Nanny's bill and then would have competitions with their friends to see who could put the most Yankee Doodle cupcakes in his mouth and chew and swallow them in the shortest amount of time. We girls would laugh when they relayed the stories, because we never once thought about putting any item on Nanny's bill without permission.

If Billy and Whitie were ever in an overt competition when Nanny was home, Whitie always won. Nanny did not allow anyone to mess with Whitie. Still, Billy picked his times carefully. We were never allowed to watch scary movies, but Nanny was always at bingo, so in reality we watched whatever we wanted. After watching the movie *Two on the Guillotine*, Billy followed Whitie around with his arms outstretched, trying to capture him to put him on the guillotine, calling out, "Melinda, Melinda," which was the name of the character to be beheaded in the movie. Whitie started crying, and Nanny dragged her big body into the boys' bedroom and reached her jiggly arm up to the top bunk bed and began slapping Billy. "You instigator. You leave him alone!" she shouted. We laughed into our pillows, so we didn't get hit as well.

I didn't have a performing talent, and while I played basketball in grammar school, high school, and college, I never was very good at it. I could shoot from anywhere and am still great at three-point shots, but I couldn't really run, jump, dribble, or play defense. The only reason I could shoot was that every day in the summer, Billy and I went to the basketball court with a clipboard and chart and practiced shooting. Each day, we played "Around the World," which required you to make every shot around the key. Then, we did the same shots from the three-point area. We didn't stop for the day until we made 100 percent of the baskets. I once made eighty-six out of one hundred foul shots in a competition and won a red, white, and blue American Basketball Association basketball signed by Julius Erving ("Dr. J"), but I never had a competitive spirit. If the basketball was on the ground, our coach believed that we should dive on top of it, grab it out of the hands of our opponent, and tie it up for a jump ball. I pretty much stood back and politely told my opponent, "Oh, no, you have it, I insist." So I didn't contribute much physically to the team, but I was recognized by my coaches for team spirit and leadership. When we had to run forty laps around the gym before each practice, I was the last to finish. At first, I was embarrassed, but then my coach gathered the team and said, "Murphy here has more strength and spirit in that skinny little body than all of you put together. She gives her all to this team." And then I felt proud.

Still, I preferred playing with words. When I was in sixth grade in Catholic school, we had a trendy, hippie English teacher named Mr. Harrelson. He had shoulder-length, golden blond hair and a mustache, which contrasted with the suit and tie he wore to teach every day. He stood about six feet tall and was so handsome because he looked like I imagined Jesus would have looked. However, we loved him, not for his looks, but because he never used the grammar book. Instead, every morning when we came into the classroom, he had a song by Cat Stevens on the blackboard. As we settled into our desk, we began to read these words in his extremely neat penmanship covering left, center, and right side classroom blackboards.

Oh, I'm being followed by a moonshadow,
Moonshadow, moonshadow
Leapin' and hoppin' on a moonshadow,
Moonshadow, moonshadow
And if I ever lose my hands,
Lose my plough, lose my land,
Oh if I ever lose my hands—oh if...
I won't have to work no more
And if I ever lose my eyes
If my colours all run dry
Yes if I ever lose my eyes—oh if...
I won't have to cry no more.

Then Mr. Harrelson read us the biography of the songwriter and asked us to discuss what the song meant. I felt I was a kindred spirit with Cat Stevens because a few times a year, since kindergarten, I'd had to leave during the day and take a bus to North Arlington for a chest x-ray because my tuberculosis test always came back positive. My teacher said that Cat Stevens nearly died from TB, so his words meant more to me. The class was so interesting because of the poetry lessons that we hated when the lunch bell rang. Then, instantly, like Pavlov's dogs, we stood, blessed ourselves, and said our prayer before lunch "*Oh, bless us our Lord and these thy gifts we are about to receive from thy bounty through Christ, Our Lord. Amen.*" Throughout the school year, we reviewed the words of Cat Stevens's classics "Father and Son," "Peace Train," "Morning Has Broken," and others. We also spent a very long time analyzing and discussing another popular song called "American Pie."

I was really proud when Mr. Harrelson sometimes asked me to put a poem that I wrote on the board. I had terrible penmanship, despite Sister Rose's best efforts, so when I turned my back to write my poem on the board, I went very slowly to use my best printing. Although I didn't have a stylish haircut, as Nanny forced me to wear a pixie because my hair was so thick and bushy, I didn't feel awkward standing in front of my peers because my uniform was perfectly pressed by the dry cleaner and my saddle shoes were spotless. Thank God, I didn't have to stand with my back to some public school classmates and have them critique my blue jeans or top, because we really only had our uniform and church clothes. Play clothes or everyday clothes were generally hand-me-downs from my sister. So, as I wrote on the board, I mostly worried about my penmanship.

Adults

Adults,
they don't give us what we want
or expect.
They give us love
but no respect
They talk about us to everyone
Because they can't
Accept the ways
we like to have fun.
They call us damn kids
Yet they want things from us
And to them
Every little thing
is a must
For them we're just
things
that happen to be
Intruders in their adult society

Mr. Harrelson asked me to explain to the class why I wrote this poem. I told them that a group of friends and I had nowhere to go at night so we would sit on the stoop of a corner store called the Milk Bar and just talk. When we did this, a police car would come every night and the officers would tell us to move along. We didn't really have anywhere else to go.

Mr. Harrelson took over and asked the class to discuss what was missing in my poem. The conclusion was concrete language. He turned to me and said, "We know the feelings that you are trying to express, but we should be able to see them, taste them, smell them, and touch them."

Even though the poem needed work, it was still selected by Mr. Harrelson to be placed on the board. Each time this happened, I set a personal goal to improve what I wrote so that my poem would be selected every time, and it was.

Even though my love of words was growing, using my words to defend myself at home was still not a good idea. Every time my mother returned from the hospital, I was caught in a terrible Catch-22. Should I continue to take her abuse for the sake of peace in the family, or should I challenge her and stand up for myself? My chest was beginning to fill with the injustice of it all. Children are people, too, and they should not have to put up with shit. Soon, the outrage began to erupt from my mouth and I couldn't hold it back. But I quickly learned that opening my mouth did more harm than good.

Each week, I was paid $2 to go after school to bring coffee from the bakery to Nanny's work. This was much easier than my previous job for Nanny. Every day, when she came in from walking home from work, it was my job to separate her toes. She rushed to her reclining chair and dropped into it, exhausted. "Please, sweetheart, my toes." She would signal to me pointing to her feet. I had to kneel on my knees and untie Nanny's black oxfords. As I did, she moaned a little. I carefully widened the shoes with my fingers and then slid them off from the heel to the toe. Then, I had to reach underneath her flowered dress and roll down each of her stockings. When her wet feet were bare, I would start with her pinky toe and slowly and carefully pull her wet, pudgy little toes apart. "Thank you so much," she would say and finally sigh her relief.

Bringing coffee sounds easy in comparison, but it was a little scary because I had a big tray of six coffees and a bag of pastries. As I walked the eight blocks to her work, I had to be very careful not to spill the coffees. Also, I had to walk past many factories and warehouses. If my walk coincided with break time at the factories, there were gangs of men outside smoking and they yelled to me as I walked. "Mira, Blondie, come here. Blondie, I have something for you. Besse me, chiquita."

I walked very fast past them and ignored them because $2 was a great deal of money to me. In those days, a bag of potato chips was only 25¢, and I could buy them and a lot more snacks for $2. Also, once in a while, if he was standing outside while a truck was being loaded, a foreman named Brownie would call me over and hand me $1. He always winked and smiled and said, "Don't tell your grandmother." When this happened, it was the best week ever.

When my mother came home from the hospital after her last episode of "being away" she told me that she would be taking $1 of my $2 in pay each week, and if I told Nanny she would rip my tongue out of my mouth. She justified this by saying that all parents were entitled to half of their child's earnings. According to her, it was the law.

This infuriated me the whole time I walked home with my pay during the first week she was back. The injustice of it all was festering in me as I struggled to keep from spilling the coffees on my school uniform. As I walked, the Styrofoam lids filled with coffee, and I tried to lean the carrier to the left and right to get the coffee to go back down the sip hole. It was like playing one of those little handheld games where you have to get the silver ball into an eye hole. Well, I leaned a little too far and one of the large coffees fell right off the tray, down my blue plaid uniform skirt and down my leg. Although the coffee was warm and sticky on my leg, it wasn't scalding hot. Still, I had to walk back the three blocks to the bakery where I got the coffee and get another cup. Fortunately, they didn't charge me for the refill. Still, Nanny would be furious if she saw my uniform.

Luckily, when I got there, Nanny was in the warehouse, and her pretty secretary, Mary, took the coffees without saying a word to me. I felt a closeness to Mary because on my last birthday, Nanny let her take me to Korvettes to select any gift I wanted. Mary helped me pick a blue poncho with red and white stripes. It was very stylish at the time, and it was nothing like what Nanny would have picked. Nanny always selected lace and flowered prints for us, and we hated them. She also begged us to take sewing lessons and dance lessons, but we wanted to play basketball.

After the ordeal of spilling the coffees and having the sticky liquid bake on my skirt and legs in the ninety-degree June heat, I finally reached home. Now, I had to get up to my room without my mother seeing my uniform skirt. As I opened the solid front door and stepped up the one step with my right foot, I heard my mother shout to me, "Did you do those dishes yet?" What the hell? I hadn't even gotten in the door from school and work. What did she do all day? Plus I had to give her half my pay? Without missing a beat, I yelled back, "What the hell do you think I pay you for?" I chuckled a bit under my breath because I thought that it was a pretty good impromptu line. My celebration was very brief, as she rushed towards me in the hallway and brought her right hand across my face so hard that it split my top lip. Instantly, I could feel the burning as my top lip separated and bled onto my tongue. I wanted to start punching and kicking her as hard as I could. She wanted that. She stood there with her hands in position like a boxer and said, "Come on...go for it." She lifted her head and her chin in a taunt. For a split second, I pictured myself kicking her fucking ass. I would pull her hair and bash her head into the oak banister that led upstairs. I would knock her down and kick her over and over in the gut until she was dead. But a priest's voice stopped my rage. "Forgive your mother."

I pushed past her and went right to the kitchen sink to wash the dishes. Caked yellow egg yolks were glued to the plastic plates that had been there since breakfast. The blood from my mouth dripped down onto the white, foamy dish soap as I finished the dishes. I let it drip, too, because I needed some concrete language. As Mr. Harrellson said, I wanted to be able to describe the smell, taste, touch, of my life. I needed physical proof that the unfairness was real.

The next day when I went to school, I was called to Sister Mary Catherine's office. She asked me what happened to my lip. I looked towards the polished wood floor. With all my might I wanted to tell her that my mother smacked me for no reason the way she always smacked me. I wanted to beg her to go and smack my mother with a ruler right across the face. I wanted her to make my mother kneel all day with twenty dictionaries across her arms. But Nanny's voice in my mind stifled me: "You don't talk about your family outside of this house...ever."

I told Sister Mary Catherine that I fell off my bike. She asked me five times if I was sure that is what happened. I could tell she was very frustrated. "I can't help you if you won't help yourself," she shouted. "I am on your side; can't you see that, silly girl? Get out of my office and get back to class."

Sister Mary Catherine would have loved to see my mother punished also. When my youngest brother, Whitie, was in first grade, he asked Mrs. McNarkle if he could go to the bathroom right before the lunch bell. She said no because the lunch bell was going to ring in a minute and then he could go at home.

In reality, Whitie couldn't wait, and he had a bowel movement in his pants. When he walked home for lunch and walked into the house, my mother was furious. Rather, than call the school, she took his soiled underwear, wrapped them in white tissue paper, put them in a big square gift box, wrapped the box in Christmas wrapping paper, taped a gold bow on top, and gave "the gift" to Whitie to give to his teacher after lunch.

When Ms. McNarkle opened the gift, she gagged and immediately grabbed the box and ran to the principal's office. Whitie said the class had so much fun while she was gone for a long time. When the teacher came back, she only looked at Whitie with a sad expression and said nothing.

My mother also wasn't very fond of permission slips or providing emergency information either. We all had to sit at many detentions because my mother refused to fill out three different colored emergency cards for each child of her five children. In Immaculate Mary School, there was always a rule that if you didn't get your emergency cards in to your homeroom teacher by the first Friday of the new school year, then you were given detention.

My mother tore the cards into little tiny pink, yellow, and blue confetti pieces and put them back in an envelope and told us to give them to the teacher. It was so embarrassing to turn them in and watch the pity flow from our teacher's eyes. When they opened their mouths to ask a question, each of us said what we were told to say: "My mother said that the cards were in by Friday as requested."

The teachers never took out their frustration with my mother on us. In fact, in fourth, fifth, and sixth grades, I was the only student in the school who was allowed to leave the building to go get coffees for some faculty members. Each day, I would wait for the clock to hit 10 a.m., and a student would enter my classroom with a note that stated Mrs. O'Brian needs to see Katie Murphy. I was called to the front of the class, and I was given the coffee order by Mrs. O' Brien and left for the remainder of that class period. When I returned, my friends always asked me where I went. Speaking a little louder than usual, I would report, "I get coffee for the faculty." This was a big deal.

Nanny was filled with pride that I was selected for this duty, but she was infuriated when my mother's behavior tarnished our family image. Our black-and-white saddle shoes were polished and inspected every night. The coffee and other stains on the outside of our uniforms were removed, and our pleats were pressed neatly so none could see what was hiding inside. We looked exactly like all of the other children running and playing freeze tag in the school courtyard each day...or else. After one too many incidents between my mother and the school, portraying our family in a negative light, there was another blow-up at home and Nanny made her phone call. The police arrived and my mother was taken away.

Trenton Psychiatric Hospital

SUMMARY OF HOSPITALIZATION

DIAGNOSTIC THERAPEUTIC NOTE:

Patient Name: Clara Murphy

This patient is a 29 year old, white separated, female patient. Patient claims she had several admissions to this hospital and received insulin and electro shock therapy. She claims that lately she has frequent arguments with her mother. She states that she was locked up with maniacs for the last eleven days at the Hudson County Diagnostic Clinic. During the interview, she was noted to be quite circumstantial, exhibited an inappropriate emotional reaction and was quite paranoid in her ideation. She reveals no insight into her condition with poor judgment. Her memory to past and recent activities is not impaired. Her treatment is to continue her on Phenothiazine namely Thorazine 100 mgs. Artane and occupational therapy.

CHAPTER 5—NOVEMBER 1969

MY MOTHER'S FIFTH ADMISSION

Admission Quote: "I am a deaf mute and have four children, but they are all in Vienna."

Six months after the last commitment, my mother was in the hospital again. This time, Nanny told them that she didn't want her back. My sisters and brothers and I realized that we should just erase her from our lives and pretend she didn't exist. This was pretty easy because by then I thought, "What does she do for me anyway?" Since I was starting seventh grade, I had more pressing concerns on my mind. Boys and girls in my class were starting to notice each other, and I didn't want to be left out. In order to be popular, I was going to need more money for cooler clothes, so I was becoming aware of my finances. Even to buy my first bra, I left Nanny a note under her pillow and set up a payment plan.

Dear Nanny,
I know that I don't have much on top, but many girls in my class now wear a bra. I was wondering if you can buy me a bra too. I will pay you back $2 per week with my coffee money. I really want to have a bra for when we change clothes in gym class.
Love,
Katie

Nanny did buy me my first bra, and didn't make me pay her back. Still, I would need money for other clothing items as well. Girls in seventh and eighth grades had started going to dances that were held on Friday nights at the courts. They wore bell bottoms and cropped tops to these dances. Nanny would never buy these clothes, but probably wouldn't know if we bought them. So we started to make our own money.

Billy and I had already developed some effective sales skills as we were hawking my grandmother's wares that fell off the truck at work from bar to bar. Kearny was known in New Jersey as the town that had a bar on every corner, so we had an extensive territory for marketing. Also, we were well known to bar patrons because the house where we lived was right next door to Packy's Tavern. Besides the entertainment of weekly barroom brawls, we benefitted by being runners or "valets" for the bar patrons. We played outside the bar, and as drunken patrons stumbled out the door, we were waiting. They were so out of it that they paid us $1 to find their cars for them. The drunken clients gave us a description of their vehicles, and we ran around the block and located the cars and then led the drunks to the cars. This was an in-demand service because parking spaces in our small town were at a premium. Sometimes, the drunks didn't even realize that they were handing us a $5 bill instead of a $1.

We began other enterprises without Nanny's knowledge. Each year, as a student in a Catholic school, we were expected to collect money and sell items for fundraising, such as Christmas Seals. Christmas Seals were basically a book of stamps that featured the nativity scene. They were supposed to be sold for $1 per book of ten pages of stamps. Billy and I went from bar to bar selling them for $1 per page. We pocketed the $9 per book and were rewarded at school for being the top sellers in class.

Billy and I also enrolled with a company that advertised in the back of *Boys' Life* magazine seeking kids to sell Christmas cards. The cards were delivered in a big box while Nanny was at work.

We sold the cards for $4 per box, sharply undercutting the true price, and kept all of the money. We never paid for the cards. They sent letter after letter to the house, but we just threw them away before Nanny got home. We knew that they couldn't do anything to underage children.

Another profitable activity was shoplifting. Every day at lunchtime, we joined other Catholic school students who crammed into the Milk Bar to buy gum and candy (both not allowed in Catholic school). While the overwhelmed clerk was assisting the five or six students in front of her, we filled our pockets with Sugar Babies, Good & Plenty, etc.

At night, we were able to go out wearing fashionable clothes because Nanny was always at bingo and never saw us leave to meet our friends. I belonged to a group of cheerleaders and boys' basketball players who hung out on corners each night. Even though I didn't quite fit in the group because I was a girl basketball player and not a cheerleader, they kept me around because of my sense of humor. I was always able to come up with some good one-liners.

Me: "Hey, want to go to a party?"

Boy: "Where?"

Me: "In your mouth, we're all coming!"

However, when darkness covered our little town, boy basketball players and girl cheerleaders would pair up and find dark corners of the park or the side of a stoop to make out. I would be left alone. Nobody wanted a girl with a pixie haircut who played basketball. Nanny made it clear that I would never have long hair. As a result, I didn't have the shimmering, smooth blonde locks that touched a narrow waist in the back that showed through a midriff top. I was never permitted to wear rose-colored blush and pink lipstick to brighten my face. Our fingernails could not be covered in bubble-gum-colored polish. "Get in the bathroom and get that trash off your fingers," Nanny insisted. I never had pom-poms. In fact, when I was selected to be an angel in the Christmas pageant and Mrs. Penza offered to let me take home the huge gold gilded wings I wore in the play, Nanny said, "Take that back to school. I don't want crap like that around the house."

While I walked home alone in my new bell bottoms and pink checkered Raggedy Ann midriff shirt I bought with my own money, I could only come to one conclusion. My mother was right. I was too ugly to kiss. No seventh-grade boy wanted to kiss me. I looked and acted like one of them. I was five feet seven inches tall already. I looked like a Q-tip. I was rail thin with no shape whatsoever, and my hair was just a platinum blonde puff on top of my head with no style whatsoever.

Each morning allowed me to forget about the loneliness and darkness of the night because I had other ways to get attention. One day, I was in Sister Arlene's math class and was called to the blackboard to complete a math problem. As I did the work at the board, I noticed that Sister Arlene had squeezed her rotund figure into my student desk and was flipping through the pages in my black-and-white notebook. She looked as if she could hardly breathe in that tiny desk, as her face was so red against the white frame of her habit. I knew what I had in my notebook. A few girls and I had written stuff about other girls in the class. Mary Beth is a bitch. Mary Clara is a jerk. Mary Elizabeth is a slut. Mary Francis smells.

When I finished the math problem, I walked back and stood next to my desk looking down at Sister Arlene with my hand on my hip. She glared up and said sternly, raising her eyebrows above her wire-framed glasses, "Does your mother know you write these things in your notebook?" Without missing a beat, I said, "Does your mother know you go through people's things when they're not watching you?"

The entire class gasped and then laughed quietly. I looked around and garnered support from my peers. Before I even knew what happened, she stood up and slapped me so hard across the face that it knocked me off my balance. I could feel the huge red handprint burning my face for the rest of the afternoon.

The incident did make me a celebrity among my peers. This was happening anyway because in seventh grade, I had begun sharing interesting tidbits about cursing and sex that I was learning from my mother's friend's husband. When she was at home, my mother and his wife enjoyed coffee on a daily basis. While they were in the kitchen, a few times, Freddie was in the living room telling me the meaning of curse words. He called me, licked his hand, and used his wet hand to smash down his long black bangs, which were part of his Beatles hairstyle. He asked me if I knew what "fuck" meant. I didn't, but I was excited to learn. Each time I saw him, he told me the meanings of all words related to sex, and I was interested because no one ever talked about sex before. One day, when he was telling me, I noticed he had something hard in his pants pocket and asked him what it was.

He said, "It's nothing."

I said, "Well, then let me see it." It was shaped like a roll of quarters.

He said, "No, you can't see it, but you can touch it if you want to."

I said, "First, let me see it."

He said, "Nope, but you can touch it."

I said, "Forget it, asshole!" I brought my fist back as far as I could and punched whatever it was really hard. He bent over in pain and began squealing and turned really red. I ran out of the house into the backyard where the boys were playing and pretended it never happened. That ended his lessons in curse words.

Over the next few years, another teacher took his place to teach me the meaning of words because I began listening to George Carlin's album at my friend Madeline's house and immediately memorized the routines. Right in the middle of religion class, I raised my hand and waved it until Sister Ruth called on me. Then I asked, "Sister, could God make a rock so big that he himself can't lift it?" Or, "Sister, say you are on a ship, right, and you didn't complete your Easter duty, and the chaplain goes into a coma, would you go to hell then?"

Listening to George Carlin's words about religion made me begin to pay more careful attention to the words we were required to say in church. Have you ever really examined the words to the Stations of the Cross? Each Friday during Lent, the whole school filed into the church, and a priest, carrying a crucifix and surrounded by an entourage of altar boys, walked around the inside perimeter of the church and stopped at each gold-gilded relief representing the steps Jesus took towards the crucifixion. As the priest paused in front of each mini sculpture, he told the story of that stop along the way. These included: Jesus is condemned. Jesus receives forty lashes. Jesus receives a crown of thorns. Jesus falls for the first time. Jesus is stabbed in his side.

On a regular basis, as we relived these horrible things that happened to Jesus, the whole school knelt in the darkened church and said in unison that what happened to Jesus was our fault.

Jesus falls for the first time:

My Jesus, the heavy burden of my sins is on Thee, and bears Thee down beneath the cross. I loathe them, I detest them; I call on Thee to pardon them; may Thy grace aid me never more to commit them.

There was such a contrast between what George Carlin was saying on the record player and the words we were saying everyday in school and church. Yet I liked Carlin's words better because we were not all Christ killers. We were just human. One of my favorite cuts on the album was Carlin's version of confession:

And all the Irish guys that were heavily into puberty...would go to confession to Father Rivera. 'Cause he didn't seem to understand the sins, y'know...or at least he didn't take them personally, you know. It

*wasn't an affront to him. There was no big theological harangue; he
didn't chew you out. He was known as a "light penance." In and out,
three "Hail Marys," you're back on the street with Father Rivera, man.
You could see the line move; that's how fast he was working.
But he wasn't ready for the way Irish boys were confessing at that
time and that place...
"Uh, bless me, Father, for I have sinned...Uh, I touched myself in an
impure manner. I was impure, impurity, and impureness. Thought,
word, indeed. Body, touch, impure, sex, dirty. Impure legs, impureness.
Touch, impure dirty body, sex, rub and covet; heavy on the covet,
Father, uh..." (Rivera:) "That's OK, man! Tres Ave Marias!"...
You'd be home in five minutes, you know?
The Irish priest, on the other hand, nice guy, but, uh, first of all, he
recognized your voice 'cause you'd grown up there, right? He knew
everyone—"What'd you do that for, George?" "Oh, God, he knows,
man!" And the Irish priests were always heavily into penance and
punishment, y'know? They'd give you a couple of novenas to do,
nine first Fridays, five first Saturdays, Stations of the Cross...a trip
to Lourdes, wow! That was one of the things that bothered me a little
about my religion was that conflict between pain and pleasure...
'cause they were always pushin' for pain and you were
always pullin' for pleasure, man.*

Since my religion teacher hadn't heard of George Carlin, she thought that I was a deep thinker and was exceptional because of my ability to question my faith at such an early age. In fact, she selected me to do a reading at the children's Easter mass. This honor was usually saved for the beautiful, angelic girls with long blonde spaghetti curls and pretty dresses. A tomboy basketball player from a welfare family wasn't usually the girl of choice.

I decided to make the most of my chance to speak to my community and to my church. So, at the last minute, I switched the reading that I was supposed to do with an original poem that I wrote especially for the occasion. I really concentrated to ensure that I added concrete language to every line of the poem.

> *'Twas the night before Easter and all through the church*
> *All the neighbors were praying, each with his purse.*
> *The priest was nestled and snug in the pew*
> *While dreams of collections came into his view.*
> *Jill in her fur and Jack in his cap.*
> *Were dreaming of baskets they soon would unwrap.*
> *There was not a mention of Christ being reborn*
> *But simply of the new bonnets to be worn*
> *Then in a flash, they left happy and quick*
> *They did not notice a man, who was lying there sick.*
> *They ate chocolate, found eggs, and each gave a cry*
> *Happy Easter to all, as the old man died.*
> *Then out came the priest, his stomach like Jell-O*
> *He looked down towards the ground*
> *and said, "God bless you, poor fellow."*
> *The priest's pockets were bulging*
> *from his collection of cash.*
> *He shouted, "Happy Easter to all,"*
> *Then was off in a dash.*

I didn't wait to see if there was any reaction to my poem. I turned and walked down the steps towards the left aisle of the church and walked out the golden doors. I didn't know then that when you use spite, you aren't supposed to spite yourself. I thought that I was going to teach the people in the congregation a lesson. Instead, I stole something so valuable from myself.

It was as if suddenly while I was reading the words I had written just the night before, I had an epiphany, deflating the only hope I carried inside my chest. My handsome God, the same one that got me through the basement, the one who I wholeheartedly believed was going save my brothers and sisters and would someday allow me to rest my weary head on his strong shoulder, was really just like Santa Claus or the Easter Bunny. He wasn't ever coming to help me. He was a children's story, and I was no longer a child.

It was time to shrug off all things related to childhood, and perhaps that meant giving up hope. I turned then full-time from the script of daily brainwashing provided in school to the brilliant wordplay of George Carlin. I knew every routine word for word. My most requested number in school was "The Seven Words You Can't Say on Television" routine:

"Shit, piss, fuck, cunt, cocksucker, motherfucker, and tits. 'Tits' sounds like a snack. I know it is. New Nabisco Cheese Tits. Bet you can't eat just one.... Remember, you can prick your finger, but don't finger your prick."

My God, my God, why have your forsaken me?

Trenton Psychiatric Hospital

SUMMARY OF HOSPITALIZATION

Disposition Summary

Patient Name: Clara Murphy

This is a 30 year old white, separated, Catholic female who was admitted to Trenton State Hospital by regular commitment papers on 11/7/69. There is a history of several previous mental hospitalizations in this hospital. On admission the patient appeared neat in appearance, had a flattened affect and was over productive. Her productions were spontaneous with irrelevancy and looseness of association. She had flight of ideas and displayed some grandiose ideas stating, "I am a deaf mute. I had an operation in Vienna six months before I got married to Dr. Ervin Winnfield. After discharge from this hospital, I will go back to school and finish my internship. I want to discover a cure to treat poliomyelitis, etc. I have four children. They are all in Vienna."

The patient was very well oriented as to time, place and person; and her memory for the past and recent events was very good. She was very disorganized in her thinking and lacked insight and judgment into her condition. However, no suicidal or homicidal tendencies were noted. The patient was placed on Thorazine 300 mgs. After a few weeks, the patient's mental condition gradually improved and the grandiosity and over productiveness gradually subsided. The patient's mother does not want the patient to return to the family home as it is too upsetting for her children.

CHAPTER 6—JANUARY 1973

MY MOTHER'S SIXTH ADMISSION

Admission Quote: "I need some treatment. I am going to kill my children."

In the summer after graduating from eighth grade, I learned that there were people in my neighborhood that had it worse than we did. I received about $80 in cash as gifts for my graduation. From bringing coffee to my grandmother's office, I was able to get that up to $100 to purchase a brand new bike that I had my eye on in the bike shop on Kearny Avenue. It was a five-speed banana yellow bike with a really thick, padded, bright yellow seat. It was beautiful and I couldn't wait to own it. When I passed by the store every day on the way to get Nanny's coffee, I stared at it glistening in the store window and made a plan to get it. I stopped in and talked to the bike shop owner. It was listed for $125, but he told me that if I could get $100 together, he would give me a discount.

Having a bicycle meant absolute freedom for any city dweller. As a family, we never owned a car, so the only way to get around, as a kid, was to have a bike. With a bike, we could go to the next town and go to Dairy Queen, Stewarts Root Beer, and other places where other teens gathered. Plus, a few blocks away was an old RCA Factory. The streets in front of it were so smooth that you could ride your bike for blocks with no hands. It was so freeing to not pedal, put your hands out to the side and let your hair blow in the wind as you coasted. Plus, a bike allowed you to escape the house whenever you needed to get away. My brothers got bikes for Christmas, but Nanny never thought to get the girls a bike. When my mother overheard my sister Becky and me discussing how unfair it was that the girls didn't have a bike, she chimed in, stating, "You will break your hymen on a bike and then we'll have to take you to Doctor Stanley's office for a certificate stating you're still a virgin."

"Yea, thanks for your input, nut job!" Becky and I rolled our eyes at each other. Besides the freedom of escaping home at any time, it was exhilarating to know that I purchased the bike for myself. It wasn't a handout or a hand-me-down. I bought it with my own money. I earned it. It was something that was exclusively mine that I got for myself. This made me raise my arms even higher when I pulled my feet off the pedals and soared down the RCA blacktopped hills. Nanny was so proud of me because she never allowed us to let others know our circumstances. Even if we were starving and a neighbor offered us a cookie, we were taught to always refuse. Nanny said, "We still have our pride."

One day after delivering coffee, I pulled up in front of my house on my new Cadillac of bikes and put the kickstand down so I could run into the house and go to the bathroom before joining all of the other neighborhood kids at the courts. I was looking forward to playing touch football because when I was the steady quarterback, a boy who was a foot shorter than me named Jimmy Mancino kissed me every time I completed a pass. I began throwing perfect spirals to get that kiss.

When I came out of my house, my bike was gone. I couldn't believe it. My heart sunk to the pit of my stomach. Someone stole it. I called the police and they filed a report, but they concluded that it was my fault for not chaining it. "You know the colored kids from Newark come here looking for bikes every day, so I don't know what you were thinking," said the officer.

"How could you be so stupid?" is all Nanny said. "Next time, you'll know better."

What a loss. It was so hard to get the money together and to get the bike shop owner to give me a break. It was so great to use the bike to get coffee and to run errands and meet my friends at new and exotic places. It was my first taste of freedom and now it was gone.

A week later, a gang of us were sitting on our front stoop drinking RC Colas after playing football. Joe shouted, "Holy shit!" We looked up and there was a bum riding by on my bright yellow bike. Instantly Joe and the other guys chased him and surrounded him. They didn't touch him because he was so filthy. His face was covered with black sores. His hair and beard were dusty and matted. His blue flannel shirt was torn at the pocket and was covered with white caked stains. He reeked of urine, and the front of his blue jeans had a big wet circle in the crotch area. His feet were covered by work boots, but the toe of one boot was complete missing and he had no sock underneath it, so his charcoal toes were exposed.

Joe got close enough to the bum to push his shoulders, causing him to fall back a few steps before he gained his balance. "Give us the fucking bike back, asshole," Joe said. I was such a slow runner that I was last to reach the circle. While I was rushing over I was so excited that I would get my bike back. But when I got close and saw the pathetic man with my bike, my anger left me. His moist brown eyes contained that vacant look that I had seen so many times in my mother's face. Among the shouting and cursing of the other kids, there was a silent space that existed between him and me in which we shared a glance. I felt some type of connection to him. I looked at the basket of my bike and saw it was filled with aluminum cans and returnable soda bottles that he must have been collecting to turn in to get the deposit. Maybe that money was going to be his food for the day. I stood between him and Joe and said, "Let's go. That's not my bike. My bike didn't have a basket." Of course, it did, but everyone shut up.

"Let him go," I said and then turned to him and said, "Sorry, buddy, we had the wrong bike." He opened his mouth revealing black gaps where his teeth should have been, but it was not a smile. He growled, "Next time, I'll call the police on you brats."

He passed my house again the following week riding my beautiful yellow bike, and, as with everything else, I just had to turn my head and swallow my feelings so that they could erupt another day.

I saw so many people with the same look in their eyes when we went to Trenton just two weeks later. Nanny didn't allow my mother to return to our house from the hospital after her fifth admission, so life was sometimes interrupted by upsetting trips to visit my mother in Trenton State Mental Hospital. These were some of the most frightening experiences of our lives. We all took a train ride from Kearny to Trenton, which was always exciting. As a taxi drove us in past the wrought iron bars up the driveway, through the bucolic grounds, nothing was more remarkable than the vast difference between the outside of the place and the inside of the place.

Walking through the maze of hallways was like entering the *Night of the Living Dead* zombie movie. Memories are so vague now, but I recall men and women strewn throughout the hallways in white coats that ended at the waist, exposing their genitals. I don't know if this is reality or the nightmare. Everywhere we walked, we were escorted by a tall, muscular black man, dressed all in white, whose sole job was to keep the zombies off us. At every turn, patients with wild hair and glowing eyes tried to pet us as we passed. There was a man who thought he was Groucho Marx. He walked around the activities room in a tuxedo with a cigar hanging from his mouth, mumbling jokes.

What was worse is that each employee my grandmother approached to find out the whereabouts of my mother seemed as dazed as the patients. After asking directions, one woman in a nurse's uniform stared into Nanny's face and said, "You can go left or you can go right. The direction you choose in life is yours." It was worse than following a yellow brick road, only the munch-kins were really tall and ugly and Dorothy looked like Janis Joplin singing after her worst binge ever.

As we passed one hallway, I noticed that the doors only had a small window. Out of curiosity, I broke my rule of only look-ing forward and peeked quickly through the window so that I could see that the white walls were padded. I heard the horrific screams of a wounded animal inside and I broke down instantly. "That's her," I screamed. "That's our mother, I know it." I began to convulse with tears and pain, and my sister Renee came over and held me until it was over. It wasn't my mother.

When we finally did see my mother in the activities room, she smiled and asked, "Did you bring me cigarettes?" My grand-mother gave her the cigarettes and she giggled and walked away to get the picture she had painted in activities class. That was a typical visit. She never once asked about us. It was all about her.

We learned to deal with these visits through humor. Whenever my mother was scheduled to return from the hospital and we found ourselves anxiously sitting in the living room on our flowered couch covers, Billy suddenly started tapping his foot in a specific rhythm and asked, "Do you know what Stell is going to say when she walks through the door?"

By the time we were teens, we called my mother "Stell" because we couldn't call her any maternal names like "Mom." We found her new name when our mother told us that when she was younger her name was Estelle and not Clara. This was actu-ally the name on her birth certificate. However, black children in her neighborhood used to tease her by saying, "I's tellin on you. I's tellin on you." So she had her name legally changed to Clara when she was old enough to do so.

So, Billy asked, "Do you know what Stell will say when she comes home from Trenton?"

Then he jumped up and started singing, "I'm feeling those good vibrations. Good, good, good, good vibrations." Of course, he was referring to the electroshock treatments. Then, he threw on a scarf and changed his voice to Carole King's and sang, "I feel the earth move under my feet!" We laughed as he danced around. Billy was about five feet eight inches tall already and was exceptionally lean. He pushed his hands through his thick blond hair and grabbed a spatula or a hair brush as a microphone. He was a born entertainer.

Sometimes Billy placed a photograph of all of the kids in our family, my mother, and our black French poodle, Suzie, on the living room mantle. He had us all sit on the couch as if we were game show contestants. With a hairbrush as a microphone, he would deepen his voice like a TV announcer and turn to us and sing the Sesame Street song:

One of these things doesn't belong here.
One of these things just doesn't fit.
Can you guess what things doesn't belong here
Before I finish my song.

He would hold his blond head erect and glance back and forth from the mantel to us. "Hmm, what doesn't belong?" He would raise his eyebrows, revealing his sharp blue eyes, and feign hesitation at each photo as if he was really considering the choice. He would drop his arms and pretend he was drumming and make a fake drum roll sound with his voice and then pick out the photo of my mother, while leaving the photo of the dog. Again, we laughed and laughed…on the outside.

Billy provided the comic relief we often needed to protect ourselves from really feeling what was happening to us. He shared many funny stories when we got home from school.

He told us that one time when my mother was just home from the hospital, somehow he and Whitie were able to climb inside a free-standing brown metal closet in the master bedroom upstairs. Like contortionists, the two boys were able to roll themselves up into little balls and store themselves on the top shelf. They hid there and kept the metal door open ever so slightly so that they could see when my mother passed by. When she did, Billy lowered his voice into a deep manly voice and called, "Clara, Clara, I can see you, Clara." Whitie then provided the echo to Billy's calls. "Clara, Clara." Both boys covered their mouths with their hands to muffle their laughter and their stomachs hurt and they shook up and down on the closet shelf.

They could see my mother through the little crack in the closet door and knew she was looking all around. In a sing-song voice, Billy started again, "Clara, Clara, I can see you in your blue house coat."

My mother raised her arms to cover her ears in sheer panic and said, "Who's talking to me? Stop it, stop it. Am I am hearing voices?"

Billy and Whitie could not take it. It took everything within them to muffle their laughter. They bodies shook uncontrollably on top of the shelf. When he got control of himself, Billy started again, "Clara, can you hear me? Oh...Clara?"

"Stop it! Stop it!" my mother started crying.

Billy and Whitie were laughing so hard now that they had to jump out of the closet before they fell out. My mother screamed as they landed just behind her. "I'll kill you, you little whoremasters!" She started chasing them. But she could never catch them as they were down the stairs before she knew it. We all rolled off our chairs laughing when they told us about it.

Another time, Billy was given about $100 from relatives and neighbors for his confirmation. He had the money on his dresser in a pencil box. When he came home from school, he noticed that money was missing from the box. He immediately went to my mother and asked her what happened. She confessed that she took the money to buy cigarettes. Billy was furious, but there was not much he could do...we thought. But the next morning, when my mother woke up and went to the bathroom, "THIEF" was written across the medicine chest mirror in red lipstick. When she went down to the kitchen to make her coffee, a piece of notebook paper was in the coffee can and contained the word "THIEF." When my mother opened the loaf of Wonder Bread to make toast, the word, "THIEF" had been carved out of the slice of bread with a knife. When she opened the butter dish to butter her toast, an index card with the word "THIEF" in black magic marker was stuck to the butter. Every where my mother turned, the word "THIEF" greeted her...in her underwear drawer, on each cup of her bra, on her tee shirt. On her left black shoe in Wite-Out was TH, and on her right was IEF. When Billy came home from school, my mother shouted, *"For Christ's sake, take your God-damn $3 back. I'm your fucking mother!"*

Billy had one response: "THIEF," he shouted. She chased him out the front door and down the stoop. "I'll kill you, you fucking bastard child! Half of that money is mine."

Again, when Billy relayed the story, he made us laugh, and we found the craziness funny for just a few minutes.

While Stell was away from home living in a halfway house, Renee entered high school. Nanny found an all-girls' Catholic high school in Newark called Newark Catholic and enrolled Renee there as a freshmen. This was great, because we never wanted to go to public high school. In Immaculate Mary Elementary School, we were always taught to run from the public school students when they came to our school every Monday afternoon for Catholic instruction. We actually yelled, "Run, run, the publics are coming! The publics are coming!" We were so afraid of them because they were unholy.

We felt somewhat superior because even as we grew older, Renee and Becky were still singing in our local church and were the best players on the neighborhood girls' basketball team. My stories were being read by my teachers in my English class. Billy was a dancer in the school's annual productions, and Whitie was voted the best-looking boy in his class. He was also the first player picked by the older kids when any sport was played at the courts.

In the midst of this, Nanny gathered us in the living room to tell us that my mother wanted to come to visit us. The visit was going to take place while Nanny was at work, and it was going to be supervised by a social worker.

The night before the visit we all gathered in the boys' room while Nanny slept and whispered about how excited we were to see our mother. "Maybe she's better," Becky said. Billy and I made a plan to go to the five and ten and buy her a set of ceramic skunks. It included one ten-inch ceramic skunk with a rhinestone collar and a chain-link leash connecting it to five two-inch baby skunks. We thought that Stell would really this because she told us that all of her life she wanted a pet skunk.

When our mother arrived on the front porch the next day and we spied her through the living room window, we couldn't believe how good she looked. Her hair had been dyed from her mousy ash blonde to a sunny blonde, and she wore it pinned up neatly in a French twist. She wore soft powder blue eye shadow and light pink lipstick. Her tweed suit with a pencil skirt showed her shapely figure. She looked like one of the movie stars in a Hitchcock film, and we felt almost proud that she was our mother. She walked in with a new air of confidence and independence as if she had gone away to charm school.

We ran to her and she gathered us up in her arms, giving each of us a hug. She told us that she was feeling wonderful and that she had her own little place. She said that she was taking GED (General Educational Development) classes and was doing watercolor paintings. She lit a cigarette and held her head high as she put it to her lips. When she blew her smoke up in the air, I was certain that she could be a Hollywood actress.

Then she remembered that she had presents. She went out to the porch, where the social worker who was monitoring the visit was having a cigarette, and brought in a bag from Two Guys Department Store. She handed Billy a GI Joe doll; Whitie, a baseball glove; Becky, new bras and panties; and Renee, a bright striped guitar strap. She looked at me and seemed so sincere when she said, "Sweetheart, I couldn't find anything for you." She added, "I promise if you tell me what you like, I will get it for you next time I visit." I really was okay with that because she was being so pleasant to us.

She stayed and talked with us for a few hours. She stood up a few times and walked to the kitchen as if she were going to put on a pot of coffee or take out a frying pan to start cooking, but she paused in the doorway and seemed to be examining the wallpaper. Green vines of ivy wallpaper ran from the ceiling to the linoleum floor. She laughed and said in a barely audible voice. "That wallpaper always made me crazy. I hate that wallpaper." She ran her hands down the rough pink tweed in her suit and smiled as if to say, "I don't ever have to put up with it again. I don't live here anymore." She turned and said, "Okay, two big ones and three little ones, come give me a kiss goodbye." She put a tissue to her face as she started crying. She stood abruptly and walked out the door. We could hear the clicking of her beautiful black pumps until she passed the tavern next door.

We were giggling with excitement when she left because the visit had gone so well. When Nanny arrived from work, we told her all about it. Everyone showed Nanny what presents they received. Nanny turned to me and asked, "Where is your present?" I hesitated for just a second too long and then said, "She gave me a big bag of candy, but we all ate it already."

Nanny wasn't buying it. She was furious. She made all of the other kids put their presents back into the Two Guys bags and put them out in the trash. She said, "If everyone does not get a present, no one gets a present. She will never be allowed in this house ever again."

One day, Nanny was on the phone using this specific business voice that she had only used before on three occasions. The first time was on the day of the death of John F. Kennedy. The second time was on the day of the death of Robert F. Kennedy. The third time was the day her chartered bingo bus crashed on the way to the shore. She told the story over and over. "The driver lost control of the bus. We were driving in the ravine."

On this particular day, she was being evasive and focused on trying to have just a one-way conversation. I guess the gist of it was that my mother was found in a terrible state and that something happened to her in her "own place." Nanny disappeared for a few days and left us to be cared for by Grandma Polski. This was her Polish mother, who spoke very little English. We were a little bit afraid of her because she went senile every winter. She called me into her room and opened her top drawer and showed me a hammer, an apple, silk stockings, and an empty margarine container and said, "I am saving all for you, my darling."

She and I had a particularly close relationship, because every time I came home when she was staying with us, I stopped at the Spa Diner and bought a brown paper bag filled with french fries. I carried them up to her room and we shared them with lots of ketchup. Together we watched *Divorce Court* every afternoon. She cried and said, "Look, that no good dirty bastard, he beats her." And she wiped her entire face with Kleenex in a big circle, and then added, "The poor thing, she is so thin."

She also loved bingo. After attending bingo the night before, she gave me a full report as we shared our fries. She'd always tell the same story. "I sat next to a no-good dirty Irish woman," and then she'd spit into her tissue. Then a glow covered her wrinkled face and she said, "But then I met a beautiful Polish woman. It was a wonderful evening." Our moments of warmth ended when she asked me to run to the store for a pound of ham bologna. I was confused. "Grandma, do you want ham or do you want bologna?" She got infuriated and said, "You son of a bitch, just get me ham bologna." I had no idea this product existed.

It was great that she helped Nanny out by making us breakfast and dinner—but it was a real spit fest when the two of them argued in Polish as they did every night. When my grandmother came home from work her feet would be kicking and twitching whenever she was arguing loudly in Polish with her mother.

After the few days away, Nanny did take my mother back into the house, but my mother wasn't the same. She was meek and quiet and rushed around as if trying her very best to do what Nanny expected of her. The house was spotless. When we came home from school, she stood in front of the ironing board in the living room, smoking her cigarette, and there were five piles of perfectly ironed and folded clothes on the couch. She would say, "Everyone, take your pile and put them away." She had a hot lunch on the table when we came home for lunch, and we all tried to answer *Jeopardy* questions while we ate. Renee was the only one that didn't come home for lunch because she was enrolled in the Catholic high school in Newark, New Jersey. The absence of Renee, who was my grandmother's eyes and ears, seemed to allow my mother to relax a bit. We all laughed and told stories of our teachers and nuns and shared jokes. We enjoyed our favorite lunches, which were English muffins with Velveeta cheese, sandwiches and tomato soup, or Ellio's Pizza squares.

One day during my seventh-grade year, I was called to the principal's office just before classes were to be released for lunch break. When I got there, my sister Becky, who was an eighth grader, and my brothers, who were in fifth and fourth grades, were already there. They were just standing in from of the principal's desk, and Becky rolled her eyes as I came in because she assumed our mother did something embarrassing again. The principal cleared her throat and said, "Children, I have terrible news for you. Your grandmother died today at West Hudson Hospital. May she rest in peace. You are dismissed."

We were in shock. Nanny died at the hospital? Not a word was uttered as we walked home. The minute I entered the house, my great-grandmother met me in the doorway with Kleenex held to her eyes and nose and said, "Katra, you have to go right away to the shoemaker. I need new soles and heels on my black shoes. Wait for them. He is going to do it right away. Here's the money," and then she closed the door in my face.

"What? Ha? Are you kidding me? The shoemaker?" I asked. "How can I go to the shoemaker? Nanny is dead." I couldn't believe that I had to go to the shoemaker. I wanted to be with my brothers and sisters. I wanted comfort. I was so lost. Each step of the three-block walk was agony. I stopped after the first block and threw up in the gutter. I had never, ever imagined that Nanny could die. I never in my life felt so alone—not even in the basement. How could I be going to the fucking shoemaker today? The audacity of it has stuck with me for the rest of my life.

At least my anger and disbelief kept me from crying, that is, until I was on my way back with Grandma Polski's repaired shoes. I was in the middle of reasoning that maybe she was worried that when she knelt down before her daughter's casket, people would see her new heels and soles and think better of her. My inner struggle to understand how a mother could think about her black shoes on the day her daughter died was interrupted by the school bell. Lunch period was over, and I looked across the street and saw all of my peers walking, two by two, back into the school. Their loud, joyous chatter filled the street, and I felt so apart from them. Suddenly, I was so much older than they were, and I longed for their innocence. I cried violently, not because Nanny died, but because I wanted more than anything on earth to be one of them.

I have only one memory of my grandmother's funeral. My youngest brother, Whitie, was so physically upset that my grandmother's nephew, cousin Willy, took him outside the church. We didn't see him again for the rest of the funeral mass. When we filed

out of the church, Whitie was waiting outside with a new basketball. When I went home and opened my journal, I was greeted by
a poem I had written about Nanny just one month before.

You were warm
if you slept with my grandmother
on cold nights
any one of us would sleep there
A soft pillow arm to rest on
the other one always around you
as you listened to reassuring
singing snores
Soothing you to sleep
Flannel warmth surrounded you
Then suddenly you panic
Will she always be?
Then calm, rhythmic snores
Shushed you back to sleep
Always.

The day after my grandmother's funeral, the extended family
gathered at our house. This included my mother's brother, Uncle
Chaz, and my mother's sister, Aunt Jennie. These relatives were
frequent guests at our house. Chaz's wife, Auntie Rose, and Aunt
Jennie used to bring our cousins to our house every Sunday. Chaz
and Rose had two girls named Jackie and Caroline. Aunt Jennie
had four children, Jeanie, Marianne, Rosalee, and Joey. All of us
cousins had fun every Sunday playing freeze tag, hide and go
seek, and one, two, three, red light. When the adults called us
into our kitchen for dinner, they put the ironing board across two
kitchen chairs and six kids could sit on one side of the table using
the ironing board as our bench.

Our fun Sundays ended after my mother's sister, Aunt Jennie,
cut her wrist in our bathroom. She stopped in one day to see my

mother, but my mother was out at the store. Only Whitie, who was six years old, was home with a bad cold. Still, my mother left him as she ran to the store for cigarettes. Whitie hid under his bed when he heard the front door open and Aunt Jennie's high-heeled shoes clicking. He stayed there after he saw the bathroom door close. From his hiding place, he could monitor the bathroom door to spy to know where Aunt Jennie went afterwards. His cough medicine must have made him fall asleep, because the next thing he knew, two policemen were kicking open the bathroom door.

Whitie covered his head with a faded blue blanket that he had pulled down from the top of the bed to cover himself even further. When he peeked out from behind the darker blue ribbon trim, Whitie could see inside the small gap where the bathroom door was opened. Between the police officer's legs, he spied dark blood dripping from Aunt Jennie's dangling arm to the green linoleum floor as she lay lifeless and naked in the claw foot tub. He thought he was having a nightmare. He fell back to sleep. He was awakened again when my mother, who must have let the officers in to help Aunt Jennie, yelled from the bottom of the steps, "Would you officers like a nice, hot cup of coffee? Would you like anything else nice and hot?"

Whitie was constantly reminded of that scene of Aunt Jennie in the bathtub every Sunday when he went to church. As he looked around the church, he saw the same dark blood dripping from Jesus's head, hands, feet, and side. He saw more blood dripping from Mary's bleeding heart; blood smeared the face print in the painting of Veronica's veil. To him, there appeared to be blood everywhere in church. Whitie rubbed his wrists incessantly trying to erase what he saw in the bathroom. His only relief from his thoughts in church was the sound of Sister Marion clicking a handheld clicker, which she used to compel her class to kneel, stand, or sit on cue each Sunday.

After Aunt Jennie was taken away by the police officers, three of her children lived with us—so that my mother was then caring for eight children. Through Billy crouching and spying on the hallway steps, we had learned that our cousin Jeanie died of pneumonia. Joey, Jennie's youngest, was placed in foster care, and Marianne and Rosalee remained with us. Unfortunately, when my mother continued to have nervous breakdowns, Marianne and Rosalee were eventually placed in an orphanage. When we visited them there on the Sundays, we were so jealous of the life we perceived they had. They performed for Sunday visitors in various plays and recitals. More importantly, every girl had a pretty pink bed, with a top sheet and a bedspread and a beautiful crucifix above her head. We all shared beds at our house, and we never had a top sheet.

At home, when Nanny was on a house-cleaning tirade and in the middle of scolding us for not washing the kitchen floor properly, she threatened us, "Do you want to go to the orphanage? I will send you two boys to Boystown and the three girls to St. Anthony's. Is that what you want?" Our mouths offered no reply, but our hearts prayed, "Please, Nanny, yes! They have basketball courts at the orphanage!"

On the day after Nanny's funeral, as Uncle Chaz and Aunt Jennie commiserated, we all sat silently in the living room. Stell sat among us as if she were one of the children. We didn't say a word because Uncle Chaz was so loud and aggressive. We didn't really know him too well. Whenever he and his wife and our cousins visited us on a Sunday, he spent the whole day at Packy's Tavern next door. He came by afterwards to pick up his wife and kids to drive them home when he was ready. He staggered in and started ordering them around, and they rushed without saying a word. Their fear was palpable.

One day, my sister Becky was invited to stay at their house for the weekend. While she was there, my Aunt Rose talked on the phone as she set the table and prepared dinner. It was amazing how she knew just how long her phone wire was. It was like a fine-tuned ballet on a bungee as she reached for forks, bounced back to the table, went to a drawer for napkins, and sprung back to the table. While she performed in the kitchen, Uncle Chaz walked in the back door from work. He put down his tartan plaid lunch box and went right to his recliner chair in the living room.

He sat there for all of one minute without acknowledging my sister or his kids. Then, like a wild animal, he suddenly leaped out of the rocking recliner chair, causing the entire recliner to tumble and make a loud thud on the floor. As he neared the doorway between the living room and kitchen, he reached his hand around the corner and pulled the beige Princess phone right off the kitchen wall. The plaster of the wall fell, leaving a cloud of dust in the doorway between the two rooms. Auntie Rose screamed as Uncle Chaz grabbed the coiled phone wire, stretched it straight, and went towards her head as if he intended to wrap it around her neck. While his children huddled together on the couch, my sister Becky ran into the kitchen and said, "Stop it! Leave her alone!" She grabbed onto Uncle Chaz's thighs, and this was enough to distract him.

He said nothing, but his receding hairline turned crimson as he simply began undoing his belt. My Aunt Rose screamed, "No, Chaz, no!" She raced to beat him to the doorway and tackled Becky to the floor and threw herself on top of her. Aunt Rose writhed on top of Becky as her back absorbed all ten lashes Uncle Chaz released violently with the belt. When he had expended himself, Uncle Chaz grabbed his keys from the kitchen counter and walked right back out of the house. Aunt Rose went into the half bathroom in the hallway between the garage and the kitchen. Her kids starting putting the furniture back in place. No one said a word as they strained to hear the water running in the bathroom and listened as Aunt Rose coughed several times.

She opened the bathroom door, smiled, and said, "Come on, kids, let's eat. I made some fish sticks tonight. Take your places. Becky, you can sit here," she said as she pointed to Uncle Chaz's chair.

With that, everyone went to the table and ate in silence. Later that night, as Becky slept on the living room couch, she heard the bed above her in the master bedroom banging into the wall over and over and over again. She covered her ears with her freckled hands and cried herself to sleep.

When Becky came home and told us this story, we were so happy that we didn't have a father. Before this, we were so jealous of our cousins because they seemed to have everything—a beautiful house, nice clothes, and a mother and father. We were learning quickly that fathers, all men actually, were stronger and scarier than women.

Now, the six-foot-tall, 240-pound Uncle Chaz paced back and forth in our living room like the lion I had seen at the Bronx Zoo. The question on his mind this day seemed to be who was going to get what of what Nanny had left. Chaz called his sister Jennie over to the large free-standing freezer that stood next to our old Kenmore refrigerator. When he opened the heavy door, even from the distance, you could see it was packed with fine cuts of meat to rival any butcher store. The two of them did a rapid inventory: eye of round, crown roasts, strip steaks, flank steaks, pork chops, spare ribs, hot dogs, hamburgers, kielbasa, sweet sausage, hot sausage, and rolls of Taylor ham. Uncle Chaz ran next door to Packy's Tavern and came back with empty cardboard boxes. He loaded them with all of the meat in the freezer and placed them on the table.

He walked into the living room and said, "Now, I'm in charge of these kids and..."

He was interrupted by Aunt Jennie.

"What I want to know is how we're going divide this money. Why did she leave her money for these kids? It must have been a mistake. What are kids going to do with money? What about my kids? We should divide this money among us."

Aunt Jennie was a tall, slender woman with dark hair and the same light blue eyes as my mother. She frequently had a glass in her hand. Her usual drink was a highball, and she drank them all day during her Sunday visits. Whenever she had visited my grandmother regularly, she said the same thing: "How are you, Mamma? You know what I need?" I remember one Christmas when my young brother, Whitie, gave Aunt Jennie a bottle of Champagne Bubble Bath as a gift. She drank some of it and didn't like us too much afterwards.

"What do you mean, you're in charge of these kids?" asked a new voice in the conversation. My brother and I looked at each other in shock. "These are my kids," my mother said, stepping into Uncle Chaz's space. Uncle Chaz forced a loud roar of laughter. "Since when?" he asked as he towered over her, his words assaulting my mother like a schoolyard bully. "You're going to take care of them? You can't even take care of yourself. You're nothing but a blood-sucking leech and you have been your whole life!" My mother shrunk and went back to her place on the couch among the children.

My Aunt Jennie said, "Chaz, forget about these rotten kids. They are ingrates. What about the money?" It seemed that Nanny had left a $10,000 life insurance policy with Renee as the beneficiary. Renee couldn't touch the money until she turned eighteen years old. Even though Renee was just a freshman in high school, Nanny had left her in charge of the funeral arrangements as well. Finally, when they were all screaming at the same time, Renee stood up and screamed one of those guttural, life-changing screams and said, "Get the fuck out of our house, now! Just shut up and get out! We don't need any of you." She turned to us and said, "Come on, let's go upstairs." The five of us kids filed out after my sister. The room was silent as we climbed the steps until my Aunt Jennie said, "Fresh little things, aren't they."

The next day when we woke up and went down stairs to the kitchen, the freezer and all of the cabinets had been emptied by the scavengers.

As you could imagine, life changed dramatically with Nanny gone. My mother had no experience handling money or living on a budget. We still received Welfare through the Aid to Dependent Children program and her Social Security disability check, but they were sent to my grandmother's brother, Uncle Ted, who had become the legal guardian. We never saw him, ever. Instead, I walked to the Kearny Post Office once a month, where he left cash from the welfare checks with the clerk while he walked his beat as a town police officer. He wanted no association with us at all. Each month, I walked up to the window, picked up the checks in an envelope, and walked back home.

In the beginning of the month, there was a wild party atmosphere in our house. My mother bought pizza, candy, and lots of junk food with food stamps. Meanwhile, she used the very little available cash for the month, which was less than $100, to buy cigarettes and go to bingo. She also bought soap, shampoo, and laundry detergent at the beginning of the month, but sometimes this didn't last until the end of the month, and no more money was available.

By the end of the month, the refrigerator was empty and we were starving. This caused so much frustration, which led to many arguments. Rather than allowing us to use milk for a bowl of cereal, which could always fill our stomachs, my mother wanted every last bit of milk to be saved for her coffee. She shouted, "Who used my milk? That milk was for my coffee." I never understood how a mother of five children could think about herself rather than her children. The girls in our family always worried about whether Billy and Whitie had milk, not whether we had it for ourselves. Seeing my brothers hungry made me feel even more disgusted with my mother every day. Her self-centered behavior was in such contrast to all I believed a mother should be for her children.

My sisters had had enough of her. Now it was one against five. Whenever my mother made a move in my direction to deride me or smack me or pull my hair, there was a wall of siblings standing between us willing to protect me. As Renee and Becky reached fifteen and fourteen years old, respectively, they made a conscious decision that any type of abuse was just not acceptable anymore.

Unfortunately, despite their valor and the risks they were taking for me, the confrontations didn't always end with me gushing with gratitude and sharing warm feelings with them. Becky, especially, was constantly trying to protect me by taking the brunt of the physical abuse herself. She was so furious with me for being a victim. She said often, "Stand up for yourself. You're such a coward."

She was right, but she was also unaware that while in the basement, I learned from God or some guy that my mother didn't mean to hurt me. I felt sorry for my mother and knew how it felt to be treated the way she was by her mother. This stayed in the back of my mind always. And, sometimes, in their efforts to protect me, Becky was willing to hit my mother, and I just couldn't stand to see that. "Don't hit her!" I would scream. "She's our mother."

Trenton Psychiatric Hospital

SUMMARY OF HOSPITALIZATION

Disposition Summary

Patient Name: Clara Murphy

This is a 33 year old Caucasian, separated, Roman Catholic, female admitted to Trenton Psychiatric Hospital for the sixth time on a 7 day commitment paper. Mrs. Murphy's behavior was brought to the attention by police because she threatened to kill her children and on occasion actually hurt them. One child, after whom she suffered post partum psychosis, seemed to be the scapegoat for most of her tyranny. On admission, patient was loud, boisterous but friendly, her mannerism was quite inappropriate at times, smiling at no provocation. Conversations showed looseness of association, she denied hallucinations, delusions, homicidal or suicidal ideations. She claimed she wanted to be back in the hospital because she wanted some treatment, although she cannot be specific. Mrs. Murphy has no insight into her illness and exhibits extremely poor judgment. Although she is in contact with her environment, she is on occasion inappropriate and often very hyperactive. Her behavior is generally very childish and self centered. She will continue with her medication Mellaril 200 mg, Stelazine 10mg, Akineton 2 mg.

CHAPTER 7—JUNE 1973

MY MOTHER'S SEVENTH ADMISSION

Admission Quote: "My daughter had sex with my boss and he fired me."

Our busy schedules ensured that my siblings and I weren't home that much. All of us were able to find some odd jobs to pick up spending money. Renee worked at bingo a few nights a week, and Becky and I babysat for different families in the neighborhood every weekend. We were all also busy playing sports, doing schoolwork, and hanging out with our friends at the local park.

My mother even got a part time job working as a waitress "under the table" to try to earn extra spending money for bingo. While she worked, it was my job to start dinner and to make her coffee. I did my best to make the coffee the same every day because she was so happy and relieved to have her coffee ready when she got home. We settled into a routine, and before we knew it, all three girls were in high school.

We all attended Newark Catholic in Newark, New Jersey. Renee was a junior, Becky was a sophomore, and I was a freshman. We took two buses each day to get to school. We were lucky to even be going there because we could never afford the tuition. Renee was a freshman there when Nanny died, and she cried because she thought that she was going to have to leave and go to a public high school. The principal, Sister Eileen, found patrons, who were alumni, to pay the tuition for all three of us. She just made sure that we knew that we were expected to demonstrate our gratitude by doing our best and giving our utmost to the overall school program—which we tried to do every day of the four years. We were so grateful for the opportunity. People frequently asked how we managed to go to Catholic school our whole lives. The truth is that I don't know. We were told that Nanny had won the Irish Sweepstakes and had donated the entire amount to Immaculate Mary School. According to neighbors, that is how my brothers continued to go there after Nanny died.

Sister Eileen, the principal of Newark Catholic, was a heroic figure in our lives. She stood at five feet eight inches tall, but she seemed seven feet tall. She dressed in street clothes, not a habit, and wore her salt-and-pepper hair short and cut out over her ears. Her oval face was warm and she smiled easily. She had a way of making you do whatever she expected, but she did it by adding a quick smile at the end of the sentence. "You will have that math book covered when you arrive at school tomorrow." Then a smile. You listened because Sister Eileen's reputation preceded her. Stories circulated that in Renee's freshman year, a student brought a gun into school to shoot Sister Eileen. According to legend, Sister Eileen walked right up to within an inch of the girl, Davette, until the barrel of the black handgun was touching the belt of Sister Eileen's black and white tweed skirt. Sister Eileen said calmly, "Davette, you will hand me that weapon right now." No smile. Sister Eileen's demeanor was the same as Clint Eastwood seething, "Go ahead. Make my day."

Davette's lower lip quivered as tears streamed from her almond eyes. She put the gun in Sister Eileen's hand and then crouched down to the floor. Sister Eileen walked over and put the gun in a locker, checked the number, and locked it. She then walked over and put her arms on Davette's shoulders and said, "Come with me, dear. You're going to be OK." The police came to Sister Eileen's office and took Davette to the hospital. She never returned to school.

Another time, a girl named Tina was threatening to jump from the balcony to the gym floor below. The word around school was that she was high on heroin and thought she could fly. As Sister Eileen got closer to her, Tina shouted, "Get back, bitch, I'll jump. I'm not playing." Sister Eileen reached out her hand with her practical white gold Timex watch glistening in the streaming light and said one sentence. "Come with me, dear." Tina listened.

Sister Eileen began each school year with a speech that started with "Today is the first day of the rest of your life." And you believed her, because in the middle of the decay of the city of Newark, New Jersey, Newark Catholic was a beacon of hope and Sister Eileen was bigger than Superman.

As if it were a new day, amazing things happened to us while we were in high school. Our paternal grandmother showed up at our house. One day when my brothers came home from grammar school, there was a short woman with wavy auburn hair and wearing a black coat with a fur collar standing on our front porch. As my brothers approached her, she said, "Why, hello, Billy, hello, George," and smiled kindly at them. They were shocked that this woman knew their names. They were both taller than she was and she looked up at them with such admiration.

Billy stepped up and said, "Good afternoon, what can we do for you?"

She said, "I am your grandmother."

Whitie said, "Our grandmother isn't here. She just passed away."

The woman smiled and said, "Yes, dear, I am aware of that. I am your father's mother."

Billy said, "We don't have a father."

She giggled and said, "Of course you do. I am your grandmother on your father's side."

Billy invited her in for tea.

She was still there when the rest of us came home from school. We were all sitting around the table having a cup of tea with sugar cookies, and our new grandmother told us that Nanny never allowed our father or her to see us. Now that Nanny was dead, she wondered if we wanted to get to know her.

We couldn't believe this. Maybe there was someone in the world who cared about us after all. Our new grandmother invited us to her house for Sunday dinner. She lived in Newark, New Jersey—in what was considered a very rough neighborhood. In fact, my grandmother was the only white person who lived in the area. When we arrived at her house, we quickly ran up the front porch steps because a group of black kids were sitting on the front porch next door. They started saying, "White devils, what you doing here?" We just ignored them because they seemed even more dangerous than the publics.

My grandmother served us an amazing home-cooked meal, which included roast beef, mashed potatoes, creamed-style corn, green beans, and applesauce. At the table, we met two new relatives. Our grandfather was a thin, sickly man who we learned hadn't been out of the house for twenty years. He had tuberculosis and was placed in a sanitarium to be quarantined. After surgery, he was left with one lung and couldn't make the climb down the steps of their second-floor apartment to ever leave the house. I felt a special connection to him because throughout my elementary school years, I had to go to get chest x-rays every six months and take medication because I was exposed to TB. I guess he was how I got exposed. We must have lived with my grandparents at one time or another as babies and we just didn't know it.

Despite his illness, my grandfather was as cheerful as ever and never stopped telling corny jokes. "What is a honeymoon salad? Lettuce alone with no dressing." Grandpa also loved to feed people. As soon as we entered his kitchen, he hopped out of his chair at the head of the table and said, "What will it be, kids? Ham, turkey, roast beef, corned beef, you name it, we got it! Pound cake, brownies, ice cream, what'll you have?" Every once in a while, he had one half of a beer and felt good and started singing "K-K-K-Katie, K-K-K-Katie, I'll be waiting by the K-K-K-kitchen door." My father's mother yelled, "Stop singing, you fool." Grandpa said, "Come on, Kate, give an old man some nourishment. Drop one of those teats into my mouth." Grandma turned beet red and threw a pot holder at this head.

Grandpa's special offering was, "Kids, how about some toasted pound cake with butter?" He made a homemade pound cake every day. I answered, "Grandpa, I'll get too fat." He barked back, "Nonsense. A woman should provide warmth in the winter and shade in the summer. A man needs something to hold onto, too. You weren't built for speed, you were built for comfort!"

Grandma's faced turned red, and she said, "George, stop it! You get to your room now!" Grandpa replied, "Only if you're comin' in for a little afternoon delight." We couldn't help but giggle, but our new grandma was furious.

We also met one of our father's brothers, Uncle Mike. He wore a work uniform and sat very quietly drinking coffee at the table throughout the visit. As he sipped black coffee and listened to his mother answer questions about our childhood, Mike's face grew red. Then he put the small china tea cup down onto the saucer with force and chimed in once in a while. "You kids were filthy. Your mother never took care of you. You were disgusting!" and then he went silent again. He was never married and still lived with our grandmother although he was forty years old. When we asked him why he never married, he said, "After I saw what happened to your father, I was determined to never get married. You kids ruined your father's life. He had a scholarship. Your father could type one hundred words per minute."

Before we left, Uncle Mike reached into his pants pockets and pulled out a wad of bills. He gave each of us $20 and said, "Get yourself some ice cream." We refused the money, as Nanny taught us to do. Uncle Mike grew furious and said, "You take this money." So we took it thinking, "Wow. What expensive ice cream."

Our Sunday afternoons at our other grandmother's house became a routine. It was so exciting to unearth a past that existed in photographs in her attic. We had never seen photos of ourselves as babies because they weren't available to us. We sat with my father's mother on her couch, which was covered with plastic, and flipped through photos of our father and his brothers and learned stories that were previously untold.

"Your mother always hated you," she told me. To change the subject, I looked up at my father's mother's ruddy Irish face and asked, "Was I cute when I was a baby?"

She said, "You pretty much always looked the same."

Then she held up a photo of me as a cherub-faced one-year-old baby sitting between my two sisters. We were all smiling, and all I could wonder is how someone hated such a cute and happy baby.

Each Sunday, we enjoyed the same menu, and we loved it because it felt like we had a family. All of our neighborhood friends always returned to their grandmas' houses for Sunday dinner, so now we felt as if we were part of an exclusive club.

It wasn't always fun to be in her neighborhood. Once when we were driving to our grandmother's house, we had the windows rolled down because Renee's car didn't have air conditioning. When we stopped at a red light, a black teenager walked up to the car and punched Billy in the face for no reason. Other times, just going from the car to the house was so frightening because the black kids on the neighboring porch continued to badger us: "Blond-haired, blue-eyed devils! Get out of our neighborhood."

Then, because my grandfather had not left the house in twenty years, he didn't realize how much the neighborhood had changed. He often asked my brother Whitie to run to the A&P grocery store for an eye of round roast. Whitie refused at first because it was eight blocks away. My grandfather replied, "Get going, boy! Don't be lazy." Whitie sprinted as fast as he could because he was so afraid of the black kids in the neighborhood. Later in life, he became a championship runner. We attribute this talent to food shopping in my grandmother's neighborhood.

Still, the introduction to this new dimension of our lives filled us with immeasurable hope. We had a father. He was alive. He had red hair and freckles just like our sister, Becky. He wasn't a garbage man. These were concrete details. He was probably coming on a white horse to save us at last. Every night, when I thought my silent prayers—even though I pretended I didn't believe anymore—the face of my handsome God now became the face of my imaginary father. I folded my hands and whispered into the air:

> *Our Father,*
> *who art in New Jersey,*
> *somewhere,*
> *Hallowed be thy name.*
> *What kingdom from? Will you come?*
> *Make our earth into a heaven,*
> *Give us this day*
> *Some daily cash or bread to*
> *Deliver us from evil.*
> *We will forgive your trespasses*
> *Now and at the hour*
> *Of your arrival,*
> *Amen.*

Yet the idea of meeting our father was somewhat insignificant compared to what was happening at school, because we loved our high school. The best part about it for me was that it didn't matter how beautiful or ugly you were because, unlike in the public schools where my grammar school friends attended, popularity was based on achievement, not looks. Since I always felt ugly every day of my life, and was in fact too ugly for my mother to kiss good night, it was great that looks didn't matter at school. The smartest, funniest, talented, and most athletic girls were the most popular girls in our school.

At the same time, we were never treated like girls. From the first day of high school to the last, we were trained to think about our contributions as women to society and not personal gain. This training was taking place in classrooms where white girls, black girls, and Hispanic girls were all best friends.

All of the hopelessness at home was thoroughly balanced with all of the hopefulness of Newark Catholic. Each day of school brought so many unique experiences. Instead of English class as we knew it before, which included diagramming sentences and constant grammar lessons, we were enrolled in communication arts.

This one-and-a-half hour class took place in a huge open classroom that was furnished with six to eight couches, trunks, beanbag chairs, coffee tables, and throw rugs. Instead of desks, all of our learning took place in small groups sitting around these living-room areas. Every semester, a team of six teachers presented sixty freshmen with the themes they were offering for that semester. Sample topics included urban justice, special education, women in society, the family, religion and society, school around the world, war, the generation gap, social status, or international studies. Students selected their top three choices for a theme, and the teachers tried to give each student her first choice. Then, smaller study groups were formed.

Within your group, you spent the semester studying the theme using different approaches. First, you read literature on the theme. Reading novels entailed reading them at home or on the couches and oversized floor pillows in our unique classroom. Then, as an individual or as a group, we could go to a resource room to find more information related to our theme. In the urban justice group, for example, we researched the law and prisons in America. Each day, the teacher spent a part of the class period discussing topics related to the theme. This was always intense because the group sat in a circle and talked quietly so to not disturb the other groups. Each person around the circle took on a new tone of seriousness as she formulated her contributions and listened carefully to other group members. Teachers were facilitators, not lecturers, who ensured that each member was involved, but no one was ever forced to participate.

After discussions, girls dispersed and sat on Oriental rugs leaning against a trunk or wall to write their daily journal. The journal could be a response to the discussion, to the book, or just your thoughts of what was going on in your life for that day. The journals were collected every Friday. The teacher read the journals over the weekend and wrote comments. Then, she selected samples to read to the group throughout the next week. It was such an honor to have your journal read to the group. It was my top priority to achieve this goal every week. I took my time to craft every journal to ensure that it evoked emotion. Nothing was more important to me during my freshman year than opening my journal on Monday and reading the teacher's comments, usually done in blue marker. I would scan the white pages, and my eyes would go right to her comments. "Great job! This would make a wonderful short story." Every comment made my heart pound with excitement because it was a shared connection with an adult I admired. Sometimes, the journal was just a little portrait of everyday life, as in this example:

"It's ten o'clock. Do you know where your children are?"asked the television in an uncaring voice. Mrs. Hayes shrugged and clicked it off with her new remote control. She put on her pink fuzzy-wuzzy slippers and walked to the kitchen, where she filled the teapot and set it on the aged yellow stove. Drops of water sizzled as they hit the burner. Her long, crooked fingers pushed back her grey hair, revealing eyes entrapped and shadowed by three wrinkles on each side of her face. "They're gone now," she said aloud.

"Everybody's gone now." She shrugged again, causing the strap on her nightgown to fall from her white shoulder to the middle of her arm. She left it there and walked to the teapot, which was desperately screaming out—as she wanted to do so badly.

After reading and writing in the classroom during the school day, my urban justice group went on off-site trips to explore our theme firsthand. The city of Newark was our great resource. We didn't need teachers to go with us. Instead, teams of students left school, traveled by public bus, and visited courthouses and watched court cases. This was fascinating, and we learned about how our justice system worked and observed the importance of a good legal argument. I returned to school and joined the discussion with the group and was so surprised that, like my classmates, on the first few days of the trial, I was 100 percent supportive of the prosecutor in a case of a young man accused of using and selling drugs. During the second week of the trial, when I heard the defense arguments, I was 100 percent behind the defendant. I came back to school saying, "The man was tired from studying so hard and working two jobs. He needed those drugs to relax." This was a fascinating way to learn, and I woke up every single day excited about going to school.

Speakers also came to our school to speak to each group about their subject. Prisoners from the Fortune Society visited us and didn't hold back in retelling their raw stories because we were female. One man shared a story about how he saw a prisoner rip another man's testicles right off his body. Listening to their stories, I couldn't believe how many men seemed to be in prison because of their childhood. Prisoner after prisoner shared a biography that included a childhood lacking caring parents and neighborhoods that offered a different sense of belonging as members of a gang.

We also visited the FBI building in Newark and learned about the day-to-day work of law enforcement officials and saw how difficult their jobs were in a city like Newark, where problems seemed insurmountable. At the end of the semester, our team had one week to create some form of presentation for the entire freshman class that allowed our classmates from other groups to experience what we learned through our topic.

For the presentation, our group dressed in black and stepped onto a darkened stage. Set design and lighting gave the impression that we were behind bars. Each of us recited a vignette detailing a life of childhood neglect and abuse that ended with our imaginary prison sentence, "twenty to life." The words on the program left our audience with something to ponder: "Are we a just society?" With me as the emcee, we held a lengthy discussion afterwards. One audience member stood and said with conviction, "The laws of our country are based on even more important laws, which are those established by God and handed down to Moses. People deserve to be punished if they cannot live by the laws."

A member of our group answered, "Is it wrong, in the richest nation on earth, to steal food if you are hungry? Is it wrong to dishonor your mother and father if they are not worthy of your respect?" Another said, "Your brother is in the army. Is it wrong for him to kill an enemy soldier who is about to kill him?"

Students and teachers both instantly stood waiting for their chance to be recognized by me and to share their opinion. It was a riveting discussion ,and every single experience in communication arts shaped my future.

For the special education unit, we had to read *Lisa: Bright and Dark* and *Flowers for Algernon*, and the short story "Silent Snow, Secret Snow." Then we visited students in special education schools and tutored them. We learned about adaptations that could be made to help special needs students learn. We watched a film that allowed you to experience what it is like to be a student with special needs. We met students with autism who were trapped within their bodies as doctors tried to unlock the mysteries of their disease. We did this in 1972, way before these topics were popular.

The one theme that was very tough for me was mental illness. I shouldn't have selected it. We read works by Edgar Allan Poe and Sylvia Plath, and we acted out *One Flew Over the Cuckoo's Nest*. We read many case studies by Sigmund Freud and were assigned the task of creating a model of our mind. I took a shoe box and glued a nude photo of a man from Playgirl magazine on the back of the inside of the shoe box. Then, I took grey yarn and made a web slightly in front of my nude male photo. On top of the web, I glued words and pictures of school, family, friends, sports, etc. Then, on the cover of the shoebox, I made a face of a girl from construction paper using yellow for blond hair, and I cut out holes for the eyes so that when a viewer looked into the eyes, they could see my "mind." When I brought the finished project into my group and had to explain my mind, my teacher asked about my choices. I told her that according to Freud, the sex drive is man's motivating force. She thought it was excellent, but had to eventually hide it in the closet because every class that day was being interrupted by classmates trying to get a peak at my gorgeous naked man and his casually displayed penis.

In later years, our group went to the movies to see the film *One Flew Over the Cuckoo's Nest*, starring Jack Nicholson. I was fine watching the movie until they started to perform electric shock therapy on the main character, MacMurphy. I ran out of the movies crying. My teacher ran after me, but I told her that I couldn't go back into the movie. I was too upset and embarrassed. My teacher was very tender as she asked me to explain, but the words gagged me as I held them back. "Never tell people what goes on in this house," echoed in Nanny's voice in my head and kept me from explaining as my teacher stood helpless.

One of my teachers in communication arts thought that my journal showed that I had potential as a writer. She was a brilliant young lay teacher with long red hair and a cool, hippy vibe about her. She was so intelligent that just being in her presence put me in a state of constant anxiety. She always made me feel as if she thought that I was as bright as she, and it just wasn't true. She believed that there was much more to me than there really was. She was only in her early twenties, but she seemed as if she could accomplish anything. What made her an exceptional teacher was that she always connected ideas from all subject areas throughout history when she taught. She would bring in artwork, foreign language, current events, and film to make a lesson come alive. Her husband graduated from Georgetown University, and when we were studying government in another group, she took us on a trip to Washington, D.C., to see all of the sights. We got to go for free because we slept in dorm rooms of her husband's friends. Since we were the type of family that never left New Jersey, the trip to Washington, D.C., and another to Boston were great eye-openers for me.

Once this gifted teacher invited me to her apartment in Greenwich Village to meet published authors and to share some of my writing with them. This was such an honor. I took the Path train after school and arrived before the guests. The apartment was a beautiful, open loft, and her dining table was set for a formal meal. When I arrived, she was just getting out of the shower and asked me to go to the market, a few doors down, to get "a really good cucumber" for the salad. I took the money from her hand and headed to the elevator. Instantly, I was filled with panic. What the hell is a really good cucumber? I was gone for an hour as I walked aimlessly throughout the market holding up the cucumber I selected. I dashed from person to person in the store asking, "Is this a really good cucumber?" Then, to a black businessman, "Is this a really good cucumber?" Then, to a blonde woman in a house dress, "Excuse me, would you classify this as a really good cucumber?" I wanted to please her more than anyone.

When I returned from the store, my teacher was visibly upset. "Where did you go? I was so worried." I felt as if I had disappointed her and that I was being yelled at, and I couldn't recover for the rest of the evening. When I looked at the table, I panicked again, because I had no idea of what fork to use. We didn't even have paper napkins in our home—never mind fancy cloth napkins and several pieces of silverware at each place setting. Meanwhile, the food was a tomato, hollowed out, with a runny egg inside and some type of yellow sauce on top. I gagged at the site of it. When the writers arrived and were all having cocktails and talking, I felt like Benjamin in the beginning of *The Graduate*. I was so out of place. While my teacher, Mrs. Levinsky, was in the kitchen preparing dessert, I quietly opened the door to the apartment and left. She never mentioned the situation to me and never treated me any differently.

I wondered if she ever knew how her few scribbled words in a notebook sustained me. I would close my journal and clutch it to my chest to allow the blue Magic Marker letters to penetrate my soul to convince me that I was worthy. Her casual notes, which she may have jotted while drinking a glass of wine and reviewing student journals, became my cherished love letters.

The way Newark Catholic handled religion class gave me hope as well. We always studied all forms of religion, and it always included a semester of community service. One day a week, instead of staying in religion class, we had to take a bus to go to perform community service at various locations throughout the city. My first community service location was a nursing home. I was sick to my stomach the entire time I was there because the institutional environment brought back terrible memories of Trenton State Hospital. I tried to push through my feelings and was given the assignment of helping patients to attend a recreation program. I went from room to room asking people, in a cheerful voice, if they wanted to go to recreation. Most said no, but then I got a big smile from a shriveled, pasty white gentlemen who was waiting in a wheelchair by the elevator door. I smiled back and said, "Good afternoon, sir, would you like to go to recreation today?" He smiled again and made a gesture with his hand for me to come closer. I walked up closer and he gestured me again to lean in even closer to him still. I leaned in and he smelled of sour milk and urine. When my ear was close to his crusty lips, he whispered in my ear, "I know you do it. I can tell by the way you walk." I ran away shocked and disgusted and never went back to the nursing home again. I had other great experiences working with special needs children and helping in the maternity ward of the hospital.

Each year, our class participated in a religious retreat at the Jersey shore. This trip was less about religion and more about spirituality, goal setting, and seeing yourself as a strong and capable woman in the context of a challenging world. Each day of the four-day weekend retreat featured a speaker who shared his or her life story with the group. Some were recovering drug addicts; some were priests and nuns who told the story of how they found their calling in life. One was a nun who left the convent and married a doctor who was a widower with six children. Their stories were always about choice, self-awareness, forgiveness, and second chances.

The most important lesson that these speeches taught me is that if I ever thought my life was difficult, there was always someone's life that was much worse. In first grade, Sister Rose used to say, "If everyone walked into a room and placed his or her cross in middle of the floor, and everyone had a chance to look at everyone else's crosses and to pick one that he or she preferred over his or her own, every person would pick up his or her own cross and leave the room satisfied." I never understood the meaning then. I wondered, "Why are people carrying crosses?" After studying communication arts class and attending my first retreat, it occurred to me that I finally understood what Sister Rose meant.

At my freshmen year retreat, I was overwhelmed with the beauty of Harvey Cedars, a complex owned by the Sisters of Charity at the Jersey shore. Seagulls greeted us with welcoming calls, and we all immediately headed to a back dock that went far out over the bay. We could look down into the water and see fish and turtles swimming by. After participating in a variety of leadership and trust activities during the first morning, I joined a discussion group in the library. There, I listened to a pretty young novice, training to become a nun, tell her story about being raised by an alcoholic father who had beat her mother to death. She told about running away from home and living on the streets and getting involved in heroin. She finally got help in a homeless shelter when she met a priest who saved her life.

She described how, at the depth of her sadness, wishing she would just die, the priest wrapped his arms around her like a loving father while she cried and rocked her and told her that everything was going to be all right. She cried in his arms until she was exhausted. He helped her to get straight and to find herself again, and she was now giving herself to God in order to help others. There was something in the warmth in her eyes and the pious glow on her face that told me right then and there that that was exactly what I needed—just not the part about becoming a nun. Instantly, I was filled with jealousy and aching longing. I hungered with every fiber of my being for a father to hold me tight and to fill the hollow, aching emptiness.

I had to admit that ever since we met my father's mother, I went to sleep picturing the day I would meet my father. I imagined that he was tall and slender, with slicked-back hair like handsome Uncle Mike. If he had tried to save us so many times before, but was turned away by my grandmother, I knew he would want to save us now. I imagined every night how life would be different if we just had a parent who willingly put his arms around me and kissed me good night. I imagined that with two jobs, he would be able to help support us financially and to take care of us just a little bit. But even if he was not rich, he would have two strong, manly arms and could wrap them around me, and I could be as lucky as the girl at the retreat. My singular focus in life was going to be finding this feeling and keeping it forever.

The retreat experience and everyday life at Newark Catholic was filling me with optimism. Every day, I was presented with the most perfect role models. Besides being the leader of our high school in Newark, which had a 99 percent college graduation rate, Sister Eileen, our principal, was a personal hero to us. As my mother went in and out of the mental hospital, as the principal of our school, she never informed anyone that we were living alone. She allowed us to sign our own report cards and permission slips. And she was also an advocate for us outside of school. Once, I was summoned to the Hudson County Welfare Office in Jersey City, New Jersey, for an audit. I don't know how I was chosen to represent our family in these situations, but it was always my job to go.

I took a day off of school and traveled by Path Train to Journal Square. Once I got to the office, I joined a small crowd of others waiting for their turn to see a representative. From 8:00 a.m. till noon, I sat and waited. The whole time, it was easy to look across the pole and rope barrier between the workers and the recipients to see that the workers were talking and laughing and not doing any work whatsoever. Every now and then, they looked over at the group of recipients and turned to each other and made comments and laughed loudly.

The recipient group was filled with various shapes and shades of women, many who had small children with them who struggled and cried as they grew restless. One Hispanic woman walked up to the ropes with her three-year-old baby and said, "I have been here for two hours. Can you tell me how much longer it will be, because I have to be home to get my son off the bus."

The thin black woman at the first desk didn't even look up to acknowledge that the Hispanic woman was speaking to her. After waiting for a few minutes, the Hispanic woman just walked back to her seat. At noon, a heavyset black woman came out to address the group and said, "We're going to lunch now. We will take more cases at 1:00 p.m."

Take more cases? They hadn't taken one all morning. A few of the weary women in the room turned and mumbled to each other, but most sat silent and numb. I had no money to leave for lunch, and I didn't want to lose my place. We had been given numbers, and I was number seven in line since the morning—lucky number seven.

At 1:00 p.m., they started to call names. When I was called into a small, cluttered cubicle at 1:30, a white woman with a red beehive hairdo motioned for me to sit down. When I did, she opened up a bag and took out a tuna fish sandwich. The over-powering smell of the onions and tuna reached me instantly. I was so hungry that the smells actually made me sick. She ate the entire sandwich with me sitting in the room and didn't say a word. I couldn't say anything, either, because we needed this money to live. When she finished, she made a big gesture to wipe her face, and the orange imprint of her lips smeared the napkin.

She asked me a few questions about whether my mother was working or not. I told her no. She asked if we received child support from our father. I told her no. Then she asked, "Why are you on welfare? Why don't you quit school and get a job like everyone else has to do, so you don't have to be on welfare?" I shrugged and said nothing until she stamped a card and handed it to me, but on the inside I shouted, "I am fourteen, asshole! You call what you do work?"

As I left the cubicle and crossed the pole and rope barrier, I kicked three or four folding chairs as I left. The next day, I told Sister Eileen what happened. She said, "Come with me." She practically ran down the senior hallway in Newark Catholic, down a secret faculty stairway, to the parking lot where a light blue K-car was waiting. She said, "Get in." She drove us to Jersey City to the welfare office and asked to speak to the director. Ironically, a man named Mr. Goodhand came out. Sister Eileen calmly told the story and finished it with "I'm not leaving until something is done about this." She handed Mr. Goodhand the card that I was given. He went into the cubicle and came out with Big Red. The agent cowered under the gaze of Sister Eileen—as everyone did. She looked at me and said, "I'm sorry that I ate my lunch at my desk in front of you yesterday. I'm sorry for what I said about dropping out of school." Mr. Goodhand turned to Sister Eileen and said, "Mrs. Olson will be suspended for three days." Sister Eileen said, "Let's go."

While we drove home, Sister Eileen explained to me, "The people working in that building are the ones on welfare. They are taking taxpayer money and aren't doing any work. They are the ones who should feel shame, not you. The difference between you and that woman is that she has a choice every day. You don't have a choice right now, but I know for certain that your children will never be on welfare." Sister Eileen took me to McDonald's for lunch, and it was a great day as we felt victorious.

Sister Eileen always stepped in to help us when we needed assistance with books or uniforms, but at the same time, she never let us get away with anything. One time, when it was snowing heavily but school wasn't cancelled, my sisters and I didn't feel like trudging through the snow to catch our two buses to school. So we wrote an excuse note to Sister Eileen.

Dear Sister Eileen:

Please excuse the Murphy girls for being absent from school yesterday as our dog sled was in need of repair.
The Murphys

Sister Eileen didn't find the note humorous. She made us come to school for four Saturday detentions. Each week, we had to polish all of the wooden banisters and wash and wax floors for six hours each day. We would never try that again.

Because we were so busy with schoolwork and extracurricular activities two buses away from home, we settled into a tolerable routine. We were all basically only home to eat and sleep, so we stayed out of our mother's way and she stayed out of ours. Then, one day during my freshman year of high school, I came home from school and began to make a package of chicken legs for dinner. When I removed the plastic cover from the package of twelve chicken legs, I couldn't believe the horrible smell. I had never smelled it before. Quickly, I took the package down the street to Mrs. Finnerty's house and asked her to smell it. She said that the chicken had spoiled and that I couldn't cook it because everyone would get sick. She threw it right into her garbage can in the alley and sent me home.

On the way back home, I worried what my mother was going to say when she came home and there was no dinner ready. I honestly didn't know what to do. So, when I got home, I dialed the phone number of the restaurant where she worked. A man answered the phone, and I asked if I could speak to Clara. He said, "Clara is busy, what do you want? Maybe I can help." I explained to him that I was supposed to make chicken for dinner and that it was spoiled and wanted to know if I should make something else. He said, "Don't worry about it. Your mother will be home soon."

I felt so relieved that I sat down at the dining room table and started to do my homework. In religion class, we were given a new Bible, and our homework assignment was to make a Bible cover. This was an unusual project for a Catholic school because we had never really read the Bible much before. As I sat at the dining room table, I covered the Bible with pink felt, and then I cut a few circles of brown felt to make a teddy bear. I made some arms and legs and then added white eyes, a black nose, and a cute little pink tongue. I then traced and cut out letters that said, "God is like a teddy bear. He comforts me."

Just as I put the glue on the last letter, I heard my mother come in the door. I stayed seated in the chair and continued my project because she usually went upstairs and changed first before she came down to get her coffee. Before I knew it, her hand smacked me so hard across the side of my face that blood spewed out of my nose all over my Bible cover. The pink felt background was now polka-dotted with blood. I was stunned, but I was so angry that I tried to stand in protest, and she shoved me back in the chair from behind and was tugging my head back and forth by my hair. I was as tall as she was now, so I should have been able to defend myself, but her superhuman powers were present. She simply overpowered me because of the leverage she had while I was in a sitting position. I screamed, "What are you fucking doing?"

She said, "You got me fired today! You little fucking whore! You got me fired. Why did you tell my boss that you wanted to fuck him? Do you think that was funny, pig? You fucking little whore!"

As she continued her verbal and physical attack, suddenly Renee ran down the stairs and screamed, "Leave her alone, you fucking bitch." My mother turned on her and said, "Don't you ever talk to me like that," and smacked her across the face.

Renee said, "You're not going to get away with this shit anymore. Leave her alone." My mother started towards Renee, but was stopped in her tracks when Renee said, "I fucking hate you. I am leaving and I am never coming back to this nut house." Renee grabbed her Newark Catholic basketball coat off the banister and went out the door and slammed it behind her.

My mother turned to me and said, "Do you see what you made her do? You're an instigator who's always causing trouble. You're not even my daughter. I hate you and I've always hated you." I ran up the stairs, slammed the bedroom door, and stayed in my room. As the other children got home from school, Stell told them that Renee ran away because I got Stell fired from her job.

They immediately came upstairs and asked me the real story. Renee didn't come home that night. She didn't come home the next day or the next night. My mother finally called the police. They asked us if we knew where Renee was, and we honestly didn't. My mother spent day and night just pacing the floors. She went to the sink and washed her hands over and over again. She poured water, drank a sip, and then poured it out, and then did it again the very next minute. She did this nonstop for the whole weekend.

It turns out that Renee was hiding out in Barricini's Candy Store in Penn Station, where her friend Yolanda worked. She slept in the store overnight and ate candy when she was hungry. When we went to school on Monday, she told Sister Eileen what happened, and Sister Eileen drove her home and had a long talk with my mother that day. Because of her fear that Sister Eileen might find out that she was the one who killed Jesus Christ, my mother cowered under her gaze and promised Sister Eileen that she would keep her hands off of her children.

Trenton Psychiatric Hospital

SUMMARY OF HOSPITALIZATION

Disposition Summary

Patient Name: Clara Murphy

This 33 year old, white, separated, Roman Catholic female was admitted to this hospital on 7 day commitment papers. According to commitment papers, patient was belligerent, having auditory hallucinations, she wanted to be left alone. She hit her 17 year old daughter for no reason. She was easily excitable and showed bizarre behavior. On admission, patient was correctly oriented to place, person and time. Her memory was fair; she was over talkative, repetitive, disorganized thinking flights of ideas. She admitted to having auditory hallucinations. She showed poor insight into her condition, her judgment was impaired.

After a month of hospitalization her mental condition improved. She seemed to be in much better contact with reality and with her surroundings. Conversation became much more coherent and relevant and she has however a tendency to be over productive. Because of her overall improvement, she has been transferred to an open ward. She will continue her present medication.

CHAPTER 8—MAY 1974

MY MOTHER'S EIGHTH ADMISSION

Admission Quote: *"I'm all right. I will stay here."*

Whether my mother was hospitalized or not became irrelevant to our lives. Renee was a senior in high school, Becky was a junior, I was a sophomore, and the boys were in eighth and seventh grades. Renee called a family meeting, and we gathered around our oval oak table. She said, "Nanny told us to stick together like glue, and we are going to do that." She added, "No one knows we are here alone, and we should keep it that way. If you open your mouths and blab about it, social workers will come and split us up and take us all to different foster homes. So just go on with life as usual."

Renee was always good at melodrama. One time, after Stell whacked her on her cheek for being disrespectful, Renee threw herself to the floor and blood dripped onto the fake brick linoleum. Her head was down, covered by her long, brunette hair, then she flipped it back, revealing sharp blue eyes, and said to Stell, "You will drink this blood." It was perfect. Any director would have yelled, "That's a wrap!"

Renee was always Nanny's confidant, so in many ways she was completely qualified to take over the lead role. She passed us a poster that illustrated rotating schedules of whose turn it was to do the dishes, sweep the floors, clean the bathroom, and shop for groceries.

Despite the schedule, it turned out that I was the one in charge of food shopping each month. This occurred because Nanny had always sent Billy and me to do the shopping since we were little. So many times, we had to stop and sit on someone's front stoop because the bags were too heavy for us to carry all the way home.

Food shopping for five teenagers was a nightmare. First, because we had to walk one and a half miles to get to Shop Rite to get good buys, then we had to take a taxi home. The other terrible part of shopping was that we had to use food stamps. Even if I had completed an entire hour of grocery shopping, had a filled shopping cart, and was next in line, I walked away from the entire basket of food if I saw someone I knew. We never wanted anyone to know we were poor. Even at lunchtime at Newark Catholic, there were so many times when teachers or nuns asked why we weren't eating lunch. We just lied and said we were dieting or that we weren't hungry. The truth was that we were starving, but we refused to sign up for the Free and Reduced Lunch Program because Nanny taught us that it was shameful to take a handout.

To make our money stretch, I bought each child his or her own box of frozen waffles, Ellios Frozen Pizza, and Banquet frozen entrees, including turkey and gravy, roast beef and gravy, and chicken parmesan. Sometimes, these individual frozen servings, which you dropped in boiling water, were ten packs for just $1. They could be described as "mystery meat," but, when slapped between two slices of bread or made into an "open-faced" sandwich, they were filling. Everyone also got his or her own box of Steak-umms. This was great because we could all trade with each other to get our favorites. I rounded out the grocery order with eggs, milk, bread, minute steaks, spaghetti, and lots of cereal.

No matter what I bought, no one was happy. I was filled with guilt and felt incompetent every time one of my brothers stood in front of the open refrigerator or freezer door and said, "There is never anything to eat in this house!"

I responded, "There is something to eat, but you have to make it."

"Why don't you make it?" they asked.

"Because I am not your fucking maid," I said. "Make it yourself!" Inevitably one of the girls got up and made them a Steak-umm cheesesteak sandwich or a pizza. The cooking situation was complicated by the fact that we were all involved in various school activities and didn't return home from school until 6:00 p.m. on most nights, so we didn't have time for real cooking.

It was around this time in our lives when we began to shoplift on a regular basis. We did it out of necessity because we had such a limited amount of money for essential nonfood items. There is an old saying that soap and water is cheap. This is simply not true at all. Soap, shampoo, conditioner, toothpaste, mouthwash, toilet paper, deodorant, powder, sanitary products, laundry detergent, dish detergent, and other cleaning supplies were the most expensive items in our budget. They also couldn't be purchased with foods stamps. Yet, there are very few items on the above list that five children between the ages of twelve and seventeen could live without and blend into a private high school. Besides the fact that we wanted to fit in, we had to keep up all appearances, because we could be separated if anyone knew we were living alone.

Also, to feel like a real family, once in a while we invited some of our favorite nuns, like Sister Juanita and Sister Maggie, over to the house for dinner. They were an odd couple that was always together. Sister Maggie was short and stocky and wore a perpetual smile. She had a quick wit and instantly brightened any room she entered. We frequently mocked her in business class because she shared tips on a daily basis, but they seemed unrelated to any work we were doing that day in class. She said, "Girls, never carry cash on your person." Or she announced, "If you go braless, you will get Cooper's Droop." When we reminded her in later years that she gave us these tips, she just laughed as if she never heard of them.

Sister Juanita, her best friend, was a perfectionist. She was an exceptional English and film teacher who worked hard to get the very best out of every student. There was no way you could ever get away with not participating in her class because she always got nose to nose, even with the biggest, roughest, black girls, and required their participation. No matter what the subject was for the day, she was enthusiastic about it. It was obvious that she loved teaching. She had the best laugh and was amused by her students every day.

We were excited when they accepted our dinner invitation, but we couldn't serve them our waffles or frozen pizza or Steak-umms, so Billy and I walked into Shop Rite or Pathmark to prepare our special Sisters of Charity menu at a "five-finger" discount.

As we passed the register on the way into the store, we selected the busiest checkout line. One of us set a screen (as we learned to do in basketball practice) while the other grabbed a handful of brown paper grocery bags and immediately held them with one hand inside a long coat. Quickly, we zipped through the grocery store and picked up the items for our special menu. This included veal cutlets, tomato sauce, mozzarella cheese, Progresso breadcrumbs, eggs, parmesan cheese, Italian bread, and lettuce and tomato. We placed these items in the shopping cart like anyone else would and then proceeded as if we were headed to the cashier.

However, right near the checkout section was a new plant and flower section, where they also sold balloons. We paused here and took out the brown paper bags we had hidden in our coats and filled them up with the food, and then walked from behind the flowers with our bagged groceries as if we had just paid. We then walked out the door and kept walking.

When we got home, I pounded the veal really thin as I had seen Julie Balaqua do a million times when I babysat. I dipped the veal in egg and breadcrumbs, browned them in oil, topped them with the cheeses and sauce, and placed them in the oven.

Sister Juanita and Sister Maggie enjoyed an Italian feast that included veal parmesan, spaghetti, garlic bread, and salad. When I think back on those dinners, I am so embarrassed that we used to beg Sister Juanita and Sister Maggie to sleep over. They politely refused, stating that they didn't bring their toothbrushes. But I wondered what our lowly house looked like to them compared to their neat-as-a-pin convent. We probably never saw our house the way they did. It must have been difficult for them to even visit or to share a meal.

In addition to food and toiletries, we also had to steal supplies that helped us succeed in school. We needed pens, pencils, paper, notebooks, calculators, art supplies, poster boards, markers, sneakers, sweat socks, basketballs, etc. We had no way to buy these items, so we had to steal them from local drug stores, five and dimes, and Two Guys Department stores.

Once in a while, we stole items to improve the house. We didn't have Home Depot then, so we went to Two Guys or Chanel Lumber for these items. For a few months, we had a great shoplifting run at Two Guys, because my brother had stolen the pricing gun from where a worker left it on a shelf in the sports aisle. Rather than hiding items we needed to steal, we just put a ridiculous price on it. We got a gallon of paint for $1.99, and the landlord was so pleased with how we painted the living room.

It's funny, but the term "landlord" was like a curse word that invoked fear in all of us. No one held more power over us, because she could easily reveal the fact that we were living without parents. Just as the neighborhood kids warned us years ago when Nanny was coming, they did the same in our teen years when the landlord was coming. Fortunately, in major cities, many people walked to their destinations, so our landlord took a bus from Nutley, where she lived, and then walked the few blocks from Kearny Avenue to our street.

Since she worked, she only visited in the evening. We would be in our rooms listening to music when our front door would burst open and a neighborhood kid would shout with great alarm, "The landlord is coming!"

We dropped everything and ran around tidying every inch of the living room and kitchen. Sometimes, we threw dirty dishes under the couch cushions or dumped them from the sink to the back porch, where she would never look at night. We quickly filled the kitchen sink with water and bleach, ammonia or Pine Sol, so that the house had a clean smell to it.

One of us put a pot of water boiling for tea, and then who-ever was home grabbed a book and a notebook, and we all sat at the dining room table and pretended we were studying. By the time she reached our porch, we had the water poured into a tea cup. We had sprayed all of the couches and chairs with Lysol. All of the windows would be opened to let in the fresh air.

She would yell in the door, "Children, it's Mrs. Calvin, are you home?" She thought we were home alone for a few hours each night because we told her that my Uncle Ted was our guardian and he was a police officer who worked the night shift. When she entered, she was greeted by the smell of a clean house. She saw at least three young adults huddled around the table doing their schoolwork.

"Your uncle must be so proud of you," she would say. "Look how beautifully you painted my house. I am so happy you are my tenants." We would give her a hot cup of tea and barrage her with questions and comments all about herself.

"Did you just come from the beauty parlor?"

"Is that a new coat?"

"Have you ever read this book?"

"Do you have a favorite poem?"

She left feeling like a queen and always complemented us on what wonderful children we were. When she was safely down the street, our friends came in and we laughed about how she looked like Baby Jane Hudson from *Whatever Happened to Baby Jane* with Bette Davis.

As our lives became hectic, we had less time to do laundry and to keep up with the chores involved with running a big household, so we also begin to steal underwear. We simply walked into Drug Fair in Kearney, New Jersey, and shoved a handful of new panties into our pockets. While store managers followed any black or Hispanic person who was in the store, they never suspected the blonde-haired, blue-eyed teens wearing uniforms to be stealing right under their noses.

After a while, we even got cockier about it. We walked in the store and actually purposely engaged the salesperson in conversation. Then we held an item up in our right hand above our heads and asked, "Miss, how much is this item, I don't see the price." As the sales person looked up to see the item, we put the item in our other hand into our pocket or under our coat. As stores became more sophisticated, we even learned to outsmart surveillance cameras by identifying blind spots so that we could steal shoes and sneakers.

Our house was the center of our neighborhood, and everyone wanted to be around us. But it wasn't because we were the "cool" kids who were drinking or doing drugs. It was just the opposite. Regardless of how many friends we made, it started to become apparent that one of us was always in charge of the group's activities. Somehow, despite the limitations of our family, we seemed to be the smartest, the funniest, and the most daring. This enhanced our self-esteem and made us love being with other people, and we became more and more skilled at charming them.

From my grandmother's example, we often gambled and had poker games at our house. Whitie, who was in seventh grade, frequently had six or seven friends over to play poker. Once while they were playing, Becky and I returned from a day at the beach at the Jersey shore. On the ride home, Becky's shoulders hurt from sunburn, so she undid her bathing suit halter top under her T-shirt while she was driving. When we entered our kitchen and Becky saw all of the seventh-grade boys playing cards, she took on a Mae West tone and said, "Hey, big boys, wanna see my new bathing suit?" Becky was extremely pretty, with flame orange red hair that reached her butt in the back. She was well built and had substantial breasts starting in the fourth grade. In fact, she got her period then. When she did, she called me into the bathroom and showed me the blood in the toilet bowl. She was crying because she thought that she got her period because she wore her black patent leather Sunday shoes on a school day. I assured her that it had nothing to do with that, but I didn't know what it was. She was afraid to ask Nanny because then Nanny would know about her shoes.

As Whitie's seventh-grade friends looked up from their seven-card stud hands at Becky's freckled face, Richie, the tallest of the seventh graders said, "Sure, I wanna see it." Without thinking, Becky lifted up her T-shirt and exposed perfectly round, milky white, high school junior girl breasts to the seventh-grade boys. As she held her shirt up, she could not understand the silence. She lowered her head from her movie star pose and saw the shock on the boys' faces. Only then did she realize that she untied her halter top in the car and that she wasn't wearing a bathing suit top. The boys roared with laughter and said, "Whitie, we are playing cards here more often. How many sisters do you have?"

There was no other house in the neighborhood where kids could play poker for money openly and glance at some breasts. But it wasn't just in the neighborhood, because even in school we were treated special. I was allowed to leave class to go to the resource center to write. It seemed I could do no wrong.

In English class, I stopped reading required novels because we didn't really have a lifestyle that allowed one to enjoy reading at home. Yet, as we sat around in a circle in our ultramodern classrooms discussing *Of Mice and Men*, Sister Clair said to me, "Can you discuss the significance of George and Lennie's dream?" I sat quietly for a moment as though I was seriously contemplating her question, having no idea of what she was talking about, and then said, "Really, Sister Claire, don't we all have a secret dream about the future that we play over and over in our heads? For example, you play the guitar and sing. Before becoming a nun, did you have a different dream? Like, did you ever think of getting married or having children?"

Sister Claire became flushed and disarmed and would then spend the entire class talking about herself. I asked her this question because she frequently brought her guitar to school, and it seems the songs she sang to the class were always love songs. She sang "Suzanne," and "The Wedding Song," and "Your Song," by Elton John.

Sister Claire, who resembled John Denver because of her straight blonde hair and glasses, said, "I often think about how my life would be different if I got married. I did have boyfriends, you know. I had a boyfriend all through college. But here's the difference. If I were married, I could be the mother of a few children. In this role, as a sister, I am the mother to so many children. That is irreplaceable."

Renee gained notoriety in high school when she wrote a complete musical that was performed by her senior class. Becky was directing the class and was portraying Bette Midler on the school stage in a talent show. Billy won a local and state speech competition and was headed to the nationals. Whitie was great in math and was so popular with all of the older kids in town because he was good in every sport. We all absolutely loved school because these daily affirmations of our value gave us the strength to go on every single day.

Still, when we went to bed at night, alone, completely aware that maybe no one loved us, the aching emptiness always returned to fill us with anxiety about tomorrow. I summed it up for Sister Claire in this poem.

My brothers and sisters,
Such royal kings and queens we are
Holding ourselves high
Robed in red royal lies
White fur confidence protects us
We roar laughter
Forgetting true pain
As our friends
Our royal servants
Hand feed us grapes
Poison lies
Giving us dictatorial powers.
We are self appointed,
And so as life goes,
We will be self destroyed.
Love,
The missing jewel
In our glorious aluminum foil crowns
Will sneak and cause us to crumble
But don't think about it now
If it hurts you
Play king and queen
There is still some time
Before we crack
Then how does it go?
All the kings horses and
All the king's men
Won't be able to put us together again
We will be alone

Condemned in a world
Filled with bodies
Grabbing and playing love
With one another.
We will be Kings
Only
Because no one else
Will be there
To take the job.

Even if we were pushy, friends loved hanging at our house. We hung a reshaped wire hanger on one side of the living room and another reshaped wire hanger on the other and used a pair of rolled-up sweat socks to play full-court basketball. No one cared how much noise we made as we thudded up and down on the hardwood floors. Sooner or later someone called a foul and we had to get the broom to use the handle as the foul line.

Our friends stole ingredients from their own pantries and put them together in a big pot of soup or spaghetti that everyone shared. They pitched in to do the cooking or helped with cleanup, and we all felt like we were playing house. When the dishes were done, we'd play pinochle or poker for money. Our favorite games were three-card monte, acey-deucey, and seven-card stud.

When the weather was warm, we played neighborhood games like "Catch, Kill, or Torture." This was a game with two teams. The one team got a five-minute head start, and then the other team came to find them and could either imprison them or torture them. If the person was imprisoned, they were placed on the front porch until a teammate could come and tag the porch to free them. If they were tortured, this usually meant that they were taken to the side of the porch and hidden from public view, so that the catcher could make out with them.

This usually ended in some laughs, and then everyone came back to our living room to relax. Renee took out her guitar and everyone sang songs and we were each assigned a part in the harmony. Our most frequently sung songs were "Leaving on a Jet Plane," "Sound of Silence," and "Bridge Over Troubled Water." But our ultimate favorite was from a corny movie that we loved called *The Singing Nun*. The name of the song was "Brother John," and everyone in the neighborhood had a part.

Renee also wrote her own songs that we learned and sung. These included:

Nosy Neighbors
Please leaves us alone,
because we don't bother you.
They watch.
They watch from out their windows.
They watch from out their doors.
They watch.

Another song she wrote that became the graduation song for her high school class was

Sitting together
No sense of time
Watching the world
Pass us by.
Finding each other
Different before
Good things happened
We've got so much
Sharing to do
Why can't we just
Live for each other
Live for each other
All the time.

Our most frequent guests in the house at this time were Brian and Carrie Finnerty. They lived just down the street from us, and Carrie was my best friend, and even though Brian was my age, he was my brother's friend. We took turns sleeping at each other's house. Their mother, Aida, always invited us to dinner and allowed us to swim in their above-ground pool. Sometimes there were nine or ten neighborhood kids in their pool, and we'd make a forceful whirlpool. We ran around the pool as fast as possible, giving strength to the whirlpool until it carried us. Then, we yelled to Kirk, a fourteen-year-old boy who once fell on the train track and got hit by a train and now had a steel plate in his head, "Kirk, here comes the Path Train. All aboard! We're coming to get you." Kirk yelled, "Cut it out, guys. That's not funny." But the forceful water empowered us to go faster and faster as we chased Kirk and all made the train whistle sound. "Woo, Woo, chugga, chugga, chugga, chugga, clear the tracks, Kirk, we're coming to get you."

Besides having a pool, the Finnertys' house was a safe place. If anything terrible was happening at our house, Mrs. Finnerty sat us down, made all of us a cup of tea, gave us a pep talk, and then sent us home. But no matter when you stopped by the Finnertys' house, Aida, who was Brian and Carrie's mom, was down on her hands and knees scrubbing the carpets with a scrub brush and a bucket of Tide mixed with vinegar. This always seemed strange to me because their old creaky house only had the thinnest, most worn, indoor-outdoor carpet in every room. Rather than getting cleaner, it seemed as if she was wearing the carpet even more with her scrubbing. When you walked in the door, no knocking required, she stood up and said, "Look at my hands. They are raw. I have been scrubbing the carpets all day." Her hands were indeed flaky, red, and chapped. I never dared to say aloud what I was thinking: "What are you doing to the carpet that it has to be scrubbed every day?" Aida took a break when I visited and grabbed herself a cold beer. After a few beers, she called Carrie and me into the kitchen and said, "Don't ever let a man touch you."

Meanwhile, for most of our childhood, Aida's husband, Jack, spent every single weekend building a deck in the backyard that would eventually connect the house to the above-ground swimming pool. The deck was level with the ground, and he added more pieces of "donated" railroad ties that he collected from construction sites around the neighborhood. Each weekend in the spring and summer, he walked around the yard with no shirt on, exposing his muscled back and chest. He had a tool-belt strapped around his jeans and his T-shirt stuffed into his back pocket. He stayed out in the grassless, often muddied yard, seeming to saw and hammer all day. Yet in fourteen years, the deck he was building never reached the pool.

Aida and Jack Finnerty both liked their beers, and they always enjoyed a little too many on Thursday nights when Jack came home with his paycheck from working at Public Service. Under his arm, he carried a case of beer and after dinner, Aida and Jack sat at the chrome-legged table and stared into each other's eyes as if they were on a first date. Aida said, "My Jack-amo, takes care of everything. Look at the beautiful deck he is building me." Almost every week, by the end of the night, the love fest turned into a pity party for Jack and how he worked every day and every weekend and how his wife and kids didn't appreciate what they had. It often ended with Jack hitting someone. Yet the same scenario continued to play out every weekend.

Brian and Carrie always had a tumultuous sibling rivalry. Brian was about five foot eight inches tall with long straight blonde hair that he wore in what would be considered a bob hairstyle today. Carrie was about five feet tall, with blonde hair and freckles and a cute figure. She was her Daddy's little girl and sometimes smacked herself and then called her parents to say that Brian was hitting her, and then Brian was grounded by his parents.

Brian got back at Carrie by giving her the "Blackie Treatment" when their parents were away. He tackled Carrie onto the ground, took Milk Bone dog biscuits out of his pocket, crushed them onto her face, and called their old, smelly, black mutt, Blackie, in from the muddy yard to lick the biscuits off Carrie's face. This action was legendary in the neighborhood. No one wanted to experience the "Blackie Treatment" among our circle of friends. Other times, Brian actually flushed Carrie's face right in the toilet bowl. I can't say that she didn't deserve it, though.

Although Carrie was my best friend, she was a year younger and was always in a competition with everyone. If you said that you got an A on a science project, she said she got four As in school that day. If you said that someday you were going to have a house at the Jersey shore, she said that she would have a mansion at the Jersey shore and a yacht. We referred to it as "Can you top this?" and after a while, when Carrie spoke, we all chimed in with "Can you top this?" She got mad and went home and told her mother.

The one upsetting thing that sometimes made Carrie and me stop talking to each other was that if she didn't like what I wanted to do that day, she said jokingly, "I will lock you in the basement!" Everyone laughed hysterically when she said this. At first, I laughed, too, but then after a while, I didn't find it funny at all. I told her to stop saying it, but she wouldn't. She knew that she could bring this up whenever she wanted and she could get to me.

Finally, I got something to bring up that stopped Carrie's big mouth immediately. One day, when Carrie and I were together in her bathroom putting on our bathing suits to go in her pool, I noticed that she had New Freedom Maxi Pads with the adhesive backing in her bathroom. These were a revolutionary product. I, too, had recently stolen this new product, and was so thrilled to say good-bye to a sanitary belt or safety pins—which a house like ours never had on hand anyway.

I said, "Carrie, you bought New Freedom, too? Aren't they great?"

She said, "Yea, but don't you find that they hurt so much?"

"No, what do you mean they hurt? How?"

"You know, when you pull them off?"

I pondered her statement and tried to picture myself removing a pad from my underwear and couldn't imagine how pain was involved and then it hit me.

I laughed and laughed and pointed my finger at her to mock her.

"What?" she said not understanding?

I said, "Oh, my God, you idiot! You have been sticking the pad to your body?"

She said, "Yea, why?" then added, "It hurts so much when you pull on it and it takes off half your pubic hair."

"What an idiot!" I said again. "Carrie, you moron, you don't stick them to your body, you stick them to your underwear."

"You're kidding!" she said shocked.

I said instantly, "I can't wait to tell everybody about this." "Everybody" meant my brother Whitie, who she had a crush on, and some of her brother's friends that hung out with us.

Carrie pleaded with me, "Please don't tell anyone. Please. I didn't know."

After laughing for a few more minutes, I made a deal with her. If she didn't ever say again that she would lock me in the basement, I would not tell anyone. She agreed that we had a deal. Of course, I told everyone, but they never told her.

After a while, when Brian slept over and my brothers went to sleep, he and I found ourselves alone in the living room. At first, we wrestled to prove who was stronger, but wrestling turned into making out, and making out turned into petting.

This happened whenever we were alone, regardless of whose house we slept in. If we were in his house, Carrie and I went up to the attic, which Brian had made into a club house. He had painted the walls and ceiling black, and he had psychedelic posters of Jimi Hendrix all around the room. He had big pillows and some beanbag chairs and a stereo. Carrie and I played cards for a while in the clubhouse and then soon, Brian came up and said, "Carrie, go to bed." Brian and I reclined next to each other on the pillows on the thick brown shag rug and talked about our dreams of getting far away from there. Some of our dreams were not that big. They included having butter any time we wanted, instead of margarine, and never having to drink powdered milk again in our lives.

Brian played Chicago's version of *Colour My World* on the record player and took the metal arm off the record holder so that the song repeated and repeated over and over all through the night. I rested on his shoulder. The smell of the beer he snagged from the refrigerator on his breath was powerful cologne that made him seem much older. He pulled me so close, and his bare, warm skin was my cozy electric blanket and I felt safe.

As time goes on
I realize
Just what you mean
To me
And now
Now that you're near
Promise your love
That I've waited to share
And dreams
Of our moments together
Colour my world with hope of loving you.

By morning, I sneaked back into bed with his sister, Carrie, and would always be there before Jack woke up for work the next morning.

Our father's mother kept in touch while my mother was "away," as she put it, as if she were on the islands. Our grand-mother thought that it would be a good idea for us to finally meet our father. Since we all loved the Jersey shore, it was arranged that we would meet him at his brother's house at the shore so that we could spend a night getting to know each other and walking the boardwalk and such.

At this time, Renee and Becky both worked at McCrory's in Newark after school. Renee worked at the pizza counter and Becky worked as a salesgirl on the floor. Even though I was not yet of age, Frankie, the owner of the pizza counter, would let me work once in a while on a Saturday. It turned out that on the Saturday we were to meet my father, Becky wasn't working, but Renee and I were. So, Becky drove our two brothers down to spend the day with our father and Renee and I planned to con-nect with them after we got out of work at 6:00 p.m.

Renee and I were both nervous wrecks the whole work day, and it seemed as if time would never pass. When Frankie said that we could leave, we both ripped off our aprons and hopped into her black and white Chevy that our Uncle Mike had given Renee just a few weeks ago. It was painted black and white because it was once a police car. Renee's car made going to work so much easier. When she wasn't available to drive me because she spent a night at a friend's house or something, then I had to take the bus. This was fine on the way to work, but if it was after work, I had to wait across the street in a park for the bus. It was often filled with homeless people. Also, everyone who worked in McCrory's told me, "Honey, you don't want to be a white girl alone waiting for the bus at night in Newark." It seemed as if the entire city was transformed after dark. During the day, the streets were filled with people in business apparel who worked at Bell Telephone, Public Service Electric and Gas, the courthouse, and Rutgers University. However, at night, some frightening charac-ters roamed the streets.

I felt sorry for a group of men who stood in the park warming their hands over a flaming garbage can. They dressed in rags and often wore gloves that had the fingers cut out of them, so that they could wiggle their fingers above the flame to keep warm. Once I bought a pizza with my pay and carried it across the street to the park on a cold winter day to try to provide the men with a hot meal. My bare legs were freezing cold beneath my short plaid uniform skirt, while my hands were almost burned by the hot pizza. As I approached four black men as they danced around the garbage can that they had lit on fire to keep warm, I noticed that their nappy grey beards hid faces that were pitted and scarred by life. Their brown eyes glared at me as I approached. Although I was so scared, I put a smile on my face and tried to remember that I was doing God's work. I said, "Good evening, gentlemen, I thought that I could treat you to a warm meal." I held the pizza up high as if I was raising a gold chalice on the altar. Their eyes followed the box as if to honor it in prayer and we seemed to be getting along well, until smack, one taller, heavier man knocked the pizza box right out of my hand and onto the ground. I was shocked and noticed that it landed upside down and cheese first. How could anyone do that to a pizza?

Just as I glanced back up, the man who hit the pizza stepped so close to me that I could smell alcohol rising from his cat-hair-covered black coat. He said, "What the fuck do you think we are? Bums? We're not bums! You yellow-haired devil!"

His words assaulted me, and as I tilted my head back, I caught a glimpse of the number thirty-nine bus swishing by. I ran as fast as I could and flagged down the driver. I rushed up the steps, handed him my bus pass, and sat in the first seat. I turned my head to see the white teeth of the circle of men as they laughed at my stupidity.

As Renee and I drove down the Garden State parkway, we shared our secret dreams of how having a father was going to change our lives. Like Lennie and George in *Of Mice and Men*, which I eventually did read, we each took turns weaving our own little story. "Someday, we are going live so easy. Maybe our father will ask us to move in with him. Maybe he has a really big house and we could each have our own room. Maybe he could take care of us from now on." One exit became the next until we found ourselves in Atlantic Highlands, New Jersey, at the home of my uncle. Renee and I rang the doorbell, and the door was opened by my brother. There was talking and laughing in the kitchen, and we walked in to find a man stirring spaghetti.

As he turned to greet Renee, he smiled. He looked a lot like my sister Becky because he had reddish hair that was slicked back in waves from his widow's peak. He had piercing blue eyes that seemed kind and lively, and his face was freckled. He gave Renee a hug. I stood behind her, and when it was my turn, he said, "Hello Katie." I said, "Hello, Pops. What happened, did you go out for a loaf of bread and forget to come back?" He laughed and said, "Oh, we have a wise ass here."

He called us all to the table and we sat down to eat a salad, spaghetti with meatballs, and garlic bread. As we talked, our father sipped a beer and laughed at our lively conversation. We were all tripping over ourselves to tell him what was good about us.

"I'm on the basketball team."

"I was the lead in the school play"

"I write poems and stories."

"I play the guitar."

He could hardly keep up. He just sort of sat back, and a smile opened his rugged, freckled face, and he absorbed it all without saying much about himself for a while. Then, we began asking a barrage of questions.

"Where did you meet our mother?"

It turned out that they had their first kiss on the front porch of the house where we were still living.

"How come you got her pregnant?"

He said, "Your mother was a beautiful girl, but she was insatiable."

"Insatiable, what does that mean?"

"She never had enough sex. Every time I got home from work, she practically ripped my clothes off."

"Then, why did you leave?"

"Because she was trying to kill me, and you too, Katie."

"Yeah, but if you were afraid of her, why did you leave your children with her?"

"Because your grandmother made it impossible for me. She hated me and blamed me for your mother getting pregnant and sick."

"Why didn't you take us to live with your mother?"

"I did, but your grandmother got a lawyer and got you back."

"Why didn't you come to visit us?"

"Because you're grandmother had a restraining order against me and had me arrested every time I went near you."

"Did you ever get married again?"

"No, but I live with a woman and her two children—a boy and a girl."

This filled our stomachs with sour jealousy and we went quiet.

He said, "How about if we clean up these dishes and go for a walk on the boardwalk."

We all carried our dishes to the sink and rushed to his car to see who could sit in the front. All of us piled into the car with our father, Becky and Renee across the bench seat in front and the three little ones in the back.

On the way to the boardwalk, he told us that he had worked as a truck driver his whole life. He said that when he was in high school at Our Lady of the Valley High School in Newark, t he won an award for typing one hundred words a minute and he was sure that he would have won a scholarship to go to college at Seton Hall. He said that he never finished his education because our mother got pregnant and my grandmother insisted that he marry her.

He said that at first he worked two jobs trying to make ends meet, driving a truck from morning till dark for Graves Trucking. He said that he came home exhausted and my mother would be throwing things. His three babies were totally neglected all day and covered in filth when he arrived. Suddenly, he burst into tears and said, "I know that you think that I should have tried harder," he wiped his eyes with a handkerchief, "but I was nineteen years old, for Christ's sake!"

As we walked along the boardwalk, we all played various games of chance. We tossed a football through a tire, had a basketball shooting competition, and put money down on Mom and Pop on the spinning wheel of fortune. He kept taking money out of his wallet to keep us playing.

While the boys tried to win some trinkets on the claw machine, the girls stood outside with our father. Next to the arcade where the boys played, there was a band and a drunken girl dancing around a poll wearing a halter top and short shorts. My father was staring at her and seemed to be waiting for her top to fall off.

I said, "Hey, you're too old to look at that."

He said, "No, it just reminded me of one time when I was at a bar and there was a go-go dancer. She said to me, 'Do you want to go upstairs and fool around?' I said sure. I got upstairs with her and she dropped her drawers and she smelled like a Goddamn fish market." Then, he lit a cigarette and the smoke seemed to transport him to another time and place.

Why is he telling his daughters this? I wondered. But I buried the thought because having a father was too good to be true and I didn't want the feeling to end. Just then, the boys came out of the arcade and we all hopped in the car and headed back to my uncle's house. There, we played Ping-Pong and pool and other games downstairs in their finished basement. The radio was on and my father came over to me at the Ping-Pong table and reached for my hand and said, "May I have this dance?"

He said, "Do you know that you are just as pretty as your mother?"

"Really?" I was so happy. This was the first time anyone had ever called me pretty. His experienced feet led me into the middle of the basement as we swayed back and forth. He pulled me close to him and rocked me slowly to the Bee Gees. I knew things would be different from now on. As we turned and turned and held each other tight, it became less and less obvious which of us really had the strength to go on.

How can you mend this broken man?
How can a loser ever win?
Please help me mend a broken heart.
And let me live again.

CHAPTER 9—NOVEMBER 1974

MY MOTHER'S NINTH ADMISSION

*Admission Quote: "I am a human bean.
I need love, too."*

Our new hopes were brought to a quick halt when our mother returned again. Now that we were all drunk with independence and power, there was no way she was going to control anything anymore. We made it clear on her first day home that Renee was going to retain control over the money, and my mother was given a small allowance for her cigarettes and bingo. This caused daily arguments, but our combined strength left my mother powerless.

After a few weeks, though, our mother was actually happy not to have the responsibilities. We had the house working as we wanted and she could basically drink her coffee, smoke, and relax. It was the first time that she did not have to be the family maid.

Having a few dollars from our part-time jobs put less strain on everyone. In fact, when she was feeling better, Stell, too, decided to get a job as a waitress at a local bar/restaurant which was just a block from our house. She thought that two days a week would be okay for her and that she could earn enough money for bingo and cigarettes. We thought this was a great idea.

With everyone so busy, things were starting to go well for us. We were all doing well in school, we basically just ate and slept at home, and we were staying out of each other's way. Then one day, Stell came home in a jubilant mood. She called us into the living room, and she was jumping up and down like a five-year-old. She said, "Guess what, boys and girls, I have a boyfriend. He is so handsome. His name is Tony and he is coming tomorrow to take me on a date." We were all so truly happy for her. That night before going to bed, Becky, the most fashion conscious and most experienced with dating, helped Stell create an outfit and practiced applying makeup and styling her hair. The next day we all made plans to leave the house because her date was coming to pick her up after work. We all thought that five kids were enough to scare any man away.

That night after the date, we couldn't wait to hear the news about how it went. When we got home and the date was over, we asked about every detail: Was he handsome? Where did he take her? What did she eat? Did she like him? Did she think he liked her? Stell was so happy. She was giddy as she told about how handsome he was. As she did, though, she kicked her leg incessantly, but it was not just a little nervous kick. She placed her left leg over her right leg and not only kicked up and down, but rocked her entire lower body so that it appeared she was actually humping her chair. We turned away in disgust. She looked away as if she were in a dream and said, "My Tony and I just stayed in and had hot coffee." Then she broke out in hysterical laughter and said, "I am a bad girl."

We ignored her response because she was being so childish and immature. We were basically happy that she was happy and glad she was going to see him again. We reasoned that the first date was just a getting-to-know-you date, like on the *Dating Game*, and he would surely take her out to a nice restaurant the next time.

My mother's new boyfriend, Tony, came to see her once a week while we were at school. Afterwards, we would come home to my mother singing joyfully as she listened to the radio and actually cooked dinner. "Hello, sweethearts, I made a cake for you today," she would say. We had to admit that the smell of food cooking was such a welcoming scent. My mother had also gotten out of her housedress and was putting on pedal pushers and a cute top every day. She was back to putting her hair up in a French twist, revealing her amazing cheekbones. She started wearing makeup and sometimes tied a pretty flowered silk scarf around her neck. The bright colors of the scarf caused her beautiful sky-blue eyes to twinkle and brought out the pretty natural rose color in her cheeks and lips.

Her new look reminded me of a time when the coal man was standing outside while a long chute delivered a half ton of coal to our basement, and he turned to me and said, "Did you know that your mother and her sister, Jennie, were the most beautiful girls in town?" Then he put his head down and shook it as if he was trying to erase something from the past. "A damn shame is what it is." He headed back to the cab of his truck. I tried to see her from an objective eye and it was true, she was really a pretty woman.

After dinner, at night, she starting walking to the avenue to window shop and greeted everyone along the way with a smile and a short conversation. When she did, passers-by laughed at her jokes and showed genuine happiness that she was doing so well. Kids in the neighborhood told us that we had such a young, fun, good-looking mother. She even became a Girl Scout leader for the local troop, and the girls loved her. She taught them to make potholders on a little loom and joked that at least she learned some valuable skill at Trenton State Hospital.

She personally walked up and down the blocks in Kearny with a pull cart selling Girl Scout cookies at every bar. Her troop won the prize for the most cookies sold. And she seemed to be almost more parental and confident at home, too. If we left our dishes in the sink or didn't pick up after ourselves, she said, "I'm not the nigger slave anymore. My master died and I am free at last." She raised her arms as if she were a speaker in a Baptist church, saying, "Yes, Lordy," and she added, "Do your own dishes, sweetie."

Then summer came and the two boys and I were home most days watching *Let's Make A Deal*, *The Price is Right*, and *I Love Lucy* reruns. Like a lot of teens, we relaxed around the house all day and then got dressed to go out in the evening. This caused a big problem for Stell, because during the summer we were pretty much dedicated to being in the air conditioning at home. On the day Tony was scheduled to take her out, my mother woke us up by banging a dust mop on our beds while cleaning because she was filled with anxiety about getting the house empty for Tony. As soon as we had our cereal for breakfast, she began begging us to leave the house by lunchtime. "Please, please," she said, "Take this money. Go to the movies. Go buy ice cream. Go bowling. Just for a few hours. Please, Tony is coming"

We mocked her by wringing our hands like Lady Macbeth and whining, "My Tony is coming, my Tony is coming." And then we'd turn to each other and say, "Fuck Tony." We commiserated and agreed on a plan to go bowling or go to the movies, but we took our dear old time making the decision so that her price would go higher.

"We'll go when we're ready," we said. This caused my mother to pace back and forth in the kitchen like a caged animal. She walked around the kitchen table in the center of the room, went to the kitchen sink, and washed her hands, then walked back around again to the kitchen sink and got a drink of water again, and then back around again to wash her hands. Her odd desperation so disgusted us. Still, we were happy to have a few bucks to do something.

One Friday, after I took her bribe and left the house to go window shopping, I realized that I wanted to take my uniform to the dry cleaners so that it would be ready for the start of school, so I went back to the house for a minute. When I got close to the house, I saw my mother and Tony on the front porch, and it appeared that he was just arriving. She rushed out the door into his arms and they kissed wildly. I could see their tongues darting in out of each other's mouths. Then they locked themselves in a deep embrace and their pelvic areas were grinding against each other hard.

As they separated, I could see that Tony was an extremely handsome man. He had a wide head and dark olive skin, and jet black hair that was neatly trimmed. He had broad, muscular shoulders with a slight belly. While I stood across the street, I could see his big tan hands moving all over my mother's backside, up her back, and across her breasts, where they landed and stayed.

My mother reached down and slid her hand back and forth on the crotch of his dress pants, and to my shock he did the same to her, right on the front porch. Without missing a beat or taking a breath, they kicked the door open and managed to move inside out of the sunlight. The door closed behind them.

What the hell? I was in total and complete shock. It was the first time it ever occurred to me that my mother was having sex with this man. I couldn't believe it. I turned around and quickly walked away. When I returned home after I thought for sure he would be gone, my mother was sitting on a kitchen chair having her coffee and smoking a cigarette. I walked into the kitchen and noticed that she was wearing only a house dress and that her hair was down and her face was red. Between smoking her cigarette and sipping her coffee, she slipped both hands between her legs and began pushing her thighs in and out, over and over again. I was so grossed out and disgusted by what seemed to be some form of masturbation. I managed to say casually, "How was your date with Tony today?"

She said, "My Tony loves me. Hee, hee."

I said, "Oh, good. Where did he take you today?"

She said, "We just decided to have coffee at home. You know how I love my coffee and my Tony. Both so creamy." Then she said, "Hee, hee. I am a bad girl," and giggled uncontrollably.

Before I realized what I was saying, I shouted, "You are noth-ing but a whore!"

She paused for a minute, sipped her coffee, took a drag on her cigarette, and said flatly,

"My Tony loves me."

Needless to say, getting us to leave for Tony was not that easy anymore. How could our mother, a thirty-four-year-old woman with five children, be having sex? Nothing could be more wrong or disgusting to us. We decided to do something about it.

First, when she begged us to leave the house, we raised the stakes higher and higher in a sinister extortion plot. She offered us $2 each, but we waited to get $5 or more each. As the time grew closer when Tony was supposed to come, she got manic and started to scream those guttural screams. "I am a human bean. This is all I have. I have feelings, too, you know. Can't you let me have this one thing that gives me joy in my life?"

We mocked her continuously, "Look, she is a bean. A human bean. A lima bean." We laughed and laughed.

She fell to her knees and begged us right there in the living room. "Please just let me have a few hours of happiness. That's all I ask. I do everything for you." She was so pitiful that we gave in after we had enough money in our pockets and couldn't take her pleading any longer.

"Look at her begging on her knees! You are so desperate."

"What has she ever done for us?"

Once, as I was leaving the house, I crossed paths with Tony on the way down the steps. He smiled and shook my hand. I paused and smile back. He had beautiful, passionate brown eyes and a bright white smile. I said, "Hi, I'm Katie, how are you?"

"Just fine," he said and flashed a perfect smile. "It's a beauti-ful day."

I said, "Hey, Tony, do you like my mother?"

He said, "Of course, I do. I like her very much."

Then I leaned in very close to him, so that my mother couldn't hear me, and I whispered. "If you like her so much, why don't you take her out, asshole?" And I walked away.

But that wasn't enough. While she was entertaining Tony on another day, Billy and I decided to go have lunch at the restaurant where my mother worked. It was a bar and grill, so teens were not usually allowed, but since they knew us, they let us in to sit at the bar and have a soda. While we were there, we worked to get some information from our waitress.

We told her how young she looked. We told her that she was so nice to my mother. She smiled and said, "You're mother is a sweet, innocent child on the inside." We got her so that she was feeling close to us. Then we pressed, "My mother seems to have a crush on a certain customer that comes in all the time. Maybe you could fix her up."

"Really? I think your mother has enough headaches without a man in her life," she said as she wiped the counter with a bar cloth.

"Yes, but she seems so lonely," I said. "She seems to think one guy is really handsome. I think his name is Tony."

"Oh, Tony. He comes in for lunch every day." She paused for a moment and said, "Tony... oh yea...but he's married, hon. He's off the market."

Oh, my God! Could this get any worse? Not only was she having sex, but she was having sex with a married man. This was like one sin rolled on top of another sin topped with the ultimate sin.

As it grew nearer to the day of Tony's next visit, my mother's legs kicked and kicked, and she squeezed her thighs faster and faster. It was impossible to watch. She said in a sing-song voice, "My Tony's coming. My Tony's coming." These expressions were followed by barely audible grunts and groans. We wished that we could gouge out our eyes and ears because we were so disgusted by her lust.

This time, we stayed strong. No matter how much she went from face to face pleading with us to leave, we wouldn't do it. What would Nanny think of our mother on the front porch kissing a married man in pure daylight for all of the neighbors to see? What would our nuns think of such a disgusting display? What kind of woman was she? Mary Magdalene?

As the time approached for Tony to arrive, she was unraveling. Her eye makeup was creating black streams down her face. Her lipstick was smudged way outside of her lips and on her teeth from wiping away the tears with her tissue. Her cute French twist, which was held neatly with blonde bobby pins, was coming undone. Wispy, wild strands of hair were poking out wildly around her face.

She started wringing her hands and talking to herself and walking back and forth to the sink to wash her hands over and over and over again. While she was at the sink getting her one hundredth glass of water, of which she took one sip and dumped the rest, the knock on the door came.

I ran to the door to answer it. Tony's smile turned to a grimace when he saw me. "Hi, Tony," I said, feeling powerful. "My mother is busy today."

Tony looked so disappointed. He towered over me and peered over my head to look into the door to try to meet my mother's eyes.

I got his attention when I added, "Perhaps I should call your wife to see if she wants to be your whore for the day." At that, he turned and started to walk down the steps. Before he got far, my mother had shoved me aside with superhuman strength, knocking me right onto the floor, and screamed, "Tony, honey, don't leave."

He looked up at her and his eyes opened wide in shock. She ran to him, trying to hold on to him around the neck, then his waist, as he lifted his arm to protect himself. He held her hands in a strong grip, not to hurt her, but to keep her from hurting herself as she navigated the concrete steps. He looked into her face and tears welled in his eyes.

He said, "I'll give you a call, Clara." Then, he carefully leaned her up against the green banister, where she sobbed and sobbed until she was curled on the steps in a fetal position. He walked away adjusting his clothes as he went.

September was just around the corner, and we busied ourselves with getting ready for the new school year. It didn't bother us at all that my mother had stopped talking to us and stayed in her room reading the Bible most of the day. We thought that perhaps it would do her some good.

Then, one day, when I walked in the front door after school, it hit me. Burned flesh. The heavy scent permeated the hallway as I opened the front door. I had smelled this stench once before when Becky almost set her hair on fire when trying to light one of Stell's cigarettes with a lighter when mimicking her. The odor grew stronger as I walked into the kitchen and saw human hair all over the faded tile floor.

"Stell?" I called as I put my books down.

No reply. Just the scratching sound of a record on the record player that has reached the end of the song.

My eyes scanned the rest of the room. The old gas stove was feathered with frizzed ash blonde hair. The salt shaker, the only piece left of my grandmother's china, was knocked to the floor, and one of the kitchen chairs, which was usually perfectly, compulsively, placed under the table, was turned over on its side. The noise from the record player beckoned me to search further. I went to the bedroom—her mysterious bedroom, where she had cloistered herself for most of the day during recent weeks.

In her bedroom, the Bible vas opened on the unmade bed. Smeared across a two- page spread of the Bible in bright red lipstick, the color she saved for Tony, were the words "Burn in Hell." On the record player, Percy Sledge's "When a Man Loves a Woman" was reduced to a recurring gentle thud as the record player needle hit the center rod over and over again.

I shuddered as my stomach hugged itself. I backed out of the room. My ears tracked the buzzing to the living room receiver, where the phone was off the hook. Just then, my brother Billy walked in from school.

"What's burning?" he asked as he entered. "Stell cooking dinner again?"

"She did something," I said. "She did something to herself."

"Nah," Billy said, waving his hand to dismiss the idea.

"Well, look for yourself, asshole. There's hair everywhere."

"So, maybe she tried to give herself a perm again."

"Shut up," I yelled.

Then Whitie walked in the door from school. "What's burning?" he asked.

Billy replied, "We're having pork roast."

"Yeah, well, too bad you don't have any pork to roast," Whitie answered.

"I think Stell hurt herself," I said again, mostly to myself, as they pushed each other back and forth joking around.

I went to the phone and dialed the very familiar number.

The Kearny police officer sounded so sad when he heard my name. He started to talk but hesitated first, to gather his thoughts. Finally, he said, "I am sorry to tell you this. It appears that your mother, somehow, turned on all of the gas jets on the stove and climbed up and sat on top of the flaming stove. She has first and second-degree burns on her thighs and arms and face."

I didn't know what to say. "Will she be OK?" I asked.

"She will be treated at the hospital and then taken to Trenton again," he said.

"Did she say anything?" I asked, almost afraid that he knew how cruel we had been.

He paused for a minute and sort of chuckled. "While she was in the back of the squad car, it was the funniest thing; she said, 'My feet are burning in hell.' I told her to put her shoes on because she was barefoot and her feet were right on top of the manifold."

He got serious again and said, "Are you kids all right there?"

I said, "Yeah, we're fine," and hung up the phone.

Eventually we were all home, and the five of us gathered silently on the worn plaid living room furniture. "Cookout, anyone?" Billy said.

We all gave him the shut-up look.

Dramatically, Renee stood up and said, "We're on our own again. We've been here before. If anyone asks, Uncle Ed is here with us. We will stick together like glue."

"Cut the shit, Renee," Whitie said and walked out, trying hard to hide the fact that he was crying.

Then, one by one, we went to separate spaces to be alone. Sounds of music muffled the sadness in every corner. Carole King sang "So Far Away" from Renee's room. Bette Midler cried "Hello In There" from the back porch. The boys said nothing as their little plastic men twirled around and around on a stick in an attempt to slam a puck into the goal as they played Sure Shot Hockey. Me, I cried silently into my pillow as the rich, tired voice of Janis Joplin covered me, soothed my back, and told me of Bobby McGee.

Freedom's just another word for nothing left to lose.

Trenton Psychiatric Hospital

SUMMARY OF HOSPITALIZATION

Disposition Summary

Patient Name: Clara Murphy

The patient claims that she heard voices telling her to burn herself. Physical examination, except for the burned areas on the face, left forearm and buttocks, essentially within normal limits. Laboratory findings unremarkable. She has been started on Stelazine, 10mg. Prolixin. 5 cc, every three weeks and Artane 5mg. Ever since admission, patient has not presented any management problem, has been cooperative and adjusted to the ward routines.

CHAPTER 10—AUGUST 1975

MY MOTHER'S TENTH ADMISSION

Admission Quote: "Nobody wants me anyway.
My son broke my arm with a rolling pin."

My mother was released from Trenton to our house just one more time in our lives. When she came home, despite her fragile state, a war broke out instantly the first time my father called because we refused to hide the fact that we wanted to see him.

"How dare you?" she screamed and her face distorted in agony. "At least I tried my best for you kids. He did nothing. He threw us away like trash. How can you choose him over me?"

We tried to explain that we weren't choosing anybody, but that we were just trying to get to know him.

One day, when I came home from basketball practice, my father and mother were sitting at the table talking and having a good time. They both tried to hide smirks as they flirted with each other back and forth. My father leaned over and lit my mother's cigarette and she said, "Let me get you a beer." Their eyes held each other in so much esteem, and it was so obvious to any bystander that these two people were still as in love as when they were 15.

As each of us arrived and gave my father any attention, things changed quickly and violently. Out of nowhere, my mother stood from the table and said, "These are my kids. You are not taking them. You had your chance. Get out. Get out or I'll kill you." With that, she grabbed a steak knife.

My father yelled back, "You are still a crazy bitch," and raised his fist as if he wanted to hit her; instead he put it through the wall. He said, "Nothing ever changes with you."

Soon we were between the two of them and Renee said to our father, "Maybe you better leave now." But my mother couldn't accept that we were in contact with him, and she hung up the phone every time my grandmother called to try to invite us to dinner. She was on the warpath and seemed to start a fight over everything. She made life miserable again.

Each day, when I arrived home from school after 6:00 p.m. because of basketball practice, I was starving because we rarely had money to buy lunch. My hunger grew as I ran forty laps before practice, completed two hours of basketball drills, and then sat for an hour bus ride. I walked in, feeling starving, and said, "What's for dinner?" Stell answered, "Nothing, you're too late. I gave your dinner to the dog." I looked to the floor and saw that our little poodle was struggling trying to eat a dinner plate filled with a whole pork chop, mashed potatoes, and creamed corn. My mother was an asshole. Yet she looked out the window daily and waited for us to come home as if she actually cared about us. Then she treated us so poorly anyway.

One day, when she was waiting for Becky to come home, she noticed that Becky leaned across the seat of a little MG convertible and kissed a black man on the lips good-bye. The black man was Richard LaChance. He was a floor manager at McCrory's. He walked up to Becky at work and said, "Hey, Redhead, do you know that if you put all of your freckles together, you would be the same color as me." This was enough to charm Becky. She also enjoyed his company because he was always singing and dancing and telling jokes. Yet, he wasn't much to look at. He was no bigger than Sammy Davis Jr. and he had the same swagger and demeanor. Renee warned Becky not to date him because she had heard from Frankie at the pizza counter that Richard and Greg, the security guard at McCrory's, had a bet with each other to see how many high-school-age white girls they could each get to sleep with them.

Each night, Frankie saw Greg waiting at the employee entrance to meet a blonde cheerleader type who had come to McCrory's, like so many, for her first job. Greg was six feet tall and extremely well built. He looked even taller in his Newark Police uniform. With his dark clothing and dark afro, he seemed to tower over the high-school-age girls talking nervously at his side.

Well, when my mother saw Becky kissing this black man in the front seat of a car from the bedroom window, all hell broke loose. When Becky walked into our house at around 6:30 p.m., my mother grabbed her by her long red hair and screamed, "You nigger lover!" She was dragging Becky all around the kitchen and was trying to hit her in the head at the same time. Becky remained bent over at the waist with her hand on her head trying to defend against the hair-pulling. She wasn't crying and didn't say a word. Billy and I both ran in to the kitchen from our bedrooms and were telling my mother to leave Becky alone.

Just then, Billy sprung into action and said, "This is it, I'll fucking kill her!" He ran immediately to the silverware drawer in an attempt to grab a steak knife. He was stopped in his tracks because I hadn't done the dishes yet, so there were no clean knives in the drawer. Infuriated by this, he fumbled in the drawer for a second, and then he grabbed a wooden rolling pin. He gripped the rolling part and not the handle and rushed to my mother's side, where she still held Becky's hair and the two were in a sort of stalemate.

Billy said slowly and calmly, "Let go of her now or I will kill you."

My mother giggled as if he were kidding. She unleashed Becky and stood up and said, "Go ahead, whoremaster, hit your mother!" As Becky tried to scramble away, my mother lunged for her arm again. Billy lifted the rolling pin high above his head and let it fall, aiming to come down on our mother's head.

I screamed, "No, Billy, don't do it. She's not worth it."

My mother raised her burn-scarred arm to protect herself and Billy came down hard on her arm. The crack of her bone surprised all of us. "Run, Billy, run," Becky and I screamed simultaneously. But we all just ran out the front door to the Finnertys' house. Once were safe there, we called our father's mother, who called our father. He met us on the street and we followed him as he walked back to our house. He knocked on the door, and when my mother opened, he grabbed her by the throat with one hand and said, "If you ever touch my children again, I will fucking kill you myself." And then he released her.

There was no fight left in her. She coughed for few minutes and said in a monotone voice. "Oh, that's a laugh riot. Your children?" Sullenly, she looked around like a child who had lost its mommy. She looked from face to face for one willing to reach out and help her, but she remained lost. No one was on her side. In frustration, she raised her voice and said, "Go ahead, you rotten traitors. You think he is better than me?" and slammed the door.

My father took us for an ice cream and then surprised us when he dropped us back on the street in front of the house and left. We stared after his car without saying a word, and then, one at a time, we dispersed to different friends' houses.

From the safety of the Finnertys' home, I could see an ambulance arrive to take my mother to the hospital. Then I knew that it was safe to return home if I wanted to do that. Still, I stayed behind to spend the night with my friend, Carrie. In the middle of the night, I sneaked into Brian's bed, and he held me in his arms while I cried. I cried for my mother because I didn't want her to be physically hurt by anyone. I wish I could have been on her side, but she was wrong. I cried for my brother because I didn't want him to get arrested. I cried for my sister because she was too beautiful to give herself to such a loser. I cried for all of us because our father didn't even consider asking us to go with him.

In the morning light, I felt better and was relieved that once again I was returning to a house without my mother. A social worker called from Trenton to tell us that because things were getting violent, they wouldn't return our mother to the house. She wasn't going to press charges against my brother and she just wanted some peace. Then, to my surprise, she added, "Your mother wants to speak to you."

Shocked, my heart leaped a little. I wondered if she finally realized that I really cared about her and would try almost anything to get her to love me. Nervously, I held the beige receiver to my ear, anticipating a much-awaited moment of bonding. Maybe she realized that I was her favorite after all. My mother's voice was in my ear and she said, "Sweetheart, could you send my green hat and gloves. I may get cold." Then a dial tone flat-lined all of my hopes.

Trenton Psychiatric Hospital

SUMMARY OF HOSPITALIZATION

Disposition Summary

Patient Name: Clara Murphy

This is a 35 year old white, married female who was admitted on a voluntary commitment paper. The patient has been in the hospital on numerous occasions previously. According to the patient, prior to admission she had a physical fight with her children and her son broke her arm with a rolling pin. Her husband also threatened to kill her. She stated that she wanted to have her medication increased but her doctor was on vacation. On admission the patient was crying and carrying on. She stated that she did not want to go back to her family anymore and wanted to stay around Trenton. She was very agitated and upset over her husband and son. She denied having hallucinatory experiences or delusional ideations. She was in good contact with her surroundings and well oriented in all spheres, memory was good for recent and remote events. Insight and judgment were poor.

Physical Diagnosis: Fracture to the right arm.

CHAPTER 11—SEPTEMBER 1976

MY MOTHER'S ELEVENTH ADMISSION

Admission Quote: "I am here for a rest."

My mother was now out of sight and out of mind. She was living in some kind of halfway house or apartment. It didn't really matter because she was the last person I ever wanted to see. At night, I would think of her all alone and pray that she was OK. But during the day, my life was moving on. I was now a senior in high school and was focused on whether or not I should have sex with Brian Finnerty. During the week, we spent a lot of time at his house watching television with his parents. Once they went upstairs to bed, Brian and I made out on the couch and went a little further each time. We didn't have intercourse because I thought that it was wrong to have sex before you were married. So, we did everything else that we could with clothes on under the blue fuzzy blanket on his couch. Then, he walked me home and kissed me good night.

Often on weekends, he told his parents he was sleeping over to hang out with my brothers, but we slept together in the same bed each night. We cuddled so tight and talked about what life would be like when we got married and had children. We were never going to hit our kids or make them eat food that they didn't like. They were never going to have to wear uniforms. We were going to live in a big house with a great backyard, and we would have a summer house at the beach.

In our junior year of high school, after we had been dating for two years, Brian was beginning to get a little impatient with me. After sleeping together night after night, he was no longer satisfied to make out or to cuddle. He was getting so frustrated because some of his friends at school were already having sex and we weren't. I tried to relieve his frustration through touching and grinding, but passion was daring us to go further.

He told me that he talked to his track coach about us. His coach was a priest who taught in his Catholic high school. His advice to Brian was to stay away from women because they were nothing but trouble. He told Brian that I was trying to trap him so that I could escape my troubled life. This didn't make a good impression on me since I was the one keeping us from having sex.

One day Brian came home from school and said that his track coach was worried that we were going to get ourselves in trouble. He saw that Brian was an angry young man and had taken him under his wing. Through tough love, he had helped Brian improve his schoolwork and become one of the state's top hurdlers.

Brian said that Father McDuffy wanted to meet me because he didn't want Brian getting trapped into a life that he couldn't handle. I agreed to meet with McDuffy, so Brian arranged that I would take the bus from my all-girl school to his all-boy school and watch track practice. When it was over, I would talk to Father McDuffy, and then he would drive us both home.

As planned, I met Brian at his Catholic school and enjoyed watching his practice. He introduced me to everyone as his "old ball and chain," and they all laughed. Brian's blond hair and blue eyes stood out in the hallway filled with mostly black and Hispanic students. It was obvious though that they all got along well and really enjoyed teasing and joking with each other.

Brian and his three medley relay team members stood in a line, wearing their short white gym shorts and the blue tank tops that featured the County Catholic logo. For an hour, they practiced passing the baton while their coach, Father McDuffy, yelled at them, "Get serious, you perform the way you practice!"

As he moved from student to student giving tips, he teased them with comments, like "Come on, move your boney black ass." I could see that his team really respected him. Father McDuffy towered over the track team in every way. He was six feet four inches tall and was as big as a tree. It's not even that he was fat, although he had a big stomach, but his arms, chest, and shoulders were well developed. He looked like the successful football player Brian had described. The thing that had most impressed me when I had seen Father McDuffy previously at a cross-country meet was that he ran the entire course, hills and all, yelling encouragement to Brian and his teammates the whole time. Since Father McDuffy was a smoker and had a big stomach, I was shocked to see him keep pace with his students.

Although I was there to see the coach, Father McDuffy avoided me the whole time I watched the team practice. It wasn't until the team hit the showers that he walked over to me, gave me a nod, and said, "You must be Katie."

I nodded my head and he said, "Follow me. Can I get you a soda or anything?"

I accepted a Coke, and then we walked to his office.

"Did you have any trouble getting here on the bus?" he asked.

We walked into his track office and he closed the door behind us. The room was an odd, rectangular room that was approximately six feet by twelve feet. Each wall had a leather love seat against it. There was a wooden desk along the short wall, and the entire room was filled with trophies and plaques. I could see that a few were for Father McDuffy being named the "Coach of the Year."

He started by asking me to tell him a little bit about myself. I told him that I was a junior at Newark Catholic and that I was on

the varsity basketball team, newspaper staff, yearbook committee, and the teacher evaluation committee.

"The what?" he asked.

I explained that I suggested to our principal that students
should be able to give teachers a report card so that they could
improve their methods. Rather than ignoring my suggestion, the
principal formed a committee of students and teachers, and
we created the school's first ever teacher report card. We were
going to pilot the program in the following year.

He said, "It will be a cold day in hell when a student grades
me."

I said, "Why, do you have something to be afraid of?" Before
he answered, I reassured him that Brian actually considered him
to be a great history teacher.

He said, "Now, you are being a smart woman." And we
laughed.

He asked me about my future plans, and I told him that I was
going to go to college to become an English teacher.

He asked, "Do you mind if I smoke?"

"No, not at all."

He lit his cigarette and tucked the pack back into the pocket
on his all-black shirt. He took a deep drag and really drew hard
as his piercing blue eyes met mine. He was studying me as if he
was realizing that he may have misjudged my intentions with
Brian. Then out of nowhere, he said, "Why don't you take off your
blouse?"

Stunned, I looked down at my white short-sleeved uniform
blouse and said, "Excuse me?" I was sure I misheard him or that
maybe I had spilled my soda on it or something.

He took another slow drag on his cigarette and paused again
and said, even more slowly and clearly, "Why don't you take off
your blouse." Even though I was caught off guard by this remark,
I felt arousal flush my face.

I leaned forward and asked deliberately, "Why would I take off my blouse?"

"To prove that you trust me."

"Why would I trust you? I just met you."

"Well, I can't counsel you if you don't trust me."

"Who asked you to counsel me?"

"I thought that's why you were here."

"No, I'm here because Brian said that you wanted to talk to me." I paused and added, "Why don't you take off your pants?"

He laughed, and his ruddy cheeks became crimson. He coughed from his cigarette and said with an indignant tone, "Why would I take off my pants?"

"To prove you trust me." Then I said, "You know what? This conversation is over." I stood to leave.

He said, "Hey, hey, Kathleen, wait a minute. Let me explain."

I said, "My name is not Kathleen."

"I'm sorry," he said. "My cousin is Kathleen. What do you like to be called, Katie, Katie, right?"

I said, "That's fine."

"That question has been proven to be an effective counseling strategy just to see how you would react. I am sorry. You passed the test with flying colors."

"What horse shit," I said, but sat back down. I tried to look angry and serious, but the truth was that I didn't want our meeting to end just yet.

He said, "The real reason I wanted to meet you is because I was worried for Brian. He is a good kid and he has really turned himself around. I don't want him or you getting yourselves into trouble and ruining your lives. Now that I have met you, I feel a little bit better because you seem to have a good head on your shoulders." He paused, thought for a minute, and then said, "Tell me, though, how do your parents allow your boyfriend to sleep at your house overnight? I am shocked and appalled by this."

"Well," I said, and hesitated, "it's because we don't live with our parents."

"How could that be?" he asked.

I started to give a shortened version of the story, and suddenly, without warning, I found myself weeping—which I prided myself on never doing. I tried never to cry in front of my mother, because she never once reached out to comfort me. She would just laugh, mock me, or hit me and say, "There, now you have something to cry about." So crying was uncomfortable to me.

Before I could compose myself, Father McDuffy stood up, took the one step to cross the narrow room, and sat down next to me on the leather loveseat. He waited for a moment to see if I calmed down. When I didn't, he gently pulled my arms and was able to guide me up until I was sitting on his knee. He put his huge hand gently on the side of my head and guided my head to his chest.

My sobs were muffled and he said nothing at all as he held me. His deep, steady breathing was next to my ear, and his huge, incredible warmth engulfed me like a favorite blanket. I stayed there for what seemed like a very long time.

Finally, Father McDuffy guided me up until I was standing between his legs and turned me towards him. I looked into his kind Irish face that looked much softer than it felt as he leaned in and gave me a kiss on the cheek, on the forehead, and on my eyelashes. He said, "You are going to be OK. I want you to come see me again next week. OK?" I nodded and grabbed the white, pressed handkerchief he passed me to wipe my eyes and face.

Just as he started to give me his card, there was a loud bang on the door. Brian yelled, "Hey, old man, what are you doing with my girlfriend? Let me in, pervert!"

We both laughed and straightened our clothes and McDuffy rushed to open the door.

Brian said, "Let's go, m' lady," and he put his arm around me and walked me out. I turned back and my eyes locked with

McDuffy's eyes. I smiled good-bye, and we both knew that something had begun.

McDuffy shouted after us, "You know, Brian, there is more to your girlfriend than I thought."

I began seeing Father McDuffy once a week, and we became close very quickly. We built an extremely trusting relationship during conversations, and sometimes it was difficult to tell who was counseling whom. In our weekly give and take, I asked him about his childhood, his relationships, and his life choices.

He told me that he was the youngest of four brothers. When his mother made his older brothers watch him while she cleaned the house, they tied him to a tree while they played football. Then, they came back and untied him before they went home and said they would kick his ass if he ever told their mother. I thought that it was funny that McDuffy grew to be as big as a tree.

McDuffy had dated one girl in high school, named Suzie Simpson, but he never had sex. He kissed her and once touched her breast after the prom. That was the extent of his sexual experiences. He became a priest because his mother was a devout Catholic and thought that the only way to guarantee her place in heaven was if one of her sons became a priest. Of McDuffy's older siblings, one was a lawyer, another was a doctor, and one worked on Wall Street. After graduating from high school four years after his brothers, McDuffy felt as if he could never live up to their successes, so he gave his mother what she wanted. He joined the seminary and pursued two master degrees and a law degree. He had been teaching in the all-boys school for eleven years.

McDuffy's apparent sadness when he talked about his lack of experience with girls deeply affected me. His face brightened when he talked about his high school girlfriend Suzie, but turned sullen as if he realized that his chances at love were over forever. I felt such empathy for this gentle giant who thought that he would never know love in his lifetime. Over months of intimate conversations alone in a windowless school basement office, I felt closer to him then to anyone. I had shared everything with him, including details about my blossoming sex life with Brian. I told him about how each week, I was willing to go further until I could scream in frustration. Sometimes, the titillating conversation enabled McDuffy to live vicariously through me. He asked for details about how it felt to be naked against each other's skin under the covers.

Once, when there was a lull in our conversation, I slowly stood up, walked over to the door of his small track office, and I switched off the light. I moved closer to him in the pitch darkness, with only the amber light from his cigarette leading my way. My heart raced uncontrollably as I slowly put one foot in front the other and was soon standing just inches from his knees. He started to ask, "What are you doing?" but I put my finger to his lips and quieted his words. He listened immediately and took a long deep drag of his cigarette. He blew out the smoke, slowly and carefully, and it circled my arms as I began unbuttoning the five little white plastic buttons of my Catholic school uniform blouse.

When I got to the last one, I let my blouse slip off my shoulders, down my back, and drop to the floor. I turned my back to him slowly and slid down the left, then the right strap of my little pink padded bra. I twisted it around and undid the hook in the front and let that drop to the floor next to my white blouse. Then, ever so slowly, I turned back to facing Father McDuffy. My bare chest just was inches from his smooth-shaven face. I stepped a little closer so that I was nearly between his legs. He made no movement to touch me, but something inside his pants reached for me. Facing him fully, I unbuttoned the side button on my pleated skirt, pulled down the zipper and let the blue Glen plaid garment fall to the floor. I now stood before this man of God wearing nothing but pink panties, embroidered with the word "Thursday."

He didn't reach out to touch me, but instead just slowly and patiently scanned my body. My small nipples grew hard as his eyes paused on my breast. I reached out and picked up his enormous freckled hand and rested it on the front of my pink silky panties. I moved it back and forth gently, and his moaning showed appreciation for the fabric. His pointer finger traced the letters that spelled "Thursday" in red thread and then traced the elastic from my thigh down to between my legs. I flushed with heat, but struggled to show nothing. His finger slowly lifted the elastic and then slid inside to feel the wetness.

This caused me to jump and to feel naked suddenly. He sensed my reaction and immediately stood up and folded his large body around mine as if to protect me. It was safe and warm there. I so appreciated the security of him. Before I knew what I was doing—as I had never done it before–I slowly lowered to my knees to kneel in front of this god of mine. As I inched lower, my right hand began to undo his zipper. Instantly, he stopped me and said firmly, "No. That's not what I want." He lifted me from the ground so easily and sat me on his lap in one movement. While there, he picked up my clothes from the floor and redressed me as if I were his baby doll.

It wasn't long before McDuffy and I were seeing each other constantly behind Brian's back. McDuffy drove us both home and dropped off Brian and me together at Brian's house. Then, I made an excuse why I had to go home and I walked around the block and McDuffy was waiting for me in his car. I got into his car and went to the diner with him. We usually had a sandwich and fries and coffee and dessert. Then, we drove down the New Jersey turnpike and found some remote place to park somewhere between Kearny and Jersey City.

While parked, we talked about our day and what was going on in our lives. I always ask him about wanting more than he had in his life as a priest. I constantly pressured him to take a chance on himself. "Have you ever looked around and seen the freaks of nature you are living with? They all seem like weirdoes and obviously you're not." He thought for a long time and then said, "It would break my mother's heart if I ever left. She would think that she could never get to heaven. She would be so ashamed."

I argued, "This is not your mother's life. It's yours." He smiled, took out a cigarette, lit it up, and said, "Kiddo, everyone is not as tough as you are."

Then, I put my head on his shoulder, and he was usually wearing street clothes instead of his black frock, and his wool sweater scratched my face. After he finished his cigarette, he flicked it out the window and turned to me and lifted my face up from his chest and we kissed passionately. The windows of his car got all steamy as I lifted myself up and wrapped one leg around each side of him. Nothing made me feel more powerful then feeling the hardness grow beneath me.

His hands moved up my blouse and weakened me to the point where I wanted to do everything for him that a woman could do. With Brian, I had refused to have sex for years because I thought it was wrong. With McDuffy, I wanted to give every fiber of myself to him every day—whenever he wanted it and as many times as he wanted it. But he didn't want that, and I felt so rejected. He was the one with control. He said emphatically every time, "We will never do that. I took a vow."

One time, I answered his rejection with, "Your vow doesn't include making out in a car with your track star's girlfriend, does it?"

He lifted me off of him, drove me home, and dropped me at my house without saying a word. For two days, I didn't get a phone call from him. On the third day, when I was leaving school with a group of friends and heading towards the bus stop, I heard the honk of a horn. I didn't pay any attention until my friend Patrice said, "I think someone is calling you." I looked over and saw McDuffy in a blue Chevy Malibu, which I didn't recognize because he always had a different car. Without as much as a good-bye to my friends, I sprinted to the car.

He said, "Get in. I am taking you someplace special." I got in the car and it took everything for me not to grab him and kiss him a million times. But I saved it for when we were away from the school.

Soon, we were on a highway heading to Sussex County, New Jersey. Once we approached a gas station, he pulled the car off the road and turned to me and kissed me so passionately that he nearly smothered me. He said, "I never want to miss you like that again."

When we got back on the road, he explained that he had a special dinner planned for me. He took me to a beautiful log cabin in a rustic part of Sussex County, New Jersey. It was his parents' summer home. Tremendous evergreen trees lined both sides of the property and the A-framed log cabin was a postcard of a mountain chalet. When we entered the home, the musty dampness was instantly erased when Father McDuffy lit a fire. He told me to sit at the kitchen table to do my homework while he prepared dinner. His instructions, alone excited me. It felt as if I had a parent who cared. I sat at the table and worked on my journal and talked to him while he cooked a supper of steak, homemade cole slaw, and corn on the cob. He told me to go rest for a few minutes while he set the table.

I went into the master bedroom and lay down on top of the country quilt. The bed was so comfortable and inviting, because we never had top sheets and quilts in our house. The smell of the fire from the living room was soothing. I glanced around at the photos of his mother and father that were on the night tables. They were so little I couldn't imagine how parents that size could ever have such a huge son. After a while, I had a good idea. I yelled, "Oh, Duffie, darling, come here a moment." He said, "Give me a minute. I'm just going to turn off the grill."

As he worked on the back porch, I could hear him moving some utensils.

I said, again, "Oh Duffie, big boy, come here."

He laughed as he walked into the bedroom and I was lying on top of the bedspread completely naked. He growled in appreciation as he sat down next to me and started tickling me on every part of my body. Just when I thought my fantasies were becoming reality, he reached into the closet and grabbed a soft pink knit blanket and covered me up. I was so confused. I turned to face the knotty pine wall. He climbed into bed behind me and held me tight in a spooning position. "I love you too much to ever hurt you. You deserve more." He held me with every inch of his body, and I felt swaddled like an infant that a father truly loved. The only sound in the room was our breathing. Then, we were startled by a knock at the door.

McDuffy quickly buckled his pants and put his finger to his mouth while his eyes commanded me to not say a word. He ran his black pocket comb through his wavy auburn hair and closed the door to the bedroom. I could hear a man's voice explaining that they had seen smoke coming from the grill and wondered if his parents were there. McDuffy explained that he just had to get away from the city, so he was coming up to have dinner. The neighbor said, "No reason for you to eat alone, Father, you are always invited to dinner at our place."

McDuffy covered well by saying that he had some term papers he had to correct, so it was going to be a late night. The neighbor stayed and chatted for a while about a black bear he had seen in the field, and then said good-bye.

McDuffy continued making noise in the kitchen, but I was so content that I drifted off to sleep thinking this was the life I wanted every day. I had never loved anyone so thoroughly. In class the following week, Sister Carrie was upset when I submitted this poem.

"Me and the Man"
I'd wait in front
Of the small deli.
Peppers and onions, and
I'd be nervous.
Anxious, waiting.
He'd walk, baggy pants
Waving in the wind.
Dry nervous mouths
Kiss, Quivering.
We were together,
Me and the man.
In his small room,
Talking, laughing, eating,
English Muffins,
Tomato soup.
Nabisco Cheese Nips
Floating in red.
Wool sweater.
I lean against.
A small pull,
put my finger through
And tickle.
We were happy,
Me and the Man.
Smiling mouth freezes.
Serious. They meet
Again, hard, wanting
Hands move, warm, comfortable.
Ring caught on my sweater.
Laugh, you clumsy man.
Just sit. Quietly satisfied.
Old spice, sweet.
Synchronized breathing.

We are alone.
Just me and the Man.
That's past.
The man's tired. Old man.
Doesn't want to hurt.
Stupid Man.
Too late now.
No one to cry to.
No one knew, except...
Well, I could close
My eyes. Grey Sweater.
Small pull, put my finger through.
We could be alone, again.
Me and....
No, nothing left for Me,
And the man.

My joy and happiness and desire to be with a grown man like McDuffy began to completely overshadow my relationship with Brian. After a while, I couldn't stand this little boy kissing me and touching me because I wanted to be enveloped by the hands, shoulders, warmth, and strength of a grown man. At the same time, Brian was changing with the times. He grew his hair long and started listening to what I thought was "druggie" music like Black Sabbath, Jethro Tull, and Iron Maiden. He confided in me one night that he had decided that he wasn't going to college. Instead, he was going to become a full-time painter with a man that he worked with part time in the summers. There was no way I was going to stay with someone who wasn't going to go to college. Then, after four years of dating, the final straw came when Brian returned home from the mall with an earring. "Are you a fag now?" I shouted. I had never heard of a man having an earring in my life.

He and I began to fight constantly, and a real breaking point with him and his family was when I decided not to go to the prom with him. His mother wouldn't talk to me for months because of this. I used the excuse that I had no way to get the money to get a dress, but I really wanted to be with McDuffy every minute of the day and could only imagine myself dancing slowly with him and singing the words of Chaka Khan.

I will love you anyway
Even if you cannot stay
I think you are the one for me
Here is where you ought to be
I just want to satisfy ya
Though you're not mine
I can't deny ya
Don't you hear me talking baby?
Love me now or I'll go crazy
Oh sweet thing
Don't you know you're my everything?
Oh sweet thing
Don't you know you're my everything?
Yes, you are.

One night, the three of us were in McDuffy's office after practice when I announced that I was breaking up with Brian. Brian went crazy and started screaming at me "You bitch! How can you do this to me? I love you!" McDuffy had to hold him back and physically remove him from the room. He drove Brian home while I waited in his office, and then he picked me up to drive me home. I snuggled next to him and said, "Thank God, now we can finally be together." He said, "We will never be together." Just like that, I knew that I had made a huge mistake.

This became just another terrible chapter in what was becoming an extremely difficult senior year of high school. My relationship with McDuffy had caused me to isolate myself from friends so that I could keep the secret. On top of that, I chased away Brian, who was probably the only person who really ever loved me. I started to do poorly in all of my classes because I couldn't even Imagine leaving Newark Catholic ever. I didn't want to graduate from high school. I wasn't doing my senior term papers or homework, and, for the first time in my life, I was getting failing grades.

I tried to use my home life as an excuse, but my teachers wouldn't have any of it. They made me come to school on Saturday to make up the work. To make matters worse, my very own personal hero, Sister Eileen, called me at home one day. When I picked up the phone, I could barely recognize her voice because she was sobbing. I was devastated. First, God was make-believe, and now Sister Eileen was human? The strongest woman I had ever met was crying on the phone asking me to give her strength. After she got control of herself, she told me that she was being transferred from Newark Catholic to become the Mother Superior at the central office for the Sisters of Charity. She was so upset she couldn't even talk. It was her duty as a nun to go to where she was assigned. Still, she cried and cried and then hung up the phone.

Despite my poor senior year grades and my relationship turmoil, I graduated and, through financial aid and scholarships, I was enrolled in the College of St. Elizabeth for fall semester. You would think that a girl in my circumstances would be thrilled to leave such a crappy home life to live in the safety of an all-girl Catholic college—for free no less. As much as home was a nightmare at times, I had never left it before. I really couldn't imagine that I would be leaving my two younger brothers alone. They were just sixteen and fifteen years old, and they would have no one left to take care of them. I felt overwhelming sadness for them, because every woman in their lives had left them. My grandmother and mother had left them. Renee left to move in with a boyfriend. Becky left to go to nursing school. Now, it was my turn to leave them. What choice did I have? Stay and work at

McCrory's pizza counter for the rest of my life? Or go to college and make true what Nanny had always told us: "Education is the only ticket out"?

On my last day of work at the pizza counter before leaving for college, my boss Frankie offered to give me a ride home. He mentioned that he just had to stop at home first. When we reached his house, he asked me to come in for a few minutes. When I did, I was greeted with his family shouting "Surprise!" At his dining room table were his wife and children, which included two daughters and his son, who were all in their twenties. There was a big cake in the center and it said, "Congratulations, Katie. Good luck in college."

While I was so touched by Frankie's surprise and the compassion behind it, I felt like such a beggar because the guests at the party were not my family. His kindness and generosity only exacerbated how pathetic it was that there was no one else in my life to wish me well as I embarked on such an important journey. Frankie proudly walked in and handed me a huge gift wrapped in blue paper covered with graduation caps. When I opened it, there was a beautiful Samsonite leather overnight bag inside. It was made of soft red leather with a spot for my name. What a great gift. It was the first time I had ever owned luggage.

While his family was busy cleaning off the dining room table, he led me to the living room and said, "I want you to listen to me good." He lifted up his black-framed eyeglasses and wiped the tears from his eyes. He said, "Do you see my three kids in there? God knows, I love them to death, but they had every advantage in life. My wife and I loved them and gave them everything. And guess what? They're not off to college...you are! Goddamn it, kid, I am so proud of you, and I beg you not to blow this opportunity. With all of my heart, I want you to know that no one deserves the best in life more than you do." With that, my boss from the pizza counter gave me a tremendous bear hug and a kiss on the cheek and sent me off into the world.

On the day I finally left home for the College of St. Elizabeth's, I could hardly fill my little red overnight bag—even though I was leaving for an extended stay. There was nothing much of home worth taking. My bag was just three-fourths full, but my soul was completely empty because of who I was leaving behind.

When the Conrail train finally reached my stop, the conductor yelled, "Convent! Convent Station, Convent next stop!" I feared that maybe I had chosen a vocation and not a school.

Trenton Psychiatric Hospital

SUMMARY OF HOSPITALIZATION

Disposition Summary

Patient Name: Clara Murphy

This is a 36 year old white, separated Roman Catholic female sent here from St. James Hospital in Newark, NJ on 7 day commitment papers. Patient has been living on her own in an apartment and was having financial difficulties particularly in paying her rent and was unable to make ends meet. She could not maintain steady employment and could not take care of herself. When seen on admission, patient was flighty, over talkative, hyperactive, disorganized and inappropriate in affect and behavior. She claimed she was here for a rest and did not mind coming at all. She was very restless, pacing the hallway most of the time and was flighty. She talked about losing her family and was very hostile and agitated at times.

At the time of this summarization, it is felt patient has improved in her mental condition, is no longer depressed, no overt psychotic manifestations and has recovered from her acute psychotic episode. It is felt that she has obtained the maximum benefit from this period of hospitalization and can be released at this time. She should continue with follow up care in a clinic in her vicinity. She was advised to do this and to continue her medication.

Book 2

Harrison fire kills woman

A 50-year-old woman was found dead in her home Friday when a fire broke out in a two-family frame house at 218 Taft ST in Harrison officials reported. A passerby noticed smoke coming from the first floor of the home in the residential area at 6:27a.m. and sounded the alarm at a fire alarm box across the street from the building, according to Harrison fire chief, Richard Brown.

Within a minute, fire and police units were at the scene and found the first floor apartment filled with smoke and a rear bedroom fully engulfed in flames.

The victim, identified as Clara Murphy, was found lying in the bedroom doorway separating the bathroom and the living room, the chief said. She was apparently dead already, but was not pronounced dead until after she was taken to West Hudson Hospital, Kearny, by police. She was pronounced dead on arrival.

A resident of the building's second floor managed to get out without assistance and was not injured. Fire reports listed the one death, but no injuries to any other residents or firefighters.

The chief said there was no evidence that the fire was suspicious, but it is being investigated.

CHAPTER 1

I sat up in my bed and began pulling on my faded rose flannel nightgown, screaming, "Get it off me! Get it off me!" I cringed as if I were burning in hell. My five-year-old son ran into my bedroom and yelled, "Mom, what's the matter?"

"I'm burning up! I'm on fire!" My face flushed as I wrestled with the cover to free myself of its weight.

My son sighed and said, "Go back to sleep, Mom. You're having one of those nightmares again. Just go back to sleep." I looked over at his confused expression as he rubbed the sleep from his eyes and tied the black belt of his karate pajamas tightly around him. He came closer to the bed and said softly, "Do you want me to sleep with you for a while to make sure you're OK?"

I made sure my nightgown was still in place, felt my hands all around the bed to check that nothing was unusual, and realized my five-year-old son, Aaron, was right. It was just another one of those nightmares. I said, "No, I'm fine. Go back to bed. I'm sorry that I woke you."

He said, "Want me to get my Ninja Turtle nightlight for you?"

"No, I'm fine, honey," I said. "Go back to bed. I love you."

"I love you, too," he replied.

As I pulled my white down comforter up from the bottom of the bed, I sneaked a look at the alarm clock on the night stand next to my bed. It was 6:27 a.m.

Until I read the ten-paragraph newspaper article that began this chapter—the perfect pathetic summary to my mother's life—I had no idea that the time had any significance. But there it was, at 6:27 a.m. that morning, my mother burned to death in a fire.

The day was April 20 and I was thirty-two years old when I received the call from my sister, Becky. At the moment the phone call arrived, I was in the front yard of my house in Pennsylvania, planting forsythia bushes and trees that I had just purchased from Home Depot. Nothing was more symbolic of a new life for me than having my own trees and bushes. We didn't even have a blade of grass in the city, and now I would have an acre of land with white birch, flowering plum, weeping cherry, and pink dogwood trees. It was a clear and sunny day. The pleasant weather was deeply appreciated after a bitter cold winter of constant snowstorms and record-setting blizzards. It was my sister Renee's thirty-fourth birthday, and I was expecting her to come to my house later in the day for a barbecue.

I put down the phone after hearing the news that my mother was dead, and regret flooded my body. Having come running into the kitchen to answer the phone and still out of breath, I had to steady myself on the kitchen counter. I imagined my frightened mother, coughing and choking, struggling to find her way from the bedroom to the front door in her drab, Pine Sol soaked, three-room apartment. Of course her life would end this way. It was the saddest example of a life lived. Could anyone else have survived such loneliness and emptiness? How does a woman give birth to five children and end up completely alone?

Again, my devastating sadness was tinged with crushing guilt. My mind immediately formed the same familiar question: Was it my fault? Could I have done something to avoid it? I had stopped talking to mother for the first time in my life just four months earlier.

My brothers and sisters had given up on her long ago, but I still talked to her on the phone every day, sent her money when I could, and went to see her every holiday. After sharing Christmas with my family in New Jersey that year, I drove to Harrison to my mother's apartment to bring her a turkey dinner with all of the fixings. My son and I struggled to carry a fifteen-pound turkey in a throwaway aluminum roasting pan so she didn't have to do dishes. In other various foil pans, we had her favorite sage sausage stuffing, mashed potatoes, brown gravy, candied sweet potatoes, a string bean casserole, and mashed turnips. As we placed everything on her little round kitchen table, I made room for the small pile of gifts we brought her for Christmas. As a divorced mom with a teacher's salary of $18,500, I couldn't buy her many presents. Yet, I was happy to bring her a new blue pantsuit, a white fluffy robe, and the item she prized above all—a carton of cigarettes. My son also picked out a small bottle of Charlie perfume in a drugstore.

As I entered her apartment, the revolting smell of Pine Sol mixed with urine from her untrained mutt instantly turned my stomach, but I put on a happy face to say Merry Christmas. My son ran up to her and said, "Merry Christmas, Grandma." She smiled at him for a moment and then looked up at me and the smile faded. Her eyes were dark and held that otherworld look that I had seen many times before. She saw me looking into her and turned away instantly. She lit a cigarette and walked to the coffee pot to pour some coffee. When her back was towards me, she said sullenly, "Well, I guess no one came to see me for Christmas."

I was so angry at my brothers and sisters for not inviting her to our Christmas at my brother's house. But my brother, Whitie, said that he went to counseling in college and that the counselor told him, "If you go to a well once and you drink from it and the water is poison, it's not your fault. However, if you keep going back to drink from the same poisoned well again, then it is your fault." He and my other siblings had had their fill of my mother's poison.

I tried to use an upbeat voice to emphasize that "we are here for Christmas" and pulled my son next to me to build a united wall of cheeriness.

She turned towards us, took a drag of her cigarette, looked through me, and said, "Yeah, like I said, no one came to see me for Christmas."

Panic and anger started to rise in my chest as I tried to diffuse her unhappiness.

"Look," I said doing my best Vanna White impersonation using my arm to point to the luxurious food and gifts we brought.

"We have presents for you."

My son added, "Yeah, Grandma, we have really good presents for you."

Slowly and deliberately, she opened the largest box, which included a royal blue pant suit I had selected to match her eyes.

When she opened it, she squished her face up like a prune and pretended to be gagging. "How putrid," she said. "You're so ugly. You have no taste in clothes. Look at you."

These words assaulted me on this Christmas Day because for some reason I was completely unprepared for them. After the work involved in preparing the food, packaging it, keeping it cool throughout my holiday, lugging it from the car to her apartment, and leaving my fun Christmas with my siblings for her, I freaked out. I rushed to the table and with one stiff arm cleared all of the presents and some of the food from her metal table. I screamed at the top of my lungs, "I hate you." I rushed towards her with plans to slap her vicious nicotine-filled mouth, but, as usual, I was impotent.

My tow-headed son stepped right between us and said, "Come on, Mom. Let's go."

The moist innocence in his blue eyes caused me to pause.

I took his hand and walked right out the door and slammed it hard behind me. I held my breath until we jumped into my white Ford Taurus. I kept my emotions somewhere between my chest and my neck until I had navigated two or three side streets and was safely entering Route 80, heading back to the beauty and serenity of the Delaware Water Gap and Pennsylvania. Then, I released it all with a loud heave. I couldn't even see the road through my tears.

My son was kneeling in the passenger seat, reaching his gentle arm over to pat my shoulder over and over again. "Don't cry, Mom, Please, don't cry. She doesn't mean it."

But I couldn't stop. Between tears, I choked, "She has been so mean to me my whole life."

My son said, "I know, Mom. Don't cry, Mom, please. It's Christmas. "

This made it seem so much worse. It was Christmas. "Put your seat belt on," I said and pushed the radio button on and stepped on the gas. I lowered all of the windows to let out the sadness and we both put our heads out into the cool, refreshing air and shouted in time with Bruce Springsteen.

In the day we sweat it out in the streets of a runaway American dream
At night we ride through mansions of glory in suicide machines
Sprung from cages out on highway 9,
Chrome wheeled, fuel injected, and steppin' out over the line
Baby, this town rips the bones from your back
It's a death trap, it's a suicide rap
We gotta get out while were young
`cause tramps like us, baby, we were born to run.

Within just a few moments, we were feeling much lighter, and one song led to the next as "Born to Run" turned into "Dancing in the Dark" and then "Born in the U.S.A."

Born down in a dead man's town
The first kick I took was when I hit the ground
You end up like a dog that's been beat too much
'Til you spend half your life just covering up
Born in the U.S.A.
Born in the U.S.A.
Born in the U.S.A.
Born in the U.S.A.

Before I arrived at home, I firmly decided that my son would never be exposed to my mother again. Then, during the first week of January, when Christmas vacation was over, I made a phone call that I had been thinking about making for a long time. I decided to go to counseling to try to deal with my feelings about the past.

I had gone to counseling before in my life when I got arrested for shoplifting a suit the summer before I entered college. My knees trembled as I stood in front of the judge because he had just sentenced a sixty-two-year-old black woman to thirty days in jail for stealing one small bottle of Elmer's glue. I got caught stealing a suit from Haynes Department Store and was expecting to get much worse.

It's funny, but I knew I would get caught that day when I entered the store to steal a suit, because my anguish felt like a premonition. When the security guard tapped me on the shoulder, I had just put the navy suit jacket in a large black vinyl pocketbook. I knew it was over. He brought me into a small office next to the children's section and asked me to empty my purse. Of course, in my purse, I had a navy pin-striped skirt that matched the jacket. He asked me if I had taken anything else. I said no. He asked me why I took it and I told him that my brother won a speech competition and I wanted to look presentable when I went with him to the ceremony as his family. He asked me for my phone number and the names of my parents. I told him that I didn't have any. He raised his eyebrows as if to imply I was lying. He said that he thought that I was not being completely truthful, and I just started crying. He went away and them he came back again with a black Newark police officer.

The black officer knelt down on one knee in front of me and focused his caring brown eyes on mine. His cushioned lips opened into a slight smile. "Sweetheart, there has to be someone you could call, because it is 8:20 p.m. If we take you to the police station, the only thing we can do for you tonight is put you in jail. You may not be aware of this, baby, but you are in Newark. You got that pretty blonde hair and those baby blue eyes, and trust me; you're not going to make it through even one night in a Newark jail. I beg you to think of someone. It's for your own good."

Tears streaked my cheeks as all my toughness melted away. I just kept shaking my head from side to side indicating that I had no one to call. They put me in the back of a police car and took me to a nearby police station. I was so shocked that I could ever be in this situation, because in school, I always followed the rules and always tried to be the best. Somehow, I thought that I was entitled to shoplift because it was unfair that my family didn't have what we needed.

At the police station, I finally thought of someone I could call. I called Sister Eileen. Within minutes, she was there with cash and bailed me out. She didn't arrive before they had fingerprinted me and completed a strip search. Never had I felt such intense shame as when I was standing nude in front of a black female police officer. Her voice was gentle and compassionate, and she seemed to apologize when she asked me to turn around to separate my cheeks for a cavity search. How did I sink so low?

Sister Eileen was furious with the police that they had preceded with the booking. "I told you on the phone that I would take care of everything. What part of that conversation didn't you understand? This child doesn't deserve a police record." Sister Eileen seemed to tower over the desk sergeant, even though his desk was elevated. He explained, "Sister, we did our best. She didn't call you until it was too late. Sister, we couldn't keep her here without charging her." Sister Eileen ordered the police officers around here and there and took me by the hand and we were out the door. When I looked over at her as she slapped her hand on the steering wheel of her K-car, I could see she was frustrated. I thought that she was mad at me, but then she said aloud, "Why couldn't I have gotten here sooner? This is all my fault. I'm so sorry." Sister Eileen never once asked me what I was doing shoplifting and never said a word about it again.

Thank God, my other savior, Father McDuffy, through connections with his brother, got me a well-known lawyer for free. When the lawyer stood up in court and told the judge the story of my life, I couldn't help but feel sorry for the person he was describing. What a sad life story. He ended with, "Despite these odds, your honor, my client, a seventeen-year-old from a completely dysfunctional home, has graduated from high school receiving the school's citizenship award, English Award, and a full scholarship to the College of St. Elizabeth. She was a member of the varsity basketball team and served on the Essex County Bicentennial Commission. She has volunteered at local nursing homes and schools for the handicapped. All of this while helping to care for her family in the best way she could. She has never been in trouble before and only made this feeble, ill-planned attempt to steal so that she could try to bring some dignity to her family as she represented them for her brother, who is a finalist in a national speech competition. Obviously, she didn't succeed because she is not a thief. Your honor, my client has been humiliated. She has learned her lesson. She has a bright future in front of her. Let's not stunt her whole future with a criminal record."

I stood under the gaze of the white-haired judge, wearing a shoplifted, beautiful, cream and yellow Gunne Sax dress trimmed with yellow ribbon. The same man who was just so harsh to the other woman suddenly looked like Art Linkletter. He looked at me as if he was glancing at a toddler, and moisture filled his eyes as he said, "Honey, you have come so far. You're going to college in the fall. That is a remarkable accomplishment. Don't give up. You're a tough young lady. You're somebody special." He added, "I'm going to sentence you to mandatory counseling, and I never want to see you in my court again. Once you complete the counseling, we will expunge your record." He and I both smiled at the same time.

The sentence of counseling was one of the best things that could have happened to me. I found it so helpful, but at the time, it was just crisis counseling focused on assisting me with overcoming the deep sense of loss I felt because I would be leaving my brothers to go to college. I was paralyzed by the overwhelming guilt and sadness for my brothers. It bothered me tremendously that we girls had body parts to give away that could "buy" us a place to live and food to eat. What did two high school boys have to give away? It was completely unfair. In counseling, we focused on getting me to college and keeping me there. Even though counseling was effective and I did graduate from college, I knew that some day, I would have to go back to counseling to deal with my childhood. As a mother, things from my past began haunting me on daily basis; I started having strange flashbacks.

Sometimes, daily sensory stimuli forced me to escape reality into the shadows in my mind. This would happen, for example, when I was filling the bathtub for my son. I placed my hand under the faucet to test the temperature of the water, and like the "Wawa" scene in *The Miracle Worker*, the water meant something to me. My mind saw flickering images of naked bodies, crying and pleading. It was a shadow and then it was gone. I also started having nightmares and woke up screaming almost every night of the week. It felt as if the spirit of a woman in a white nightgown was trying to tell me something, but the message was so horrific, that I woke up screaming before I ever received it. Meanwhile, I had to admit that I failed at every intimate relationship I'd had by cheating on every man in my life.

I found a counselor in Bangor, Pennsylvania, via a phone book and began going on a weekly basis. After months of weekly appointments and getting to know each other, my counselor was already getting a little frustrated because I had so few memories or details of my childhood. From an extensive questionnaire and personality assessment, he strongly believed that

I had been sexually abused. Yet I couldn't help him confirm or deny this assessment. In fact, I had blocked out so many memories that I couldn't recall much about my childhood with my mother. All I could remember was that we were really bad children who tormented her on a regular basis and she left whenever she couldn't take our abuse anymore.

It had always been my plan to one day try to get better medical help for my mother when I could afford it. Before I stopped talking to her, I had her sign a release form to obtain copies of her hospital records. I still had the form in my possession so, a few months into my own counseling, I mailed it and had the records sent to a psychiatrist in my counselor's professional building.

When I arrived for my weekly appointment after the counselor received the Trenton State Hospital records, he looked at me with complete awe and disbelief. He seemed furious as he started a discussion immediately without any normal pleasantries. He said, "I want you to really concentrate hard and to remember your childhood. If you had to make your most reasonable guess about how many times your mother was hospitalized between your first birthday and your eighteenth birthday, what would you guess?"

I tried to concentrate. He added, "Don't just talk right away like you always do. Sit and think for a moment." I sat and thought for a moment, uncertain where to look and feeling overly conscious of him looking at me. As I pretended to think, I could only really think about how good looking he was. He looked exactly like Al Pacino in *Serpico* before he had the long beard. He was giving me a look like he was reading my mind and said, "Come on, no screwing around, really concentrate."

I finally guessed that she went to the hospital five times. I was thinking that the first time was when I was born, a few times when I was in high school, and when she burned herself on the kitchen stove.

He leaned across his desk with such intensity, verging on anger and said, "Do you believe it was twelve times? And that is not even counting hospitalizations in local facilities."

"You're full of crap," I said instantly.

"I'm full of crap?" he said. "We'll see who has been full of crap all this time."

With that, he opened his top drawer and walked deliberately over to my side of the desk and plopped the folder down.

He said, "I received a copy of your mother's hospital records, and there is a lot that you haven't been talking about."

Before I could say a word, he opened the folder and flipped through section after section of papers, all marked with Trenton State Hospital across the top. Just seeing that name made me quiver and gasp.

As if he was winning some great debate, he started reading out dates, 1958, 1959, 1961. Each word he spoke was like a knife in my chest as he seemed to be growing more and more intense. I was feeling defensive and asked, "Why are you doing this to me?"

He looked at me, exasperated. "Why am I doing this to you? How could you have wasted months of this valuable time in counseling without even mentioning the extent of your mother's mental illness?"

I stood up standing eye to eye with him and shouted, "How was I supposed to know she had an illness? I don't remember." He went back to the other side of his desk to watch safely from his leather throne.

He began reading my mother's first quote on admission, "I am eighteen years old. I have three children and I am a very bad girl."

I was so intrigued to hear this new portrait of the mother that I really never got to know.

Then, he read, "schizophrenic, catatonic state." From studying psychology in college, I knew what those words meant, and they had never meant so much to a person before. He passed me a box of tissues from his side of the desk, and I wiped my eyes and blew my nose.

"You mean it wasn't us? We weren't evil kids? I remember us being really mean to her."

He smiled and said, "Oh, that you remember. It wasn't you, knucklehead."

In between my blubbering and sniffling, I tried to form a sentence.

My handsome counselor locked his beautiful dark brown Italian eyes on mine and whispered beneath his soft, luscious mustache, "Come on, say it, it's right there on your lips."

I sniffled and said, "Say what?"

"Come on," he pushed as he went to my side of his desk, a barrier he hardly ever crossed. "Say it."

After wiping my nose and clearing my throat, I said meekly, "It wasn't my fault?"

"There you go," he said. "Now say it like you mean it."

"It wasn't my fucking fault!"

And we both started laughing.

He said, "Take a few minutes to make yourself presentable and get out of here. You done good, kid."

CHAPTER 2

Eventually, my counselor gave me the records to hold and to cherish. Regardless of where I moved, I kept these voluminous hospital records in a most sacred place in a fireproof file. The beautiful, melodious words "schizophrenic, catatonic state" were music to my mind for the rest of my life. It meant that my mother had an illness. It was that simple. I was not the cause of all of the strife in our home.

It's hard to believe, but until I read these words with my very own eyes, I thought that my brothers and sisters and I were such horrible children that we caused my mother to go away. This distortion of my childhood became even more real to me as I became a mother myself and discovered how hard it was to take care of one child, never mind five children all one year apart. When every kid in my son's preschool class had on green clothes for "Green Day" and my son was wearing blue, I drove away wondering how my mother kept five kids washed, ironed, and dressed. My son barely got out of the house with two of the same socks on each day. Plus, I thought I remembered us having hot, home-cooked meals. My son was fed a constant diet of chicken fingers and french fries and pizza. But it is amazing how time allows you to sweeten memories because, in reality, our childhood, too, was filled with takeout food.

Still, as I beat myself up mentally while driving to work each day about what an unorganized mother I was, I pictured my mother washing and ironing clothes, cooking, cleaning, making beds, etc., and couldn't believe what a horrible life she had.

She was a slave to us, the house, and my grandmother. I reasoned that anyone in her circumstances needed a rest and a little vacation in Trenton once or twice in a lifetime while raising five wild children.

My mother's tangible hospital records became a touchstone for me. A few times a year, I opened my beige flame-resistant file box and rubbed my hands across them to remember that I wasn't a horrible child. This very act of hand touching paper allowed me to feel such sorrow for my mother and reaffirmed for me over and over, whenever I needed it, that it was not my fault—but also that it wasn't her fault either. What a gift I was given. Anyone who has experienced some type of trauma in childhood will tell you that you can never trust your own memories. The hospital records that punctuate my story provided me with daily evidence, first, that I had not imagined it all, and second, that I was not the cause of my family's dysfunction.

After several months of reviewing the mental hospital records, my counselor helped me to finally realize that my mother's illness was not just something I could "love" away. He said my siblings were smart to have given up, but that I held on to the hope that if I tried really hard, day after day, week after week, year after year, that maybe she would come around to loving me. I believed that somehow I was just not doing enough. He helped me to see that her severe illness couldn't be taken away with any amount of kindness. I wish I had not given up just when I did.

Then, two weeks before she died, my mother started leaving messages on my answering machine. "Katie, a message just scrolled across the bottom of my television saying that Clara Murphy killed Jesus Christ and that they are coming to take me away. You have to come help me."

I hit erase.

You have ten new messages. "You're not my daughter. Your father was a nigger. I hate you. I never loved you. You're so ugly. You're a filthy whore."

Finally, I unplugged the answering machine.

Then, my sister called with the news that my mother was burned to death in a fire. My mother's funeral was a blur. Again, we just put one foot in front of the other in the procession and got through it. My sister Becky wanted to use the opportunity to stand up in the church and indict every person we ever knew in our lives to ask them, "How come you never helped us?" But the funeral director wisely told us that we wouldn't be in any condition to speak and that our only goal should be to simply get through the day. He was right.

I continued to go to counseling for two years after my mother died. The counselor wanted to hypnotize me to see if I could remember what happened in the basement, but I refused to participate. I didn't want to know what happened. I explained to him that throughout my childhood, whenever I was hurt and cried, there was never anyone there to hold and comfort me. When I cried in front of my mother, she mocked me. I told my counselor that I couldn't recall such terrible incidences and cry in front of him if he was going to sit there with a desk between us and look at me while I cried. I might as well be standing in his office completely naked, having a cavity search, because that is how vulnerable I would feel.

He contemplated this for a while and said, "With all of my heart, I wish that I could be the person to hold you and comfort you. I know that's what you need to feel safe enough to explore these memories. The last thing I want is for you to feel rejected by this, because what I say right now will never change as long as you come to counseling with me. No matter what happens in this office, I will never touch you. What happened before with Father McDuffy was very wrong, and it was not counseling. That was an irresponsible adult not having any boundaries. We have boundaries in my office, and I will never touch you." These words did feel like rejection, and I hated him for that, but for two more years, he kept his word and never touched me.

Another significant breakthrough my counselor helped me to experience was that I was not as ugly as I thought. If fact, he thought that I wasn't ugly at all. He said that if I were truly ugly that it would be an important part of his job for him to help me to accept that fact and to deal with it. He said that it was simply not the reality. He also said that I could gain perspective by just examining my life experiences. He asked me about the boyfriends I had throughout my life. "Do you think your boyfriend in high school, the priest, your husband, would have all asked you out if you were so hideous looking that they had to turn away?"

This helped me to see myself differently, although I have to admit that there was such safety in ugly. For years, I saved so much time and money by not focusing on what was in the mirror and trying to be sure that what was in my heart was not ugly. I considered it a huge waste of time or money to style my hair or put on makeup or get dressed nicely. When I tried, I gave up instantly because I felt as if I wasn't worthy of spending time or money on my appearance the way other girls did. Ugly girls worked on being smart and gracious. Janis Ian's "At Seventeen" was my personal anthem because I thought that I had learned the truth way before seventeen.

I was emotionally transformed from the years with my counselor, and I was so grateful for the time we shared. In the beginning, he had explained to me that counseling was like driving the same road to work every day of the week. "Then, one day, your car breaks down and a friend comes to pick you up. You drive on the exact same route to work that you drove every day, but this time you are sitting in the passenger's seat. From that new perspective, it's amazing what things you've never seen while you were in sitting in the driver's seat."

Allowing him to be in the driver's seat while I took a cautious look back enabled me to see, for the first time, that I was not the cause of my mother's illness or all of the havoc in our family. Of all of the things I had learned in life so far from examining great works of literature as an English major and an English teacher, no theme was more important. As a thank-you gift, I wrote this poem that is still framed on his office wall.

<u>Trusting My Counselor</u>
Other men, I have met in shadows
But you sit within the gray of me
Without touching, yet reaching
Me so thoroughly
Something, glistening in your eyes
Smoothes over my tense body
Caressing a child, somewhere, whose
Body aches for flannel warmth.
Your smile tickles this kid, inside
More than the tenderest series of
Other men's kisses whispering
Moist secrets along my neck.
The surprise birthday candles of
All the years I missed
Burning joyously together could
never emit the warmth
I feel for you.
And a million rides on the newest
Red Schwinn bike down
The steepest city hill with
My hair blowing like endless rows
Of apartment laundry
Would never compare to the
Exhilaration and freedom I feel
Laughing for forty minutes
With you.
Thank you for not wanting to touch…
you have reached every inch of me.

CHAPTER 3

Leaving counseling somewhat unsatisfied because I had never felt safe enough to cry aloud to release the pain of childhood was a risk. The poison my brother spoke of was still in there, slowly destroying me. But I felt as if I would be OK, because otherwise my life was going well. I was a successful teacher and the parent of a wonderful son, who was five. I had a good support system and was dedicated to ensuring the cycle of abuse was broken. The most important person in my support system at the time was my ex-husband, Stephen. I had met him while on summer break from college when my sister Becky arranged a secretarial job working with her at a trucking company in Port Newark, New Jersey.

Looking back now, I know that I married him for all the wrong reasons. First, he was the absolute worst person I had ever met. He was selfish, obnoxious, and antisocial. This sounds crazy, but I had learned from my twenty years of Catholic school that love could change everything, and I thought that if he only had someone to love him, he would be a better person. I was also so excited that with him I could have any food I wanted and would never go hungry. Finally, I reasoned that if a man, any man, thought someone like me was tolerable, I'd better marry him and not let him get away.

My sister Becky and I were the only two females who worked for a car-hauling company in Port Newark. In the company, she served as the office manager and the real person in charge. There was a general manager and a dispatcher, but they were mostly absentee bosses. The entire office included just three rooms.

The main room had two desks across the room from each other and facing each other, one where my sister sat to do all of the billing and the other desk where I sat calculating mileage. Then there was an office that was shared by the general manager and dispatcher. Lastly, there was a driver's room, where fifty-two owner-operator truck drivers waited to select their loads for the week via a seniority system.

My sister basically ran the place because she worked for the two guys, Gerry and Joe, who went out for a three-hour liquid lunch just about every day of the week. The day started at 6:00 a.m. with Gerry opening the driver's window, where he placed a clipboard listing the runs that were available for the day. In seniority order, the men lined up and sign up for the trips that they wanted to take.

"I'll take these two Lorraine, Ohio, trips," one would say

The next guy yelled, "Don't be so fucking greedy. Take one load at a time. Leave some work for the others."

After the drivers had their trips, my job was to use a big book of maps to determine the mileage of the trip. The drivers got paid for each load per car and per mile. Sometimes they came back from the road trip after a few days with their bills in their hand and yelled at me. "Do you think I'm driving a fucking plane? Do you know how many mountains there are in Pennsylvania? This mileage was wrong. You have to recalculate this."

Before the guy finished complaining, he would be surrounded by three other, bigger guys. "Don't ever let me hear you curse at these girls again. This is a college girl here, not like the trash that you married." Inevitably, the disgruntled driver would take off his Peterbilt cap and look down sheepishly and apologize.

When the guys walked away, Becky and I laughed at how the drivers protected us and thought that we were innocent. Most of the time, when Becky and I were on the phone in the office, we were really just talking to each other about the drivers. We commented on which driver was cute or ugly, which one was an asshole or a gentlemen, and if one passed by our desks, we immediately switched to our fake secretary voices.

Each morning, our desks were filled with containers of coffee and several egg sandwiches that drivers left for us before they went on their trips. The sandwiches were from a grease wagon that sold food from a trailer in the port. Also, when Gerry and Joe, our bosses came back from lunch each day, they usually reached under their trench coats and took out a glass of rum and coke for each of us that they carried out of the bar for "their girls." My sister and I never knew how they carried them all the way back to the office without spilling a drop.

The bosses had such respect for us because Becky was great at her job and because I was in college. Joe said, "Next year, I think my boy is going to go to Lehigh University. I hope he'll do as well as you're doing, because I want him to be a lawyer. He'd better." The bosses would take turns coming back from lunch completely wasted. They would say, "Ladies, I'm so embarrassed. Please forgive me. I'm drunk once again and cannot drive home. Could you give me a lift? The Mrs. is going to be awfully upset with me."

Becky and I would load the big guy into her lime green Volkswagen beetle, while I drove the boss's car to his house. We gave him a lift to the house, and he was a perfect gentleman and laughed and sang the whole time. Then, the boss leaned over and said, "I love you. I only hope my daughter turns out to be as good as you."

One day, when I was working, Stephen, the driver who always defended my honor, came over to the desk and said, "Excuse me, darling, are you a damsel in distress?"

I looked up and saw a balding, white haired man with a pleasant face standing at my desk with a bouquet of flowers. After smiling and being so pleased to see flowers, the next thing I noticed was that someone had sewn a different color flannel onto the sleeves and tail of his flannel shirt to make them longer.

He saw me looking at this and said, "My mother added extra material to keep her baby warm."

"Your mother?" I mocked, "How old are you?"

He said, "I'm forty, but any man that takes care of his mother so well would take care of his girl also."

Each day, he brought me flowers or a cupcake and pulled up a seat and sat at my desk and talked to me. When drivers approached me to talk about their mileage, Steve served as a mediator and recalculated their mileage for me and chased them away with strange words like, "Get going, you Mississippi sapsucker! Can't you see we're busy here?" Guys had a great rapport with Steve and laughed at his jokes. Steve said to guys with a mustache, "Get away, you walrus-faced fruit. This is my girl."

I began to enjoy the attention, and he made my day go so quickly.

When Steve was on the road, I tried to learn more about him from other drivers. There were rumors that Steve was very wealthy and that he was connected to the mafia in some way.

One driver added, "I seen Steve take out three guys with his bare hands. He knows karate and was a hand-to-hand combat expert in the military."

One of the few black drivers told this story: "One day, I was taking a load of Hondas to Florida and Steve was also. When we stopped at a truck stop, three white guys jumped me. I was taking a beaten. I was on the ground just trying to protect myself from the kicks and the blows. Before I knew it, they stopped, and I looked up and the three guys were down and Steve was standing over them. He didn't even have a weapon. He helped me up, dragged me to my truck, and we hightailed it out of there."

These stories intrigued me because there seemed to be something exciting about this guy. Every day, he invited me to go on a date with him and I refused. But one day, he invited me to go to the Meadowlands Race Track to see harness racing with him, and I couldn't refuse. It sounded so exciting. It wouldn't be long before I would be heading back to the nuns at St. Elizabeth's, so I accepted.

In a fake British accent, Steve said, "I will be taking you to the prestigious Pegasus Restaurant for dinner where waiters and waitresses will be placing our bets, so dress accordingly." I told him that there was no way he was coming to my house or getting my address, so I was going to take a taxi to meet him at the track.

No date I'd ever had before had required me to get so dressed up. My brother Billy went to Bamberger's Department Store and bought me a sharp crème-colored suit with a long, flowing, pleated skirt, a tailored blazer, a silk brown-and-white blouse that tied, and brown leather high-heeled shoes. He charged $230 on my brand new charge card I had just gotten a month earlier.

Even though it was a spring evening, I topped this suit with a full-length white rabbit fur coat. I bought this coat during my last year at the pizza counter. Every day, on the way to and from work, I passed a Bond Clothing Store, and the coat was on a mannequin in the window. "I must have this," I thought. It was pure white and looked so soft and touchable. "I need that coat for my future." The coat was $179. I put the coat on layaway and paid it off over a year's time. When I finally picked it up, I put it on over my basketball practice clothing and wore it on the bus with high-top orange Converse sneakers. I felt like a million bucks. I didn't care what the other passengers thought. My date with Steve was going to be my first opportunity to wear the beautiful coat on a real date.

After taking a long time to get dressed, I was ready to leave for the date when I noticed that I had a run in my stocking. It ruined my whole sophisticated look. I didn't have any other pair of panty hose in the house, and my two sisters had long since moved out, so I walked from our apartment in North Arlington to Two Guys department store, picked up panty hose, put them on in the store's bathroom, and then called the taxi to pick me up at the store to take me to the Meadowlands.

The taxi took forever, and I was so afraid that Steve would think I had stood him up. I didn't want his feelings to be hurt. I waited and waited, continuously looking out the store door for the familiar red car that was usually sent by the North Arlington Cab Company.

Finally, after eight more minutes of stressing, a red car pulled up in front of the store. I immediately ran from the store front, opened the back door of the car, jumped in the back seat, and said to the driver, "Jesus Christ. You're so late. What took you so long?"

The middle-aged driver in the front seat resembled Archie Bunker wearing a tweed cap. He turned around towards the back seat with a really confused look on his wide face and said, "I'm sorry, honey. I'm not a cab. I'm waiting for my wife."

"Oh my God, I'm so sorry," I said. I quickly opened the door to get back out of the car. Just as I touched my brown high-heeled shoe to the ground, a heavyset, middle-aged woman wearing a flowered muumuu starting yelling from just outside the store door. "You son of a bitch!" she screamed. "Who is she?" She crossed the front of the car to the driver's side window, where the little man yelled, "Honey, I never saw her before in my life!"The wife lifted her packages above her head and started smashing them down on the driver's side window in hopes of landing one on her husband's head. "You're full of shit," she screamed.

As this was happening, I ran as fast as I could, breaking the heel of my left shoe and tearing my stocking on a rock. As I did, the North Arlington Cab finally came up on my left side and I flagged him down.

"What's your hurry?" he said.

I asked him to take me to the Meadowlands Race Track, even though I was sure that I missed my date. After paying the fare, I hobbled inside and I couldn't believe how many people were there. I had arranged for Steve to meet me in a big lobby where people placed their bets. I was looking around for him, and there were so many men wearing flannel shirts with bald heads and white hair on the side.

I was about to give up when a handsome and distinguished, well-dressed man wearing a navy blue suit and a yellow polka-dot tie approached me and said, "Oh, my damsel in distress, I thought you'd never arrive." Steve gave me a big hug, and I could tell he was so happy to see me.

I told him what happened with the taxi and we laughed and laughed. He said, "I don't know if they'll let you into the Pegasus with one shoe, but we'll try."

That night, we ate, drank, and gambled all night and had a great time. He took me home and kissed me on the cheek good-night at the door like a perfect gentleman. He said, "This time, I will be a gentleman," then added, "Next time, I will ravage your bones." We agreed to meet for lunch the next day, and we did every day that he was in town until I went back to school.

Whenever he was on the road, he called and talked to me about his trip. Before the end of the conversation, he added disgusting comments, like "You or your sister should leave your panties in my mailbox for me to have something wonderful to welcome me home." I'd hang up on him, but my sister and I both laughed hysterically at how nutty he was.

I went back to college in September, but every weekend, I escaped the world of St. Elizabeth's when Steve sent a taxi for me. I took a taxi to a hotel in Jersey City, and Steve had a hotel employee meet me at the door, pay the driver the outrageous $50 fare, and escort me up the stairs. The whole thing felt so intriguing.

I was thrilled to have a break from St. Elizabeth's because I never felt as if I really fit there. The small classes allowed me to get the most out of the outstanding education, but socially, I believed I was beneath the other girls. Because of my family history, I entered the school through a program called the Equal Opportunity Fund (EOF) Program. This required me to attend a summer prep program. My nuns at Newark Catholic Academy were so furious that I was put into this program because it was designed for students that needed academic remediation. Still, the counselor at St. Elizabeth's thought it was a way to get more money towards my tuition.

When I entered the new world of college with only fifty girls in the summer program, there were only three white girls in the program. I got to be good friends with the black and Hispanic girls and was called on to help them with their summer papers. Meanwhile, they immediately started helping me get some style by redoing my hair and makeup and lending me some of their clothes. We were all united by our fear of this new world. However, when the actual school year started and I was already in this group, it made it difficult to fit into the mainstream of the college, because at St. Elizabeth's nearly all of the students were white and middle or upper class.

The Equal Opportunity Fund group was definitely separate from the regular students, and we always felt as if we were less than they were. They didn't make us feel this way; our inferiority complex did. The typical student had many material goods, and we didn't. My roommate and I had an austere room where our panties were hung to dry on the bathroom towel racks because we didn't have enough money to do laundry. Other girls, the typical students, had beautiful matching comforters and curtains, carpets and artwork, and their parents came on the weekend to clean their rooms. We couldn't compete and always felt like poor white trash compared to them. Even when I did make a connection with the general population of St. E's through a philosophy class or literature class, my EOF friends said, "What, are you dropping us now to be one of them?" I replied, "Of course not, I hate these bitches." But on the inside, I wanted more than anything to be part of that white, middle-class group.

Every weekend, Steve erased my feelings of inferiority and made me feel like a million bucks. He had presents hidden for me around the hotel room, and I enjoyed a treasure hunt to find them each weekend. Under the pillow, I discovered a stuffed animal. On the nightstand, there might be a small jewelry box, and in the bathroom, a bouquet of flowers.

All weekend, we stayed in the room, alternating between sleeping, having sex, and playing pinochle. Then each night, we went for a nice dinner to great places in both New Jersey and New York. Most times, I asked Steve if I could order big dinners to go so that I could drop them off to my brothers at the apartment where they were staying. He never objected. In fact, he admired my loyalty to them and always told me that my good heart was going to get me hurt someday. We spent lots of time in Atlantic City, and he let me be a big spender, playing blackjack or roulette. He never worried about money, and he seemed to know people and get us special treatment wherever we went.

Sometimes, when Sunday rolled around, I didn't feel like going back to school because I hated the feeling of being inferior. In our Catholic grammar school and high school, I never felt this way because our uniforms provided enough cover. However, at St. Elizabeth's, I had never felt poorer in my life. In classes, I participated in all of the discussions, and my high school had prepared me to be way ahead of my peers as an English major. But my limited wardrobe, my empty dorm room, and my closeness with my black and Hispanic friends on campus kept me segregated and allowed me to fully understand what it was like to feel less than others.

I'd have my head on Steve's shoulder and be wearing only my panties and would say something like, "I think I will quit school. I never want to go back. I'll stay here with you." Within seconds Steve picked me up and threw me in the hallway of the hotel and locked the door to the room.

Mortified, I banged on the door with my fist. "Let me in, you idiot." He laughed on the other side and said, "Are you going back to college?"

"Yes, Yes," I promised. "Hurry, please, Steve, someone will see me."

He made me wait just enough time to panic. I banged on the door furiously.

"Are you sure you're going back to college?"

I pleaded, "You asshole, please let me in."

He yelled things like, "No, you can't give me another blow job. I'm exhausted," really loud to embarrass me in case someone was passing by. Or "No, I cannot have more sex with you. You have worn me out."

As people passed by, I covered my breasts with my hands and grew even more furious. How could anyone do this?

Finally, he let me back in the room. I packed my stuff in a frenzy and he'd be laughing as he tried to give me money for a taxi. I said, "Keep your fucking money, asshole," and rushed out the door to take the train back to school. All the way, I swore that I would never come to see him again.

I always came back the following weekend, though, because the rendezvous in the hotel was so exciting compared to college. At St. Elizabeth's I talked to a friend for a few minutes while in the library, and one of the many girls named Mary turned around to me and said, "I am telling Sister you're talking in the library." Shocked that a college woman made such a statement, I replied, "Shut up, virgin." The girl picked up her books and ran away, and my friends of color and I laughed like crazy. I couldn't wait to get out of this strange new world.

My weekends with Steve definitely helped me survive my college experience. I had to stay because tuition was free for me, thanks to grants, but it was torture to see that, during the late 70s, this institution treated its students more like frightened little girls than competent woman of the future. Once in a Shakespeare class, one venerable nun made a fellow classmate stand for the entire class period because she did not join in the beginning prayer. If a student came to a college class a few minutes late, some nuns stopped the class right in the middle of a lecture and asked, "Do you want to explain to everyone why you could not be here on time?"

Still, for every old-fashioned, strict nun, there was one that really opened your mind with an outstanding discussion and individual attention. Sometimes there were just eight girls in a class, so every student was engaged in learning at all times. When the teacher lit a spark through a great question, the place was magical, and you left the classroom exhilarated and excited to discuss what you had learned with one of your peers. Unfortunately, my group of friends told me to stop living in the dream world of philosophy. "There ain't no money in being a philosophy major. What are you going to do, sit under a tree and philosophize?"

Each weekend, Steve and I enjoyed our relaxation at the hotel. More and more, we spent less time having sex, because Steve was just so tired from driving so many long trips. He worked so hard because he dreamed of being a property owner on the scale of Donald Trump.

We usually went to the same place for dinner because Steve liked to be in the situation where he walked in and the maître d' knew his table, his drink, and his special order. We started our meal in the same way. Steve ordered a glass of scotch on the rocks, and I ordered rum and Coke. Then they brought me a salad topped with six jumbo shrimp, with cocktail sauce on the side. Steve had either fried calamari or scungilli salad. I was so disgusted by the little squid tentacles that he stabbed with his fork. I'd ask, "How can you eat them?" He'd reply, "Because I like the way they tickle my tonsils on the way down." I was disgusted by this.

Even though I was twenty and Steve was forty-two, at first we always had things to talk about. But as we spent more and more time together, one conversation got very tiring, and it seemed we had it every Sunday at breakfast before I went back to school. I was his audience as he talked nonstop and outlined scheme after scheme of how he was going to get rich. I could repeat his plans word for word, and my head ached from having to listen to his plans after drinking all night.

To start, he had already bought his first six-family brownstone apartment house in Hoboken. Next, he planned on leveraging that apartment building to buy another, then another, then another. Finally, his big plan was to play a part in the redevelopment of the Hoboken waterfront.

On some Saturday afternoons, we met some characters at the Italian American Club in Hoboken. Here, Steve was immediately offered a bowl of pasta fagioli as a man in an apron set up a table for Steve as if he were someone important. There, Steve took on a whole new speech pattern and talked with his hands as if he were Italian—even though he was 100 percent German. Italian guys walked up and whispered in his ears, and he whispered back, and then they both took a drink of wine and said, "Saluda."

When I asked Steve about the Italian guys—who they were and what they did for a living—he put his pointer finger up to his nose and pressed down on the tip of his nose, making it go to the right side. "What does that mean?" I asked aloud. Steve shushed me and asked, "Are you stupid?" Insulted, I protested, "No, I'm not stupid. Does that mean they sell cocaine?"

"Jesus Christ, you're just a kid. It means they have crooked noses."

"What's a crooked nose?"

"Shut your mouth."

I sulked the rest of the night until we got to the car, when Steve explained that having a "crooked nose" meant that the man was connected to the mob. "Oh, I see. I understand," I said, but went silent after Steve added, "Don't ever embarrass me like that again."

For some reason, I could tell that these guys were playing Steve and that he just didn't really fit into their crowd. But he became furious if I mentioned any concerns. "What do you take me for, a moron? Big college girl thinks she could tell me how to run my business. Keep your mouth shut and look good. That's your job!"

Once Steve gave one of the guys $10,000 in cash that he said he needed for hush money to pay off some politicians to get the appropriate permits to begin building on the waterfront. That night, Steve and I went to the Hoboken waterfront with a pizza and a bottle of wine and sat on a blanket on the blacktop and ate. We looked at the New York skyline, and he told me where he planned to put the apartment buildings and the high-end shopping mall and pointed it all out to me. I had heard it all before, but I really enjoyed the pizza and the view.

Just once I asked, "Do you think you could trust these people, Steve?" He got very upset with me when I added that something didn't seem right. He said, "You're too naive. This is how business is done. You're a kid, what do you know? You live in a make-believe world that doesn't exist. You think everyone is nice. I'll show you nice. You just go back up there to the convent and leave business to me."

But ultimately, I was right. The guys used Steve and took his money and he got nothing for it. I remembered that I had the business card of one of the men who took Steve's money that night. I knew he worked as a dentist. He had given me the card one night at the club when he said, "What are you going to college for?" I had answered that I wanted to be a teacher or maybe a writer. He said, "Listen, if you ever want to dump that loser you're with, give me a call. I know some publishers. I can work a deal for you." Then, he winked, and I thought he must have a crooked nose.

After the group took Steve's $10,000, I took the number out of my dresser drawer and I called the dentist at the office.

A woman answered and I asked for the dentist. She said, "This is his wife, can I help you? I'm the receptionist."

I said, "You better tell your thieving husband to give Steve his $10,000 back."

She said, "Who is this?"

I said, "Tell him he's not going to get away with taking Steve's money. I'll write to the newspaper, and you can see what happens to his dental practice then."

"Who is this?" the wife asked again.

I said, "Your faggotty husband could not even lick the bottom of Steve's balls. Trust me. I'll make sure you will lose your business. Your husband better stop harassing me."

When I told Steve how I looked out for him, he was furious. He said, "You have no idea who you are messing with. Don't ever get involved in my affairs again!" He took me back to school and did not say a word and didn't call me for a long while. When he finally did, he said, "It's only money. I didn't lose anything valuable. I'll just take three extra trips to Ohio next week and I'll have the money back. You, my darling, are irreplaceable, and I admire your moxie."

"What's moxie?" I asked.

He said, "You got some big balls on you."

I wish I could say that I sped through my college years and completed my training to become an English teacher in no time at all. Instead, I quit school several times along the way because I needed money to survive. When I quit in my sophomore year, I got a job typing bills for a trucking company that delivered steel. All day, I had to type "20,000 pounds of stripped steel" over and over again. What a nightmare. I thought that I would rather shoot myself then do this for a living forever. Thank God, St. Elizabeth's welcomed me back. After a few experiences working in the "real" world, I finally dedicated myself to my classes and stopped worrying about the "us versus them" mentality that existed among my EOF peers and the general population.

I learned quickly that the other students were warm and wel-coming and that all along, I was the one isolating myself.

After I graduated from college, I moved in with Steve in his apartment in Hoboken. He took me on a shopping spree and brought me three new suits for job interviews. I immediately looked for jobs to put my English degree to work. I saw an adver-tisement for a job as an editor in New York. I had to submit some writing samples and was thrilled when I was called for an inter-view. This was going to be my big break.

I got all dressed up and took the train to the interview. When I finally found the towering office building in New York City, there were fourteen people waiting for the same job. The receptionist asked me for my resume. I said, "What is a resume?" She said, "You're kidding, right?" I was so embarrassed that I just ran out of the office and went back home.

Then I got a job writing articles for a newspaper company that published small newspapers. I was assigned to rewrite Asso-ciated Press articles for a Jewish newspaper. After a few weeks of reading articles and then developing stories for the Jewish audi-ence, my boss came over to me and said, "Why do you insist on putting an upbeat ending in every article?" I said that I thought it would cheer up the readers. I added "This stuff happened a long time ago. I thought I could focus on the positive." She looked at me in shock and said, "This is not going to work out."

Then, I got a job as a collection agent in a company that made bio stimulators. These were small machines that sent elec-tric pulses through the body to relieve chronic pain. My job was to call people who were severely injured in accidents to collect money from them for the bio stimulator and then to make notes about what type of payment arrangement I was able to make. From the first day I arrived in the office, the other women said things aloud like, "Oh look, the college girl has arrived." And they seemed to hate me because I had a degree. I never thought a college degree would be viewed so negatively.

For the first week, I called the clients at home and listened to the details of their horrible medical injuries and sad financial stories. When I went home, I told Steve about them, and he said, "They don't really have to pay those medical bills. Nothing will ever happen to them."

This information empowered me, and from that day forward, I told every client I called that I had to call because it was my job, but that I wouldn't pay the bill if I were them. This gave them some relief. I absolutely hated the job. It was such a waste of life. When the boss called me into his office just before lunch, he told me that I didn't look happy. He said, "Look, I really put my butt on the line hiring you because my boss said that you were overqualified for the job and that you would never last." He added, "I'm hoping he wasn't right."

I smiled at him and told him that I was just making the adjustment to office life and that I appreciated him hiring me. I leaned forward, looked straight into his eyes, and said, "You have nothing to fear. I will never leave. I really need this job." A few minutes later, when I went for lunch, I headed back down Route 80 to Hoboken and never returned. I never answered the phone either.

Life was not going the way I planned. I didn't really want to get a teaching job because I was twenty-one and the high school students I would teach were nineteen. I was intimidated by them during student teaching. I hated office work. Being a writer was much harder than I thought. What is a freaking resume? So on my ride home, I thought that maybe it would be best if I just got married to Steve. I would never have to work. I could just stay home and be a wife. As I pondered this, I thought that life wouldn't be that dull because he was an unusual character.

One time when he was driving his truck, someone was tailgating him the whole time, so right in the middle of the highway in Pennsylvania, he slammed on his breaks. The tailgater crashed into his truck and his car went up the ramp of the car hauling truck and crashed into a new Honda secured on the bottom.

When the state trooper came to the scene, Steve said a herd of deer were suddenly in front of him in the middle of the road and he had to stop so that he did not damage the cars. The other driver was ticketed for not having control of his vehicle.

When Steve had a dispute with his tax lawyer, Steve called a florist, had a huge funeral display of flowers made up, put "Beloved Son" across it, and sent it to his tax accountant's mother. The accountant took off to Puerto Rico and took Steve's tax records with him.

When one of Steve's tenants did not pay his rent and Steve had taken all legal avenues to have him removed and was still forbidden from removing the tenant in the middle of winter, suddenly the tenant ended up hit by a car and in the hospital. "The road was very icy. It was a terrible accident," Steve reported.

Once, Steve bought a new bed from 1-800-NEWBEDS. He didn't like it. He called the company to take it back. When they did not come for weeks to take it back, he charged them $100 per day storage for keeping the mattress and threatened to sue them for pain and suffering. They paid it.

His ethics were iffy, but exciting. He seemed to have completely different rules than I was used to. They included "pay yourself first" and "always use other people's money." He was always transferring balances from one credit card to the next and seemed to be able to buy whatever he wanted. When I got home that day, I asked Steve to marry me. He was thrilled. My friends and family were concerned because I was now twenty-one and he was forty-two, but I told them that age did not matter when you were in love. I didn't really feel any love, but I thought it would come eventually if I worked at it.

The minute that we agreed to get married was the minute that I realized that I was making a huge mistake. It was as if my eyes opened for the first time and I began to look at Steve differently. For most of our relationship, when we got together, it was in a hotel where we had no responsibilities. When I did move in with him, he was always on the road and I was left hanging out in the apartment by myself. But once we decided to get married, he began to stick around. This allowed me to see so many things that I didn't before. First, I was so disgusted by the hair in the sink when he shaved. I had never lived with a grown man before. Never in all of my life had I walked into a bathroom to see a sink filled with little tiny hairs. The same is true when it comes to the bathroom. Never had I experienced anyone being so thrilled with himself after having a bowel movement. He would walk out of the bathroom rubbing his stomach with his hand and say, "Ah, that was a great one. There is nothing better in life."

He was also in love with his penis and was constantly looking at it in the mirror and posing with it. When I awoke in the morning, something warm and wet was tapping me on the cheek and he was saying, "Look who wants to say good morning to you." Other times, he walked around with his hardened penis like a flagpole in front of him, saying, "Ah, look at it. I could cut glass with it," and then he tapped it on the furniture. While I was looking in the mirror pointing out all of my figure flaws, he stood in front of the mirror in his tightie whities, sucking in his round gut, saying, "Jesus Christ, I'm Adonis!"

Whenever, I talked seriously about dreams for the future, like, "Someday, I would like to open an alternative school for troubled teens," he replied, "Someday, I'd like to have a room filled with titties that I could just rub my toes across."

Meanwhile he was always working on a new scheme. He formed his own church in order to find a way to pay fewer taxes, and he called himself "Reverend Rick and the Sisters of Salvation."

And the closer we got to getting married, the less he felt like going to work. He came home with all types of new injuries and then filed a lawsuit against his company. First he had a cut over his eye, then he broke his wrist. Who knows what would happen to him next?

What was the most heartbreaking reality of life with Steve was that my fantasy of eating all of the food I wanted, as I had in hotels and fancy restaurants, was gone. In reality, Steve had such strange eating and drinking habits. He ate wheat germ, bean sprouts, and whole wheat bread that was so natural, the wheat crumbled in your fingers when you picked up a slice. A few times a day he drank apple cider vinegar and honey mixed into a glass of hot water because "it's good for the constitution. It eliminates toxins." Then, he drank ginseng tea a couple of times a day. The smell was terrible, but he endured it because, he said, "I have to keep up with you sexually." On top of that, he carried a shoulder bag filled with bottles and bottles of vitamins that he took every day. He also rubbed vitamin E oil on his face before he faced the bitter cold winds that hit him when he was on top of the rig unloading the cars. To keep him warm, every day I made a Thermos of coffee with honey in it. Who drank coffee with honey? Sometimes he'd make me breakfast and wake me up to tell me that he made steak and eggs. This sounded great, but when I went to the kitchen and saw the color of the meat, I knew it wasn't steak. It was liver and eggs. He explained, "You're too thin. You have to build up your blood." He was so furious when I turned my nose up to his breakfast and just had toast.

I also couldn't stand the thought of living in Hoboken. The renters in Steve's apartment building were all in their seventies. This meant that he had to keep the heat on eighty degrees day and night. Meanwhile, they had all been accustomed to coming up and visiting Steve's mother, who had died only a few months before I moved in. So, when I started cooking homemade tomato sauce, Lena from downstairs smelled it and made her way up the stairs. She walked in the door without knocking and said, "What the hell are you doing? Put a lid on that pot. You can't make gravy without a lid. Yes, I will have some coffee." She sat down in my seat at the table, had her coffee, and then she headed downstairs.

Five minutes later, Nancy from one floor up came downstairs and said, "What the hell are you doing with a lid on that pot? You can't make sauce with a lid on the pot. It has to boil down. What's wrong with you? Are you a polock or what?"

She marched into the kitchen and took off the lid off the pot, gave it a few stirs, and sat down. "Yes, I will have coffee, and do you have any sugar cookies?" Then she got up and walked to the kitchen sink. Under the kitchen sink, she grabbed a Maxwell House Coffee can and brought it to me and opened it up. In the can was a high-gloss white paint. She said, "Steve's mother, Vilma, painted the window sills once a week so that they looked nice and clean. I think you should do this now in her honor. They're getting a little dusty."

"Sure," I said.

She said, "She kept the paint brush in the pantry in a baggie." Then she finished her coffee and started out the door. As she did, Lena came back up from downstairs and said, "What the hell is going on here? I thought I told you to put a lid on that pot."

Nancy yelled back, "What are you talking about? You never made a good sauce in your life."

"Sauce? No Italian I know calls it sauce. What part of Italy are you from?" The two of them started cursing and spitting on the floor, and I was stuck in the middle.

Steve laughed at me when I relayed the story of the neighbors, then he grabbed a bag of unsalted potato chips and unsalted pretzels from the pantry, took out a liter bottle of Coke and squeezed it so all of the fizz came out, turned to me, and said, "Let's watch a movie." Who wants potato chips without salt and soda without fizz? What was I doing here?

I mentioned to Steve that I really wanted to move out of Hoboken because I hated living in an apartment with no privacy and all of the roaches and stuff that went with it. He said that he had a solid plan to turn each floor of his six-story brownstone into condominiums that would sell for $1 million each. I laughed in his face. "Who would pay $1 million for this shithole neighborhood?" I said, looking around. I told him that I would not marry him if we had to live in Hoboken. I thought it was a slum. He looked very sad but agreed to go house shopping. Who knew Hoboken was about to experience a Renaissance? Steve knew, but he let his little head do the thinking.

CHAPTER 4

Eventually we were living in a beautiful center hall colonial house in South Orange, New Jersey. The house had six bedrooms, a library, and a formal dining room and formal living room, both with fireplaces. The house had four bathrooms, with European tiles and shower stalls with seven shower heads. There was beautiful carved oak woodwork throughout, and carved pillars and eagles decorated the four fireplaces. The house had French doors, a maid's quarters, a stone patio, and a huge backyard. I guess I had a fantasy of moving my whole family into that house, and most of my family members stayed with me there at one time or another.

Unfortunately, we had a huge mortgage with 18 percent interest on the house. This was fine when Steve was busy, because he was paid well for every load of cars he delivered and he really hustled. Then the oil crisis hit, and suddenly Steve had no work. He was sad, but he welcomed the rest. For all of his adult life, he had pushed himself beyond human boundaries to drive back and forth from New Jersey to Ohio as many as three times in a week to increase his income. Eventually, it caught up with him, and he was definitely burned out. The phone rang and Steve answered it and said, "No, not this week." When he hung up, he'd turn to me and say, "An independent guy had two loads to Ohio they thought I would take, but we have a lot to do in the house." Steve had never turned down work before. When he was busy, I got up at 3:00 a.m. to pack him a Thermos of coffee with honey, a bag of apples, a block of cheddar cheese, a case of water, and a gym bag filled with vitamins. Like many drivers, he hated to lose time stopping for food or a bathroom. These items made it possible for him to sustain himself. Once we were married, it seemed as though he did not want to leave ever again.

We spent our days playing Monopoly. Every time Steve got into trouble in the game, I gave him a loan and let him go by erasing his debt. Every time I got into trouble, he made me sell all of my properties and would bankrupt me at every turn. He'd say, "When are you ever going to learn? You're too soft." Even though it was just Monopoly, Steve was always right. He said to me constantly, "Can't you see that this person is using you?" He told me a story that has applied to my life many times. He said that there was a blind man on a corner, and every day, when a businessman passed the blind man, he gave him a quarter. The blind man was always grateful. Then one day, when business got really bad, the businessman didn't have a quarter for the blind man and he had to pass by without giving him anything. The blind man said to him, "You son of a bitch! Where's my quarter?"

Steve was an expert on saying no to people and on making sure that he always looked out for himself. His ability to stay isolated from everyone was painful to me, though. Because he drove a truck for so long in his life, it was as if he were in the truck even when he was still at home. He was always in his own little world, drafting plans and sketching his big ideas. He never talked and rarely wanted to do anything outside of the house. Steve was disconnected from anything and was perfectly happy on his own. This was not a good thing once we had a baby. Even in the hospital, when I was in labor, Steve decided that it was taking too long and he was tired, so he went home to take a nap. The next day after our beautiful baby boy was born, my hospital roommate's husband arrived first thing in the morning with flowers. Steve strolled in later in the day with nothing and seemed bored by the whole affair. He asked, "When will you be home to cook dinner and stuff?"

When he did have work, Steve came back from being on the road and slept for days. Then, if our son, Aaron, cried while he was trying to sleep, he started screaming, "Shut that kid up!" Of course, there was no way I was going to allow him to see our baby as a nuisance.

What helped keep me somewhat sane during this time period was that Father McDuffy kept me company whenever Steve was on the road. He was my son's godfather, and because of his own large family, he had so much experience with babies. I called him if Aaron was fussy and he advised me to fill the sink with a little warm water and let it soothe the baby. It always worked. Also, even when Steve was home and I was going stir crazy being in the house all the time alone, he'd tell me, "Call your girlfriend, McDuffy, to take you out. I'm tired. I work for a living."

Steve babysat while I got dressed up to go to the track and dinner with McDuffy, and Steve was just happy to get rid of me. Since I was twenty-four and he was forty-six, he was constantly annoyed by the television shows I liked, by my music, and by my liberal ideas. As much as I thought he loved me and missed me, he couldn't stand the fact that when he came home from driving for eighteen hours in one day, I couldn't wait to talk to him. As soon as he walked in the door, I was thrilled to see anybody, and I'd start telling him about my day, sharing my ideas for the house and for our son's future. He would pause, smile with his unshaven face and say, "Hey, diarrhea of the mouth, shut the trap!" I was so hurt. I'd shut up and not talk to him for days, and he was thrilled by that. To him, that was the perfect relationship.

When I talked to him again to see if he wanted to go out to dinner or dancing or to a movie, he said, "Please, darling, I love you, but you're killing me. Call McDuffy and let him take you out. I'm tired." Then he sat in bed and watched movies, sketched condominiums he would own, and only came out of the room to have a meal I fixed for him. When I thought about it, this is exactly what he did all weekend when we were staying in hotels.

Somehow, it seemed fun then. He didn't really know how to be part of a couple.

With Steve's blessing, Father McDuffy and I went out and had a great time. We didn't do anything special, but we always ended the night by going to the diner for a bite to eat. Then, on the way home, we kissed and cuddled like two high school kids on a date, and it seemed to be enough affection to keep both of us content. Sometimes, McDuffy took my son and me to a Yankee game, to the zoo, and to other events, and we pretended to be a perfect little make-believe family.

Then, as the gas crisis grew worse, Steve's car-hauling company eventually went out of business. We were forced to sell our big house in South Orange at a loss and had to move up to northwest New Jersey, where we brought an old farmhouse for $35,000. The farmhouse was the exact opposite of our center hall colonial in South Orange. It was filled with dingy old flowered wallpaper, wood-burning stoves, and needed many repairs.

While reading the local newspaper one day, I saw an advertisement for a teaching job in a nearby school district. We needed the money since Steve was not working, so I applied for the job and thought that Steve could provide child care.

I was lucky enough to get hired, but it was obvious to me in the first week that Steve was not going to be adequate child care for our son. When I came home from work in the afternoon, my son, Aaron, was never cleaned, dressed, or fed. Steve would say, "I'm no Goddamn nursemaid. Do you see a teat on this body?" I was furious with him. Then, a colleague at school told me about an elderly German woman who provided child care in her home. I began taking my son to her and she potty trained him, taught him table manners, and was warm and loving.

With nothing else to do at home, Steve decided to take on some home improvement projects. When I came home from teaching, he'd show me a huge hole in the wall between the living room and kitchen and tell me his plans for making an eat-in kitchen. Months later, the hole was still in the wall and nothing was done. I was too embarrassed to let anyone in my house and started wondering how Steve was adding to my life. He didn't support me financially, he offered no emotional support or affection, and he didn't help with my son.

After just one year of teaching and being surrounded by people who were my age, my feelings totally changed for Steve. When I went to work-sponsored Christmas parties, I couldn't invite Steve to attend because I was embarrassed because of his age and personality. With the many young teachers who were my age, we had so much fun drinking and dancing after work on Fridays. It felt great to be young. More than once, I found myself giving a good-night kiss in the car on the way home to a young male teacher.

It became clear to me after just two years that getting married to Steve was a huge mistake. He was too old for me, so the people who warned me that I was looking for a father figure were right. It took all my strength to finally tell Steve that I wanted a divorce. I told him that it was not his fault, that it was just our age difference. I added that he had been nothing but good to me and that I didn't want any money from him or child support, because I planned to make my own money. I told him that if he just helped me by taking care of our son the best he could, then we could go on being parents together and best friends.

Steve didn't say a word after I told him, but left immediately for a delivery to Maine. I reasoned that he must have known it was coming, because he knew I was never alone. Through some type of weird rationalization, I thought that it was okay to continuously go out with other men if I was just honest about it with him. So, throughout the two years we were married, when Steve was working and called from the road, I told him the partial truth about my day. I'd say things like, "McDuffy took me out to dinner tonight, and then we went to the track." Or, "This nice male teacher from school and I chaperoned a school dance."

Or "Another guy from work took Aaron and me to a basketball game." Steve never seemed to mind and felt relieved that I was being cared for without being a burden to him.

My most frequent date throughout my marriage remained Father McDuffy. And although we never consummated our relationship by sleeping together, we ended each night in each other's arms. We continued the seemingly innocent kissing and touching we started years ago. He figured that if we never had sex, then he never broke his vow. I realized that he was the man that I truly loved.

In fact, I was thrilled for him when Father McDuffy's mother died and he was free of his promise. He finally left the priesthood, but he could never be with me even if I wasn't married. His very wealthy family would be in shock if he ever married "white trash" with my past. So, I was so proud of him when he was fixed up by a friend with a thirty-nine-year-old woman who was never married. He was forty when they got married and they are still happy today. I was excited to see him leave the freak show that was his home in the rectory. I call it a freak show because McDuffy's main job was driving other priests, in the middle of the night, to rehab centers and to new parishes because they were involved in some terrible activity. Father McDuffy was nothing like them in my book. He was an outstanding teacher who had motivated so many young men to succeed. I wanted him to finally enjoy his freedom, but had fantasized that one day I would enjoy it with him. He will always have a special place in my heart. He may have crossed a boundary, but his physical affection sustained me through many difficult years.

It was time for me to move on as well. After I told Steve that I wanted a divorce, on the way home from his car delivery in Maine, Steve stopped to see my sister Becky in Massachusetts and told her that he was going to kill my son and me when he got home. My sister counseled him for a few hours, and then called me and told me to run. But I knew that Steve loved me and would never hurt me, so I stayed. When he walked in the door, I walked up to him and said, "Kill me. Go ahead. Kill me. But you know and I know that your son and I are the only two people on this earth who care if you even wake up tomorrow morning." And Steve knew this was true, because he had alienated every-one in his life. He never had a girlfriend before me and never had one after me. With his mother gone, he had lost the only person who saw the good in him besides me.

Steve and I have remained close friends throughout our lives. He picked up my son every weekend all through his grammar school and high school years, so I had the best life because I got to be a mother all week and then I was able to go out and enjoy the single life on the weekends. I was never much of a partier or drinker, but I had a great group of young teacher friends, and we played games and had parties at each other's houses.

For years, Steve was invited to my house for every holiday. Every Christmas, he arrived with a Santa Claus hat on and car-ried tons of gifts for my son and me. If I ever needed money, as a single mom who was terrible with personal finances, I borrowed it from Steve, and he charged me 20 percent interest to pay it back in one week. It was a bad deal, but so many times that money sustained us.

He constantly invited me to dinner at his house, and he and our son would spend the whole day making a menu and pretty terrible food. But when I walked into the disheveled home, our son had a napkin over his arm like a waiter and they lit candles and treated me like a queen. Once when I came in and said that I was starving, they served me one piece of sausage, one tablespoon of rice, and a small portion of corn. I kiddingly said, "This is it?" Steve went to the other room and came back with a magnifying glass. He said, "Here, look through this when you eat and then you'll feel full."

When I went on a weekend trip with a girlfriend, Steve and Aaron picked us up at the airport and had a tray full of hors d'oeuvres waiting for us in the car. And because Steve's house was always a disaster, he let my son hammer nails into any wall he wanted to or paint any color paint on any wall. He let him practice wallpapering anywhere, and none of the patterns even matched.

As Aaron got older, every day was not so magical, though, because when my son was old enough to play baseball and basketball on little league teams, Steve was such an embarrassment. When my son was batting, Steve yelled, "Throw the bat at the pitcher!" This nearly caused a riot with parents on the other team. Steve also yelled, "He throws like a girl," to Aaron while the other team's pitcher struggled to strike him out. At basketball games, when Aaron was playing defense on his little team of eight-year-olds, his dad shouted, "Poke their eyes out!" Once during halftime, Aaron's basketball coached asked, "Who is that asshole yelling in the stands?" It was Steve, and Aaron was so embarrassed

I yelled at Steve to shut up. Then, as loud as he possibly could, he stood up and screamed in the gym, "I divorced you! Don't tell me what to do." I sat down wanting to crawl under the bleachers in embarrassment when everyone turned and looked at me.

Throughout the rest of my life, whenever I dated anyone else, I had to tell them that Steve came as part of the package. More than one boyfriend walked out because Steve usually sat at my kitchen table and smoked a cigarette. My current boyfriend might say, "Steve, there's no smoking allowed in the house." Steve simply blew rings of smoke into the air that hit the boyfriend in the face. Since Steve could easily take a bat to another man's head and feel no remorse, I tried to stand between the two men and create peace. But I always took Steve's side, and very few men could tolerate that. Still, my loyalty to Steve trumped my loyalty to any new boyfriend. Despite his bizarre idiosyncrasies, Steve gave me the best gift of my life—my son, Aaron. Also, I truly believe in my heart that I would never have graduated from college if Steve hadn't thrown me out, naked, into the hallway when I refused to go back to school. At those times in my life, I needed tough love. Steve was the perfect guy to provide it. For those things, I will always be grateful to him.

CHAPTER 5

The year that my mother died was a terrible year personally, but professionally I was named Teacher of the Year by my colleagues. I was thirty-two years old and teaching English to high schools students in a county vocational school. Trust me, though, this award was not given because of my great organizational skills or my dedication to the school rules. I used to joke with students that in order to get their grades, I tossed their papers down the steps in my house. Where they landed decided what grade they received. The highest step resulted in an A and the lowest step in an F. While this was not exactly true, my classroom management and paperwork skills left a lot to be desired.

The truth is that I earned a teaching award only because my own amazing high school teachers had modeled for me how to go the extra mile to reach my students. Teachers had saved my life, and I felt a real debt to repay to future students. Vocational students had been tossed aside as "dummies" by their teachers from the past. It seemed that I had a real knack for getting my vocational school students to like English. When I was selected for the job from a pool of fifty applicants—many of whom had a master's degree—the principal said that he picked me because he thought that I might make English fun for a change. He and I had spent most of the interview laughing about our own student teaching experiences.

My student teaching involved working with Mr. Marconi at Lincoln Elementary School in Bloomfield, New Jersey. He was a sixty-one-year-old man who diagrammed sentences every day

of the week. I was shocked that he gave out paper and pencils in the classroom each morning and then turned to me and
said, in a voice that was just above a whisper, "These Goddamn
Chinks and Spics do not even come to school with pencils."

At around 10:00 a.m. each day, he stopped the class and
said, "Boys and girls, I have an important lesson to teach you
today." The kids groaned because they had experienced the
lesson every day. He made elaborate hand gestures as he took
out his props. He placed a pack of Marlboro cigarettes, a silver-
plated lighter, and a white monogrammed handkerchief on the
desk. He took the cigarette and lit it in front of the whole class
and took a deep drag on it. He closed his eyes as if he were overcome by the pleasure of the smoke and sighed with joy. Then, he
remembered where he was and said, "Now, listen up, people,
because I am about to show you something amazing." The boys
and girls rolled their eyes and turned to each other mumbling,
"Not this again."

He smoked almost half the cigarette, while the students
waited, and then he took the handkerchief and said, "Now,
watch this very closely." He brought the handkerchief up to his
mouth after taking the biggest drag on the cigarette and blew
into the handkerchief. He held it to his mouth for a moment to
build suspense and then he said, "Now look at this." When he
turned the handkerchief around to face the class, he revealed a
yellow ring on it the size of his mouth. And then he said, and the
class repeated in unison, "This is what cigarettes do to your lungs.
Don't ever smoke!"

He finished his cigarette while the students took a mini-recess
and talked, then got back to his diagramming sentences. He
made the kids laugh all the time by telling a boy who was talking
while he was talking, "I will kick you right in the balls..." and after
everyone laughed, he added, "Of your eyes."

He told stories of the "big war" and got down on the floor and
crawled down the center aisle on his elbows and belly and said,

"There we were in the trenches." The kids were so intrigued and they loved him.

After being in the classroom as his student teacher for four weeks and basically acting as his aide, I got up the nerve after class one day and asked him if he thought that one day I could do something other than grammar with the kids, like write poetry.

He shook his head and said, "You want to do poetry? Poetry, huh? Grammar is not good enough for you. The old man is holding you back, right? Go right ahead. What the hell does an old man like me know?" The next day he called in sick and he didn't return for the rest of the school year. He used all of his sick days and then retired that summer. I took over the class alone for the rest of the student teaching experience.

Once I was hired to be a teacher in public school and had my own classroom, I understood the challenges Mr. Marconi faced. From the first day of teaching to the last, it was obvious to me that I was not in Catholic school anymore. Not only did I go from Catholic school to public school, but I went from the city to the most rural part of New Jersey, where most students were the first in their families to graduate from high school. I would never have believed that the state where I was raised had beautiful rolling farmlands. We barely saw a blade of grass struggling to grow between sidewalks in my neighborhood.

On the first day of school, I got my students settled and then started them off with a game called "Getting to Know You Bingo." I began to review the squares on my "Getting to Know You Bingo" board game I had created the night before. Each student was free to walk around the room and get signatures of classmates who fit the description in each of the nine squares. Then, the first one to fill his or her bingo card and yell "bingo" would get a prize.

"You gotta be kidding me," was the first response yelled aloud.

I pushed on and reviewed the squares.

Find someone who plays a musical instrument.

"Yeah, like Carl," one boy said. "He plays the skin flute."

Find someone who likes to write poetry or songs.

Find someone who knows a lot about cars.

Find someone who plans to play a junior varsity sport.

Find someone who has traveled more than one thousand miles.

Find someone who was on the honor roll in eighth grade.

Find someone who has more than two siblings.

Find someone who hopes to go to college someday.

When I mentioned that the prize was a big bag of mini Halloween candies, like Snickers and Milky Ways, the students were all up and immediately trying to fill their bingo card.

"Bingo," one student yelled, and then another and another.

It was my plan to review the names aloud in order to get some conversation going and to enable the kids to make new friends and get to know each other a little bit better.

Of course, the joke was on me when I started reviewing the first winning bingo card aloud and it took me a few seconds to catch on. There I was on the first day of school saying sentences like, "So, I see that Dick Hurts likes to play the horn, who's Dick Hurts? Oh, and Mike Hunt likes cars, where's My Cunt?" The kids were rolling on the floor laughing.

"Very funny," I said when I finally got it, but by then the bell had rung and they were out the door.

The next day, when I was handing the class our first book, *Flowers for Algernon*, a student approached my desk. She was a girl who, according to the principal, was never permitted to go to the bathroom because she had already been caught smoking three times in the first week of school. She flipped her long highlighted brown hair to one side and said, "Can I go to the bathroom?" I wanted to set the precedent immediately that my class was important and that students were not going to be permitted to leave, so I said very sternly, "No, you can't. You will never go to the bathroom during English. Go between classes. Now, just take a seat."

She threw her head back as if she had whiplash and clicked her tongue on the roof of her mouth, making a surprised sound, and said, "I have to take a *fucking piss!*"

The class reacted with a "Whoa!"

"Excuse me?" I said, shocked. "You have to do what?"

"Take a fucking piss," she repeated, tossing her long, straight hair to the other side, doing her best Cher impression.

"Okay, then," I said and reached into my top desk drawer to take out the yellow discipline referral slips that I was given in my folder on the first day of school. I said to myself, "At least we're starting off the school year with a bang."

"Let me make sure I have this right," I said out loud. "Dawn, sweetie, what is your last name? Oh, never mind, I have it here. I want to make sure I get this exactly right for the office. Now, say it again, real slow now, because I want to make be sure to capture this moment accurately."

The class was giggling and Dawn was getting a little red.

I made exaggerated arm movements like Ed Norton warming up to play the piano and then started writing with my pen, "I... have...to...take...," I said slowly as I wrote each word. "Ah...I'm sorry, hon, what was it again that you were going to take?"

"A *fucking piss*," she said boldly.

"Oh, yeah," I said, "that's right. How could I forget?" Again, the class was chuckling. Then, I spelled it out, "A f-u-c-k-i-n-g p-i-s-s." I made a big hand gesture again, but then paused to ask the class, "What do you think, an exclamation mark or a period?"

Jeffrey, from the back of the room, said, "Well, it was more of a statement of fact than an exclamation."

Nicky, from the left of the room, added, "She really didn't yell it or exclaim it, but it is a pretty bold statement."

I asked the class, "Okay, raise your hand if you think I should put a period." I counted eight hands. Then I said, "Raise your hand if you think that it should be an exclamation mark." Then thirteen people raised their hands. I said, "Exclamation marks have it. Good job, class." I put a giant exclamation mark on it and handed it to Dawn. "Okay, you can take this with you to the office and...enjoy your vacation." She was suspended from school for ten days.

Later in the month, I had to be a substitute teacher for a period for a gym class. While there, I basically watched while the kids played volleyball. It was such a shock for me to see girls scream and giggle when the ball came near them. This is something I had never experienced in all-girl schools. I reasoned that it must be something that is only done for the boys.

The teachers, not just the students, took some getting used to as well. At the end of the second week of school, I was walking to my car with a huge pile of notebooks that I had planned to review over the weekend. The notebooks were student journals, and although I didn't grade them, I thought I would review them weekly and use them as a way to get to know and communicate with my students.

As I walked through the parking lot with the pile of notebooks blocking most of my face, I heard a booming male voice ask, "What the hell do you think you're doing?"

I assumed that a kid was smoking in a car or something terrible was happening in the parking lot and that I failed to see it, because I was accused of missing many of these activities in my first week. Instead, this man rushed towards me. He was about six foot two with a beet-red face and brown Larry King glasses. He repeated himself, waving his finger right in my face.

"What do you think you're doing?" Then, he folded his arms across a maroon, Mr. Rogers cardigan sweater and said, "Don't you ever, ever take work home from this place!"

I didn't know why I needed to say anything, but I felt as though I was a kid caught stealing.

"I'm an English teacher," I said. "I have to do work at home."

"Never ever," he added. "You work until 3:00 p.m. precisely."

I just stepped around him, causing the top two notebooks to fall on the ground. I yelled back over my shoulder. "If I need your advice, I'll ask for it."

He bent down and picked up the two notebooks and slammed them hard on top of my pile, causing my knees to buckle a bit.

"Do you know who I am?" he asked. Without giving me a chance to say "Mr. Rogers," as I was thinking, he answered, "I'm the president of the teachers' association, and you are setting precedent for every teacher that comes after you."

"I've got to go," I said. I dumped the notebooks in the car and sped past him. He stared me down as I drove away.

As the year went on and I stayed after school to help my students with their work, other teachers would stop me and say, "What are you, an asshole? Why are you staying after school with those kids? You're not getting paid for that. You're setting a precedent."

Other teachers, who did not graduate from Newark Catholic, where we sat on the floor to read our books, would say, "It seems like kids are having too much fun in your room. Are you following the curriculum?" Or "It is not our job to motivate these kids. Just teach, and if they don't get it, tough luck."

One teacher actually went to the principal to tell on me for teaching *Of Mice and Men* because it was not in the curriculum. I saw her backing out of Mr. Stinehart's office, saying, "I just thought you should know what is going on in there." Mr. Stinehart would find me and say, "That's a great book. Keep up the good work."

Other teachers complained that my classroom was noisy and that I had no control over the class. While it's true that I had students sword fighting, or re-enacting the stoning scene in "The Lottery" with crumpled paper, or serving as loud jurors when having a mock trial similar to the case in *To Kill a Mockingbird*, my principal didn't complain. Mr. Stinehart said, "When I first came in, I was getting concerned that it was a little noisy in here with all of these groups...but when I went from group to group, I could not believe that they were all talking about English."

Sometimes, he did get angry with me for good reason. Once when he came to evaluate me, I had selected two students and prepped them by saying that they were going to have a fight in class. The purpose of my lesson that day was to demonstrate that every writer has a different perspective. I thought that I would stage this fake fight, and then when the students left the room, I was going to ask students to write what happened, and then I would prove that everyone saw the same situation differently.

Well, our evaluations were always a surprise, so I got really nervous when Mr. Stinehart came into the class in the first few moments and sat down with his evaluation binder. I didn't want the students to get in trouble for fighting and I didn't want the principal to overreact. So, I asked him to step into the hallway with me and explained that I had asked two students to stage a fight. He turned beet red and said, "You will do no such thing. You will never encourage violence in my school." He walked away angry and came back on another day. I cancelled my staged fight.

The most welcoming and fun person on the staff was the assistant principal, Mr. Gregory. He was about five feet five inches tall and was bald. You couldn't see him in the hallway or at lunch without him having an inappropriate joke to tell, but they were usually pretty funny. His best line was when I was rushing in late one day and he stopped me at the front door of the school and whispered in my ear, "You look hot today."

Wishing to return a compliment to the old guy, I said "You smell good, what do you have on?"

Mr. Gregory said, "I have a hard on, but I didn't think you could smell it!"

We both laughed and headed to our stations.

He and I both had another big laugh during my first year of teaching that solidified a beautiful friendship. I shared my classroom with a nursing teacher who taught a Licensed Practical

Nursing course at night. My side of the classroom was composed of rows of desks. Her side of the classroom contained six hospital beds filled with nude mannequins who had IVs attached to them. The room was also filled with models of the human heart, lungs, and other body parts. It was bad enough that every day when I walked into the room, the mannequins had been placed in sexual positions, but then something worse happened.

One day, the sweet little nursing teacher, who was in her late fifties, was about five foot two, with round glasses and mousy brown hair, and who barely whispered when she talked, asked if she could speak to me.

I left my classroom of twenty-three freshmen and told them to continue reading while I was gone for a minute. Once we were in the hallway, Mrs. Roberts, the nursing teacher, folded her tiny hands across her chest and said in a very serious tone. "We have a problem." Knowing how well respected she was and that I was new and making lots of mistakes, I panicked for a minute.

I said, "I'm so sorry. I'm sure it can be worked out. What is it, Mrs. Roberts?"

She said, "Someone stole my vagina."

"What?" She usually spoke as if sugar melted in her mouth so I assumed I didn't hear her correctly. "Excuse me?" I asked and put my hand to my ear to signal for her to repeat what she said.

She said, "I believe one of your students stole the model of a vagina that I use for my nursing class." She added, "My vagina was here last night when I locked up, and your students have been the only class in the room today."

With all my might I muffled my laughter in the back of my throat. "Oh my God, I am so sorry. I will look into it and get back to you right away."

As I turned the door knob to my classroom I thought, I am looking into her vagina. Great.

As I closed the door and reentered my classroom, I bent over and started laughing so hard that I couldn't catch my breath.

Tears were dripping down my cheeks as I laughed uncontrolla-bly. My class stared at me as if I was losing my mind. I squeezed my legs together as if I were going to pee my pants. Then I got control of myself and raised my hand to quiet the class, but more to gain my own balance and composure.

Then, with the most serious face I could muster and a mono-tone voice, I said. "Someone in this room stole a vagina."

The class had never seen me more serious. There was a moment of silence.

But just one moment later, they all lost it and laughter was roaring throughout the room. I couldn't help but join in. I tried to be serious again and added, "I don't care who did it...but I want that vagina back on this chair by 3:00 p.m. today. My job is on the line."

I was forced to ignore the comments like the one from Alex: "Hey, it's been snatched!"

Fortunately for me, Mrs. Robert's vagina was returned and placed on my desk that day as required. After that one moment of joy that we all shared, I never had a discipline problem with my class again.

As the years went on, it seemed I had a real knack for reach-ing the tough students. On the first day of each new school year, I held up the thick, modified vocational school literature book that might as well have been called "Abridged Literature for Morons" and threw it in the trash. With a great deal of ceremony, the book made a deafening thud as it hit the small metal cylinder and I said, "With few exceptions, English will be used to communicate every significant moment in your life. That's why it is important to you. And when you read certain works written in English, you will become a member of a certain exclusive educated club. It's as if you know a secret that others don't know. All of you belong in this club and I am the gatekeeper that can get you in."

Then, through the magic of reading chapters out loud, watch-ing videos, acting out scenes, and other methods, I helped them tackle *To Kill a Mockingbird*, *The Crucible*, *Of Mice and Men*, Shakespeare, and more. I loved to see how proud the students were that someone expected them to learn and to understand these works. Other teachers shared stories about how much my students suddenly loved English class. Once, the automotive teacher was listening to two students who were in the grease pit under a car. The one student, who only attended the vocational school on a part-time basis but had academic classes in a traditional high school, said to his buddy, "We're reading *Macbeth* in English class. It's so stupid and boring. I hate it." A student from my class named Brian answered, "Well, maybe you just don't understand it."

The lessons were not always easy, and sometimes the students missed the point. For example, one time, during the reading of *To Kill a Mockingbird*, Jeanine, a six-foot-tall girls' basketball player with a cranberry red Rod Stewart spiky haircut, raised her hand and said, "Don't you think this is unfair? How about that Eddie Murphy makes more money than my father and Eddie Murphy is black."

The twenty-three white students in my very rural class seemed to nod in agreement, endorsing this as a credible question.

I paused momentarily and then asked very seriously, "Jeanine, is your father funny?"

"No."

"Does your father make movies?"

Jeanine said, "No, he's a truck driver."

I asked, "Is your father in any aspect of the entertainment business?"

Jeanine said, "No."

"Then why in the world should your father make more money than Eddie Murphy?"

Jeanine said, "Because he's white."

This was far from the strangest interaction of the year. These sincere inquiries were ongoing. Earlier in the year, other ninth-grade students were reading the book *Harold and Maude*. In that novel, the writer described that the main character liked to go to churches to paint smiley faces on the Madonna statues because they looked so sad.

Upon hearing this, Michelene, who usually dressed in an *I Dream of Jeannie* shirt and harem pants and who once asked me to change her B+ to an A because then her mother would allow her to get her belly button pierced, raised her hand.

"There was no Madonna when they wrote this book," she stated as if catching the author in a major error.

I chuckled and said, "Michelene, they're not talking about Madonna the singer, they are talking about the Blessed Virgin Mary. Churches often have statues of her, and they call her 'the Madonna.' "

Upon hearing the word virgin, just as would typically happen with words like "come," "balls," "suck," etc., the eyes of the entire class lit up and heads popped up from resting on elbows everywhere.

Surprised, I asked, "Haven't you ever heard of the Blessed Virgin Mary?"

Michelene said, "No," and the rest of the class nodded no as well.

Even more surprised, I instructed, "Raise your hand if you have ever heard of the Virgin Mary."

Only one person in the room raised her hand.

"Okay, Irene, why don't you tell the class about Mary?"

Irene told the story about how Mary was approached by an angel in her sleep, who told her that she was going to become the Mother of God. Then, without having sex, she became pregnant with Jesus, the Son of God. Then, she told her husband, Joseph, who was a carpenter, that she was pregnant. He took her on a donkey to Bethlehem to have the baby in a barn.

The entire class roared with laughter.

"You got to be kidding me," Anthony shouted. "She had much to drink at a party, got knocked up, and was afraid to ⌐ her parents."

Michelene added, "Couldn't she come up with a better story than that?" With so many rules regarding separation between church and state, I had to decide it was best if I did not try to explain any further. After all, what explanation could I really offer?

CHAPTER 6

My school administrators always appreciated that I rarely sent kids to the office for disciplinary issues, but preferred to handle them myself. My most fun and effective method of discipline was always the special eraser treatment. Whenever a student, usually a male, said anything inappropriate, usually about females, rather than writing a discipline referral, I began to chalk up. I took bright, yellow chalk and ran it across the eraser over and over until it was totally covered. Then, I whipped it at the violating student as hard as I could. I always aimed at the wall just slightly above the student's head, so when the eraser hit, it showered the student in yellow powder. The class cheered. The perpetrator laughed. I forgot the incident.

I stopped using the eraser method when it went awry during the first day of school one year. I was teaching my first period of senior English. Almost all of the students in the class were students that I had taught in their sophomore year as well. The room was filled with the excited chatter of old friends meeting again. Then, Benny McMahon, a 280-pound, good-natured student from the welding shop, said deliberately, "I can't believe you're still here, because you know that women should be home barefoot and pregnant." This was a joke that he knew would push my buttons.

The whole class froze and looked to the front of the room. All the students near Benny began to shuffle their feet in front of them, working to move their desks backwards as far from Benny as possible. As if in slow motion, I grabbed the eraser and the yellow chalk and began chalking up. It was a familiar dance for the group and the class started going "Benny, oh, Benny, you in trouble, boy!" I chalked and chalked and said nothing.

Because of Benny's size and weight, because he was wearing his favorite shiny black welding class windbreaker, because I loved Bennie and Bennie loved me, I threw the eraser as hard as I possibly could, right at Bennie...not above his head the way I would usually do it. The eraser sailed across the room, buoyed by the same crowd enthusiasm as if it were a fastball at the World Series. Just as it neared Benny's desk, a new kid, a Chinese kid who spoke no English at all, struggling to assimilate in an American school, lifted his head from writing. Just as he raised his eyes, the speeding eraser immediately connected with his temple and folded his neck back and to the side, like the magic bullet Kevin Costner followed in the fabulous *JFK* movie—back and to the left. The room was silent. I rushed to the new Chinese boy and tried to brush the chalk from his hair, his face, his navy sweater, and, yes, even his pants.

"I'm so sorry," I said again and again. "It's just a game." But the boy said nothing. The bell rang and he was gone. He left school that day and never returned. I stopped at the office several times to inquire about his attendance. No one ever had an answer. Several months later, I was told that he had immediately returned to China. When other teachers wondered aloud about what could have happened, I just bowed my head. I knew it was time for a new discipline method.

Other times, students waited for me to do something and I did nothing. I had a great class after lunch every day and we always had interesting discussions because everyone was upbeat, except one boy named Anthony. I tried to engage him, but he just sat in the back of the room and glared at me as if he hated me.

Finally, one day, I said, "You know, Tony, I'm sick and tired of you bringing me down during this class. Everyone is trying hard to participate except you. What is your problem?"

Without skipping a beat, he screamed like a maniac and grabbed his hair and started pulling it. "It's the fucking pork!" he shouted at the top of his lungs. "Every morning. Every lunch. Every dinner. It's fucking pork, pork, pork. I can't stand it. It is driving me fucking crazy. Just once in a while could I have a *fucking hamburger or something? I've got to get the fucking pork out of my life!"*

Holy crap. What was that? The classroom full of students was as shocked as we watched him with our mouths wide open. Finally, when he put his head down on his desk and started crying, I said as softly and as gently as I could, "Anthony, what is it about the pork?"

It turned out that his family owned a pig farm, and every day before school and after school he had to take care of the pigs. His family also ate pork for every meal because it was free. He even had to bring a ham sandwich for lunch every day. He didn't have money to buy a different lunch. Every day from that day forward, the students in that English class bought Tony a different lunch. And I was so surprised when, at his graduation ceremony, he called me to the stage to present me with a rose for being his favorite teacher.

Thank God, my administrators overlooked it even when I was completely wrong. One day, I had PMS so bad, and these three girls in my class wouldn't stop talking to each other. They were really good kids and were really excited about an upcoming dance. I corrected them several times, and then my last nerve was fraying and I finally kicked them out and told them to go to the office. I never sent kids to the office, so the assistant principal thought that this was unusual. Within a few minutes, Mr. Gregory was outside my classroom knocking at my door. I stepped in the hallway and he said, "What the hell are you doing? You can't send me three kids to the office at once!" Then he started walking backwards to where he was headed next. In an instant, I said, "Fuck you, you fucking bastard. Don't tell me what to do!" Then,

I threw the pencil I had in my hand at him and the point landed right in his bald head. I started walking right toward the door and said, "I quit."

He chased after me and said, "Wait a minute, nut job. What's wrong with you? Come back here." He hugged me and I put my head on his shoulder and I just started crying. "I have PMS," I said. He started laughing and said, "Jesus Christ, you could have taken out my eye. Now, now, just go to the bathroom and get yourself together and I will take over your class until next period."

I was beginning to think that it was time to leave teaching when I just couldn't relate to students any more. I recognized this when I asked students to bring in a song to play for the class. We were going to listen to the song, review the words, and evaluate the song as poetry that represented them and their feelings. I bought in Gloria Estefan's triumphant and optimistic *Coming out of the Dark*. More than half of my students brought in songs along the lines of Metallica and their depressing *Fade to Black*.

After a week's worth of eight full periods a day of listening to songs about suicide and dying, I looked out at the pale, pasty students with black hair, black lipstick, black nails, black shirts, black jeans, and black boots, and said, "You know what? You think life is so hard?" I mimicked them, "Duh, life sucks! Why don't you just go home tonight and kill yourselves, for Christ's sake. Get it over with. You don't even know what a problem is! What is your biggest worry? Your joystick on your Nintendo will get stuck? You are the weakest generation. You believe in nothing. You stand for nothing. You care about no one but yourselves. You cannot even handle a pimple, for God's sake. So just go home and get it over with!"

I stopped myself from saying more while I tried to pull it all back by adding, "Tonight's journal entry topic will be defining the meaning of life." However, I knew right then that I was having more trouble controlling my temper and my words and that eventually I would get in serious trouble if I didn't think about leaving teaching.

What kept me going over the years is that my best friends were on the staff. I had a great time with most of the students, but it was the memories of times shared with my friends that were invaluable. My best friend, Patty, held herself to the highest standards as a professional educator and as a Catholic. Her constant support and reminder of what it meant to have integrity gave me a goal. I could never be the kind of person she was because I was completely undisciplined, but she certainly was the ideal best friend. She supported me through many rough times as a single mom. Even a simple thing like getting to the cash register at Macy's and having my credit card rejected would be fixed by Patty. She'd just step in with her card and let me pay her back when I could. She *never* compromised on her principles and values, while I compromised every day. Yet, we had great fun having drinks after school on a Friday night and sharing many a lunch hour.

Staff members had so much fun creating fun events each year, like the student/faculty basketball game or softball game. When we did, the teachers went out of their way to be some type of crazy cheerleading squad or to create little skits to entertain the students. Students loved it so much that we were asked to repeat the performance at the sports banquet and other gatherings.

One year, one of my best friends, Dave, a male gym teacher, and I performed Abbott and Costello's "Who's on First?" routine for the student body at an assembly. Dave and I got to be close friends when he walked into the gym and I was shooting foul shots in a black dress and high heels. He said, "Excuse me, but no street shoes are allowed in the gym." I immediately kicked off my heels and we played a few games of HORSE. He won because I could never do a layup. We began meeting each other every day in the gym to compete and ended up missing each other so much when one of us was absent. We truly loved each other as friends and spent each summer together working out at a local gym, playing basketball with my son, and alternating having parties for our group of friends.

The principal, Mr. Stinehart, who hired me and had tolerated my antics was retiring after twenty-seven years. During his last three years of employment, Mr. Stinehart served as the superintendent of the schools, so we didn't see him as often, but I definitely had a warm place in my heart for the man who hired me from among fifty applicants. His secretary, who planned his retirement party, asked if Dave and I would do the "Who's on First?" routine at the party.

In front of an audience of close to 150 colleagues and their spouses, Dave and I stood on a makeshift stage while people sipped their coffee after dinner. Dave looked so different in a suit and tie, because he wore a sweat suit every day. I was dressed in a cream shift dress and high-heeled shoes. We were being flooded with laughter as we focused on providing just the right emphasis on every line.

Dave: Well then who's on first?

Me: Yes.

Dave: I mean the fellow's name.

Me: Who.

Dave: The guy on first.

Me: Who.

Dave: The first baseman.

Me: Who.

Dave: The guy playing...

Me: *Who is on first!*

Dave: *I'm asking you who's on first.*

Me: *That's the man's name.*

Dave: *That's whose name?*

Me: *Yes.*

In the middle of the intense concentration needed for the perfect delivery of the routine, suddenly my eyes were drawn to an almost heavenly beam of dusty light that seemed to be coming from the ceiling like a spotlight. This surreal glow highlighted the face of a man in the audience. I had never seen him before. He had jet black hair, a dark black mustache, and a full beard. He had a beautiful olive complexion, and even from afar, I could feel that he had the smoothest skin that I wanted to reach out to touch. The contrast of his dark skin and his white shirt was beautiful. He had broad, athletic shoulders and large hands that he used to smooth his beard as he talked. The glowing, heavenly light encircled him, and he was the only person highlighted among the many guests in the restaurant. Remarkably, I didn't miss a single cue from Dave as I delivered every line of my skit perfectly. Yet, inside my chest, my heart was leaping and my soul was shouting other far more meaningful words: "This is the man I am going to marry!"

Dave: *The pitcher's name?*

Me: *Tomorrow.*

Dave: *You don't want to tell me today?*

Me: *I'm telling you now.*

Dave: Then go ahead.

Me: Tomorrow!

Dave: What time?

Me: What time what?

Dave: What time tomorrow are you gonna tell me who's pitching?

CHAPTER 7

It turned out that the man in the audience was our new super-intendent of schools, Dr. Diforno. I didn't see him again until the first day of the new school year. I was mesmerized as he circled around our first day of school meeting tables in a crisp white shirt, perfectly tied yellow and blue power tie, and Glen plaid suit, talk-ing about his goal of creating a "paradigm change" in teaching methodologies. I had never even heard such words before and I was in love with them. I walked around the whole day saying them to myself—"paradigm change." The first free moment I got that day, I looked them up in the dictionary and I was so excited. We were going to have a paradigm change in my school and in my life.

After completing the tours for new freshmen students that day, I happened to pass our new superintendent in the hallway. I smiled and said, "That was a great speech you gave today on paradigm change. I was very impressed." He was even more deli-cious close up. His arms and legs were so powerful that I imag-ined he could crush a woman of even my size. In his face, I could sense that he was looking into my blue eyes and admiring the waves I had curled into my shoulder-length blond hair. He smiled and was about to speak, until I added, "You're so handsome." Then he flushed and seemed embarrassed and immediately left the building.

That day I had learned other exciting news about the new school year when I was called into the office to see the principal. Last year, while in his office to discuss improving recruitment, I had asked him to let me write a grant for the Geraldine R. Dodge Foundation to create a school of performing arts. I thought this would help the vocational classes with attracting a different type of student. Happy to have anyone volunteer to do extra work, the principal give his blessing. It turned out that we were awarded the grant and were beginning our first year of the new program. Throughout the spring, I wrote other grants, and we won them. This was exciting, because it was really difficult work and the odds of winning the grants were very slim. The principal said for this school year, the administration decided that they were going to free me from teaching for a few periods per day to continue to research and develop grants.

On the day before the Christmas break, Dr. Diforno called me over to his office building. My heart was racing as I walked in. He barely looked into my eyes when he said, "I was wondering if you would consider writing this grant for us over the Christmas break. I know it's your vacation and I have no right to ask you because I can't pay you, but it is something that would put our school on the map." I instantly said that I would gladly do it. Are you kidding me? I would have licked his black oxford shoes if he had asked me.

The grant was offered by the New Jersey Department of Education and it was for $200,000 to create an interactive television classroom in the school. I had no idea what this even meant. So, I had to spend the first part of my Christmas break learning about the benefits of having interactive television in schools. I searched to find plans for existing interactive television classrooms. I learned that small schools like ours were able to offer Japanese and Advanced Placement courses to small numbers of students because one teacher at one site could teach students in three different school sites through the interactive television network.

Over the Christmas vacation, I put every ounce of love I had into the proposal because I wanted to impress the new superintendent. I wrote it over and over again to make sure it was perfect. When it was finished, it was more than one hundred, pages including a statement of need, program description, project activity plan, floor plans, and the budget. However, I couldn't complete the entire budget because I didn't know under what category I would put the cable needed to complete the room.

On the first day after Christmas vacation, I couldn't wait to get to school to bring my finished grant over to the new superintendent's office. To begin our celebration, I stopped and bought two piping hot cups of Dunkin' Donuts coffee to warm up the cold January day. Before school even started, I went over and put the proposal on his desk with such love. It was as if I was placing myself on his desk and asking for his approval. That is how much of myself I put into the project.

As he flipped through the one-hundred-page document, Dr. Diforno's face wrinkled as if he had smelled a bad smell. It was the exact face my mother had made when I brought her the last Christmas gift I ever gave her. He got to the page of the budget that wasn't finished and just tossed the proposal down on his desk. He said, "This is not even finished yet. It's due tomorrow."

I was shocked. I had worked so hard for no pay over the Christmas vacation to make him love me, and this was the thanks I got? It would only take him a few minutes to go on the computer and add the missing budget information. I lifted his cup of black hot coffee and said, "Fuck you, you fat bastard!" Then, I aimed the coffee right at his head and let the coffee cup go. He ducked and the hot coffee splashed on the paneled wall behind him and dropped onto the credenza behind his desk that held books, including *Sample Letters for School Administrators*.

"I quit!" I said, and walked out into the blustery wind.

He followed me to my car, and at first I considered running him over. Then, he asked me to open the window. When I did, he said, "What the hell is wrong with you? Are you crazy?"

I started blubbering and said, "I gave up my whole vacation to do that proposal for you and I did my very best."

"I'm sorry. I appreciate it. I don't know why I said that. Please come back."

Of course, that was enough for me, because my tears were also due to the fact that I knew I could have lost my job.

When I went back into his office, I helped him to clean the coffee. Then when I sat down, he asked if I was okay. Then he explained, "I didn't mean to say anything negative. I couldn't believe that you really did it so quickly and it looks perfect. I guess that I am so jealous that you can do this in one week and I could never do it in a year."

I said, "Jealous? Why should you be jealous? You should be happy that you have dedicated people who work for you." He apologized again and I apologized to him again also. Then he added, "If you ever have an outburst like that again, you will be fired. Do you understand me? It is totally inappropriate."

I did understand, but the twinkle in his dark brown eyes made me think, "Punish me, please."

The coffee stain, which ran down the paneled wall, remained there until he retired years later.

CHAPTER 8

Certainly, in my quiet moments at home alone, I realized that throwing hot coffee at my boss wasn't normal behavior and could easily get me fired. I really needed my job to care for my son, Aaron, who was now nine years old. Fortunately for me, before my principal who hired me and then became superintendent retired, he told me that the single most important thing he had ever done as principal of the school was to hire me. This was a great compliment, and thank God my willingness to always do extra enabled them to forgive my shortcomings.

In my various roles as class advisor, boys' basketball coach, girls' basketball coach, newspaper advisor, cheerleading coach, Kiwanis Club advisor, and dance chaperone at large, I had demonstrated my commitment to my students. Also, I was able to continuously demonstrate my ability to elevate the language arts literacy test scores of vocational high school students on standardized tests. However, throwing hot coffee at the superintendent made me realize that I truly still needed help overcoming my past. I was not in counseling, but I had to do something to help me with dealing with authority and to begin having better relationships with men.

While I was not one to have one-night stands, I constantly had long-term, inappropriate relationships with men who were not mine and were not available. These relationships lasted years and had already involved a priest, the husband of a neighbor, the husband of a good friend, and married coworkers. Because of the depth of my needs, in all cases, they began as very intense friendships. While they had little to do with sex at first, I always offered sex as a way to keep myself safe from real feelings. Feeling cheap and used by someone who wanted me for sex was so much more comfortable than feeling loved. I knew that I had these types of relationships because it was easy never to get very close to unavailable men. I was so afraid to actually trust anyone and was much more comfortable thinking that I was ugly and would be alone for ever than I was thinking that someone could actually love me and cherish me. When a man told me he thought I was attractive, it felt like such a lie. It was painful to even hear because it was in direct contrast to what I had heard throughout my childhood. My mind immediately screamed, "Liar!" to any male or female who complimented me on my looks. I instantly distrusted a person who thought I was attractive and secretly believed that their praise was motivated by them wanting something from me.

After combing through a book store, I purchased the book *Healing the Child Within: Discovery and Recovery for Adult Children of Dysfunctional Families*, by Charles Whitfield. I completed many of the exercises in the book and found them to be extremely helpful. While my brain could understand what I was going through and needed, I was still so empty inside and was constantly reminded of the pain associated with not being loved by my own mother. I desperately wanted someone to hold and comfort my inner child and give me the compassion and love that I never had. Yet I was my own worst enemy, because I usually prevented myself from getting this by interjecting sex into the relationship. I knew I needed to trust and ask for more, but I couldn't do this alone.

This aching emptiness was exacerbated by the fact that I was divorced and living without a partner, with an empty side of the bed next to me. Each night, I wished that I could wrap myself up in my own arms to comfort and protect myself, but I couldn't. I was also troubled by horrible nightmares in which I saw a woman in a white nightgown floating above my bed, trying to tell me something. Whatever she tried to tell me was so horrible that I woke up screaming every night.

I tried to seek out help for this recurring problem through a means other than counseling. Despite having great counselors in the past, I couldn't get true relief because I couldn't cry in front of them. I could never discuss any issues that would allow me to empty some of my grief. If I could only reach my subconscious, perhaps I could get some answers to what was haunting me. I had too much control to allow myself to tap painful memories willingly. Instead, I went to a hypnotist and told him only my name and that I was having nightmares every night. He hypnotized me and taped the session for me to have later. Here is what happened.

While I was hypnotized, he asked me to float above my body to see if there was any illness in my body.

I said that there was not.

He asked me to look to see if there was anything wrong with any organs in my body.

I said that there was not.

He asked me if there was any damage to the aura surrounding my body.

I said that there was not.

Then, he asked me if there was anything unusual about my body at all.

I said, "I am not in here alone."

He thought for a moment and said, "OK, you're not in there alone. I am going to ask you to take a step to the back and let the person who is in your body come to the forefront. Tell me when you have done this.

I said, "OK."

He said, "Can you please tell me who you are and what you want."

I said, "My name is Clara. I am her mother."

The hypnotist asked, "Why are you here?"

"I'm here to protect her. I was cruel to her as a child and I want to be sure she is safe because I'm better now."

He said, "Clara, I want you to go toward the light now and leave your daughter alone. She is safe. She no longer needs you. Thank you for your protection."

As he said that, I felt a weight being pulled from within my chest and separating from me. It was extremely painful, and I woke up crying hysterically. I guess I had never really grieved for my mother because life required me to just put one foot in front of the other and to keep going. Now, I felt all of the sadness of a lifetime come over me, and a deluge of tears erupted. I didn't have the dream again for a long time. Yet I still do not know if I was being haunted by my mother or if my own guilt was haunting me.

Still, I felt even emptier. One of the suggestions in the inner child book was that if you didn't have a real parent to assist you with the exercises, you could find a surrogate father that could hold and comfort your inner child. One day at school, my body went into autopilot as I picked up the phone and asked to talk to the new superintendent. He told me to come over to his office, and he assumed that I wanted to talk about a new grant project. When I walked in and sat down, I began immediately. I told him about my life in approximately four sentences. My mother was mentally ill. She locked me in the basement. She died setting herself on fire. I have a lot of pain and need someone to hold me while I work through it.

He looked right into my eyes and didn't blink as he said, "Get out of my office now." He put his head back down and continued working. That was it. I felt so rejected, and I hoped to never see him again.

Then, a few weeks later, the superintendent called me to his office again. He never mentioned my strange request, but announced that he was recommending to the board that I be made a full-time grant writer and given the title of special proj-ects coordinator. I would also work on public relations projects for the school as well. I was thrilled about the new job as he filled me in on all of the details, but I was so distracted by his animal mag-netism. It again immediately assaulted me, because I thought that he was somehow startlingly good looking. Yet he looked like a cross between Barry White and Mr. French (from *Family Affair*). Mr. French was so good to Buffy and Jody.

The superintendent's gentle, curly, jet-black hair blanketed a soft, yet manly face, highlighted by brown eyes that were as dark as chocolates. His dress was impeccable and his clothes seemed tailored to emphasize his physique. It was obvious from his shoulders and back that he had been an athlete at one time. His glaring white shirt contrasted sharply with his olive skin, but matched perfectly with his Sean Connery salt and pepper beard that complemented his black pinstriped tailored suit. And although he was a big man with a protruding round belly, he seemed to move effortlessly across the carpet, as though cha-chaing around the desk and the trash can, to point out some grant applications to me. The diamonds in his twinkling gold pinky ring acted as supercharged conductors of electricity when our hands actually touched by accident. Wow, something was knocking me off my feet, and it wasn't the new job.

As I walked back to my seat to hear all of his big plans, I put my right hand on his dark-stained massive oak desk to steady myself. As I did, he placed his hand on the small of my back to guide me into my chair to discuss the goals of the job. His over-powering body heat penetrated my back and moisture literally dampened me. I had never been so aroused by a touch in my life...and I was basically at a job interview. My face opened into a permanent smile like a pageant contestant with Vaseline on her teeth. I giggled playfully at every sentence he said, but I couldn't help it. Before him, I was being reduced, ever so quickly, to a simmering, spineless love soup of surrender.

Still, I managed to speak words and to answer his questions. Thank God, I could always talk. Somewhere along the connective beams that were flashing between my eyes and his, I mentioned years of experience, the Teacher of the Year award, coaching basketball, coaching cheerleading, advising the yearbook, the school newspaper, and the Kiwanis Club.

I knew he felt it, too, because as I spoke long ribbons of words that neither one of us listened to, his eyes were ever so subtly dipping down to my business-attired breast, where his eyelashes were teasingly licking my nipples ever so faintly. He didn't try to hide it...at all. It was deliberate, but not disgusting...obvious, but not offensive.

While discussing standardized test scores and core content curriculum standards, I could feel my nipples grow harder until I knew that he could see them through my silk blouse. He continued his quiet form of questioning and seemed to thrust his feet against the floor to secretly roll his regal high-back burgundy-upholstered chair away from the conference table. His words touched on increasing parental involvement and community support, but he ever so gradually opened his powerful thighs, exposing a noticeable protrusion erupting from his pressed pants. When he finished gently massaging the words into a formative question, he folded his hands across his white dress shirt belly and interlocked his fingers.

As I spoke of creating a district newsletter, my eyes watched disbelievingly as his folded hands, gold ring catching the sunlight, inched brazenly downwards, slowly, slowly, until they were pressing on the throbbing bulge for just a barely noticeable moment. Then he raked those intertwined fingers up across the mound, very tenderly, until his hands were back on his stomach. The protruding bulge grew even larger.

I was feeling lightheaded and heavy at the same time as I focused on the outward answers. Meanwhile, the reality of the stringent questions juxtaposed to my stomach twisting, my heart pounding, my nipples aching, and my groin arching forward seeking fullness was so surreal.

As if my thoughts were loud enough to make him awaken to reality as well, he abruptly said, "I'm very impressed with you. I don't think we have to go any further. If you would like this new job, I'd like to offer you a contract. If you don't mind waiting outside for a few moments, I will contact the principal and tell him that we have a deal. I would also like to take you to the graphic arts room to show you our new logo, masthead, and some other ideas for improving public relations."

I stood and walked toward the door, catching my stocking on a sharp piece of wood, opening a big hole through which my calf fat immediately popped through like a pork sausage. I shook his hand, and it was like dipping my hand in a hot paraffin wax and then wrapping it in moist gloves. "I'll wait outside," I said. "Thank you so much. You won't be sorry."

I waited for him to join me on a walk to the graphic arts classroom. As he led me through the polished hallways of the school, I almost expected passers-by to kneel and kiss his ring. It was amazing how much power he wielded and that I had never noticed before. The middle-aged red-headed secretary smiled and shouted, "I love your tie." A guidance counselor leaning back in his chair jumped to attention as we passed his office. In each hallway, people who seemed to be milling around quickly looked busy. It was as though they could not raise their eyes in his presence.

As we worked our way through each hallway, I was careful to keep the appropriate distance from the Dr. Diforno and let him lead the way as he walked. Still, I couldn't help notice that size wise, we were perfect for each other. At five foot ten, he was just slightly taller than my five-foot-eight frame. And although I was nearing 167 pounds and he was a solid man, we walked briskly with enthusiasm and seemed to time our strides perfectly. Ours seemed to be the only footsteps in the hallway. His highly polished black wingtips and my strappy cream sandals created a perfect harmony as they echoed in the empty halls. Something good was coming.

The whole time we walked, he spoke with a certain Lionel Richie smooth tenderness that he didn't use with the other employees. With them, he spoke directly. To the janitor, he said, "Get the glass on these doors cleaned." Period. To the principal, he said, "I have to discuss something with you today at 4:00." Period. To the guidance counselor, he said, "Follow up with that parent and get back to me." Period.

With me, he explained things softly and patiently without being condescending. As his face became more and more animated with each computer lab or classroom, it was obvious that this school was something he was very proud to show off. This building was his new candy apple red Corvette. He pointed out the empty classroom that was the shell for the new interactive television classroom. He showed me stockpiles of hand-held computers to be distributed to every ninth grader in the upcoming school year. All of these were the result of my successful grant writing. Even I was so impressed with how we had changed things. He had the ideas, and funding from my grants made them come alive. We were a great team.

As we entered the graphic arts classroom, he lowered his voice when he noticed about a dozen kids working at computers. He gave a nod to a male teacher, who was working with one of the students. He gently leaned to my neck and whispered, "I have the new school logo right over here." Although I understood the words, I hardly heard a thing because his Eternity cologne instantly freshened the air. I tilted my head towards him to take a deeper breath. I wanted it to last. At the same time, his sexy, whispering breath seemed to awaken the soft flesh of my bare neck as though it was a dripping ice cube slipping across my skin.

He hastened me through a door into a small closet like room that was the camera room, where art students shot the negatives

for the logo and masthead. We were closer to each other now...
though not touching...and although I wanted to hear the explanation for the strong chemical smell in the room, I was frozen in
my awareness of our closeness. He, too, seemed to struggle to
stay in the proper and politically correct zone of discussion. For
some reason, he began to detail the photo development process, but his words were slower and punctuated as though they
were caught on his tongue like fuzz from pajamas.

I could hear the deep intonations of the male teacher's voice
in the outer classroom giving instructions to the students about
packing up their supplies and closing their computer files for the
day. Suddenly, the superintendent opened a second door within
the camera room and somehow, without ever touching me anywhere, he guided me into its secret, smothering darkness.

It was the dark room and the chemical smell or the complete
blackness that immediately took my breath away. I was unsure,
not frightened, but the sudden and rapid shiver of my breathing
revealed my shaky uncertainty. Then, his overpowering heat was
upon me. Although I saw nothing, no matter how hard the lenses
of my eyes struggled to focus, I knew he was very close.

His cologne drifted up my nostrils and the sun-shower sprinkles
of his whispers warmed my ear as he said, "I don't want to be
your Daddy. I want something totally different. You have been
driving me crazy." And then his mustache painted a kiss on my
neck. "You have a perfect body...a women's body...and I can't
resist you."

I froze when I heard the bell ring. I could hear the modulat-
ing voices of the boys and girls as they filed out. My heart raced
and I feared they could hear it. Then, as though my hearing was
sharper because my eyes couldn't see, I actually heard the
teacher turning the lock on the door. The graphic arts room was
now empty.

That simple click in the lock activated some sort of brain-
erasing machine in my mind. I didn't care that I was in

school. I didn't care that I was just promoted to a new job. I didn't care that this man was my boss. I didn't even care that I was wearing my big white panty girdle. I simply released the tension in my body and relinquished my mind completely and succumbed to the darkness.

At first, it was as though the sheer blackness had paralyzed both of our limbs. Our lips met without any hugging or touching of bodies in any way. Our heads connected as if they were magnetized bobblehead dolls. They just found each other. Neither one of us was clear what would constitute crossing an invisible line of correctness. Yet there we were, softly and slowly kissing that high school kind of sweet kissing and freeze-framing every moment so that it could be replayed in our minds again and again.

When his tongue gently entered the warmness of my cushioned mouth without feeling like a penetration, but a subtle, gentle unraveling, it forced him just a half step closer. There, I could feel his growing excitement against my silky skirt. I parted my legs slightly to embrace it and to clandestinely caress it with my pillow thighs. With ever so slight adjustments, I could feel it almost parting me until I could rub against it in a pleasurable, barely noticeable motion. I stayed right there on that hardness, sipping his experienced tongue, conscious of my breasts fitting perfectly against his developed chest. It could have been seconds, minutes, or hours, it didn't matter. Every fiber of our bodies was engaged and alive as we became lost and slipped deeper into arousal. We enjoyed all of the securities of work preparation—minty breath, perfumed neck, oiled, scented body, smoothly shaved legs, and a perfect hole in my panty hose.

His thick finger found that hole and he used the opening to savagely rip the pantyhose from my leg, lingering only to appreciate the amazing Skin So Soft prepared inner thigh. Before I knew it, his finger was inside me, filling the aching, heavy emptiness. I gushed with appreciation.

Without a second thought, I too broke the invisible correctness barrier and heartily reached my hand around his thick arousal. Feeling its power, I was compelled to kneel, although the cramped space didn't allow my knees to ever touch the ground. He pushed air through his lips, not as a sigh, but to get control of his own breathing as I lowered his zipper and reached for his hardness.

My face was burning from passion, exhilaration, fear, and the overwhelming photography chemicals all at once. I slipped my warm mouth down over him until it assaulted the very back of my throat again and again. I would have gone deeper, bringing him into my empty chest and my heart if I could have, because I was ravenously hungry to please this powerful man—not because of who he was, but because of who he thought I was. I had never been described as beautiful in my life.

With some force of lifelong gratitude that I had built inside of me, I did please him. I knew from his whispered gratitude that I had drained the awesome power I had witnessed in the hallway right out of him and into me. He pulled me up and lowered his own head against my shoulder to be held like a baby seeking the comfort and nourishment of my breast. This is what I was originally seeking from him, but now his inner child was in my arms.

For some reason, the harsh light of the door opening didn't bring the shame that I had expected. Instinctively, we both tiptoed across the art classroom as stealthily as elephants in a circus ring. He placed his finger to his lips to quiet any talking, although I had no idea of what to say. He led me to a back door, where he used his overfilled key ring to let me out of the school building.

"Watch your step on the gravel," he said. Then he took out a pressed white handkerchief, embroidered with his initials in black, and wiped my lips, and then gently under my eyes where my mascara had probably smeared. He kissed me on the forehead, like his baby, and said. "Thank you. Congratulations on your new job."

Although I was filled with joy temporarily, I was instantly filled with worry. What had just happened? I went through my classes in a haze, hoping that no one noticed that I ditched my pantyhose. I couldn't wait to get into my car at the end of the school day. In the safety of my car, I pressed the radio's on button and was greeted with Luther Vandross amplifying my continued emptiness.

Let me hold you tight
If only for one night
Let me keep you near
To ease away your fear
I'll be at your side
If only for one night

The song ached with passion, and Luther twisted the words so gently as if he was braiding need and want together expertly. Although the song was about just one night, it already seemed to be begging for an answer to a lifelong anguish and hunger.

I won't tell a soul
No one has to know
If you want to be totally be discreet
I'll be at your side
If only for one night

I closed my eyes, and with the warm 3:30 p.m. sunshine heating me, my mind allowed me to feel his lips on my neck, kissing away my new tension. I recalled his scent, and it immediately affected my stomach and chest. I knew the aching that Luther was singing about. What I would give for just one night.

Your eyes say what I need from you
And my knees are shaking too
And I'm asking….Let me hold you tight
If only for one night.

When I got home, the phone was ringing.

His voice immediately melted into a whispered softness.

"I want you to have my private number. I'm going crazy thinking about you."

I didn't know how to react, so I brushed the comment aside because it was so new to me. "I don't know if you'll be crazy about me tomorrow," I said.

He shushed me the way Christopher Robin's mother would have, and said, "Can you come have lunch with me tomorrow? I planned something special."

I couldn't believe his words, but I smiled a huge smile alone in the house, "OK," I said. "You're the boss. That would be great."

He gave me directions to Spring Lake, which was a state park about a half hour from the school. I had been there before because it was a popular place for outdoor activities.

Although it was March and cold, spring seemed to be around the corner, and the air was filled with such great possibility. As I pulled into the parking lot, I noticed only two other cars were there. One appeared to belong to an elderly man, who was just locking the door and getting ready to walk his sandy-colored cocker spaniel. He smiled and waved to me as I pulled into a parking spot.

From the champagne colored Cadillac, I could see the superintendent was reaching next to him in the front seat and then emerging with a warm smile. He was even more attractive than I remembered. He was wearing a sophisticated black suit, with a crisp white shirt and a red speckled tie.

I shyly walked up to him and he hugged me as though we had been lovers for years. "I cannot stop thinking of you," he growled as he hugged me tight. "Look, I got us a picnic."

I tried to speak, but I was a little overwhelmed, so I just grabbed one of the bags from his hand to help him carry it. When I freed his one hand, he immediately reached down for mine and we walked toward some picnic benches.

He took a roll of paper towels from his bag and put one sheet down to act as a placemat for me and quickly put the food bag on top so it wouldn't blow away. Then he put another on the bench and said "Here, sit down. I don't want you to ruin your nice suit."

I listened and did everything I was told.

From the other bag, he brought out sandwiches. One was turkey and cheese on a bagel and the other was ham and cheese on rye with mustard, according to their waxed paper wrapping. I picked the turkey because I didn't like mustard, and he said, "Great, because I was really dying for a ham sandwich on rye today." Then he placed down small plastic containers of potato salad, pasta salad, and cole slaw and two diet sodas. I said, "Know what would be great? If you put some of that potato salad on your ham and cheese sandwich."

"Oh, yes," he said, as if I discovered the key to life. "A sloppy Joe. You're my kind of woman. I love a woman who knows how to eat."

We both laughed. While we talked, sailboats and geese occasionally drifted by and seemed to be dragging on the earth so that it could slow time just a bit. As we ate, we shared histories.

He said that he had started college intending to go medical school, but was told by his advisor at Seton Hall that he would have to switch his major or get kicked out because his grades were so low. He majored in education and couldn't get a job when he graduated from college because of the draft. Employers feared he would be leaving for Vietnam. He started having panic attacks constantly and was rushed to the hospital over and over because he thought he was having a heart attack. It was just stress, but it was enough to get him out of Vietnam.

He was able to get into the union through a relative and worked construction for a few years. Dr. Diforno went to school at night for his Master's degree and teaching certification and then started as an elementary school teacher. He married his sweetheart that he started dating in eighth grade. "When I started teaching," he added, "I was paid $5,250 for my first year. Thank God things have improved slightly after all these years."

He had two children, but felt like he was just a walking wallet. "My kids are all grown. They don't even want to kiss me or want to be seen with me anymore. They only know me when they want money. I love them all so much, but when we have a family event, I always feel so disconnected, as if I am on the outside looking in. Maybe because I have always worked two jobs, so that their mother can be home with them." He seemed to grow very sad at hearing himself say this.

"Come over here next to me," he said. I went to his side of the table, but as I went to sit, he pulled me in between his two legs and looked up at me. "You're so beautiful." This felt like a hurtful lie, but I didn't want to ruin the day. It just confirmed for me that he was dishonest and was only using me. As if to hide my embarrassment, I leaned my head down and began kissing him on his mustached full lips. His skin was so warm and smooth and he smelled so good of Eternity and spring freshness. I felt compelled to please him, but as I reached my hand near his zipper, he stopped me instantly.

"Look at me," he ordered. "Come on...look at me," he said now in his superintendent voice. "That's not what I want from you. Do you understand me? I can get that anywhere. The minute you walked into my office and started talking so fast and were so enthusiastic and so smart and so beautiful, I knew you were someone special."

These words were too much to take, and I started crying as if he had assaulted me. I thought he thought I was just a desperate fat girl, a pig, a slut, a whore, especially after what I had done in the art room. I was expecting to be that again for him because it was better than being nothing to nobody. I knew how to feel ashamed. I knew how to feel humiliated and rejected and ugly. I had no idea of how to just enjoy the feeling of being special and loved. Because I thought I knew so much, but never knew that, I just rocked in his arms while the sun slid down behind the rust-colored tree line.

The last thing he said in that embrace was, "I'll give you butterfly kisses with my eyelashes, like I used to give my daughters." Then, he lovingly kissed each of my eye lids gently. We sat quietly while two geese drew circles in the blue green water. The ripples they created spread far beyond where anyone could see.

We held hands, swinging our arms playfully on the way back to the car, until the superintendent froze. He immediately broke his grip from my hand and plunged behind the nearest tree. I put my hand over my eyes, like a salute, to block out the setting sun. I saw a woman rollerblading back and forth in the parking lot near our cars. The woman kept her head facing my direction, regardless of which direction she was skating. I suddenly recognized the roller blader as a teacher from another school district that we had met at a meeting earlier in the year. Awkwardly, I slowly inched my way behind the tree next to the superintendent and instinctively whispered.

"What's the matter?" I asked. "Are you worried about your job?"

"My job?" he said, elevating his voice. "I'm worried about my wife."

CHAPTER 9

Dr. Diforno and I found ourselves both chaperoning a trip to New York City to see the play *Phantom of the Opera*. Although we didn't get to sit near each other on the bus, we had a few hours to spend before the play seeing sights in New York City. The students were told to stay within a certain radius and to be at the theater a half hour before curtain time. Meanwhile, I pretended that I left my glove on the bus, so I could escape my fellow English teachers and meet Dr. Diforno behind the bus.

After hustling away from the group, we spent our time seeing Rockefeller Center and the FAO Schwarz Toy Store, then headed to St. Patrick's Cathedral so he could light a candle for his mother. It was a rainy day in New York, so entering the vestibule of the church provided instant relief from the bitter cold. The church door was so heavy, but as it slammed behind us, it sealed out the real world. The scent of the burning candles and musty incense helped us to escape to another time and place. Dr. Diforno hooked his arm around mine and we both starting walking slowly up the aisle. It felt the way I imagined a bride felt when her father walked her to her groom. Without planning it, at the same time, we genuflected, blessed ourselves, and he led me into a pew on the right side. Instantly we both knelt down on the brown vinyl kneeler and made the sign of the cross. Without saying a word aloud, at the exact same moment, we both began sobbing uncontrollably. We turned and dropped into each other's arms, shuddering and soaking each other with grief.

The awe-inspiring beauty of the cathedral, with its gilded altars and grand murals, was a sudden and dramatic reminder that we both had ugly, open, gaping holes in our hearts. The crushing emptiness of our souls became apparent as they filled with grief. Losing religion, whenever it happened, wherever it happened, why ever it happened, didn't matter, because it felt as if it just happened that day in New York. It was as if just as we passed through the magnificent church doors, a police officer had plowed into us and blurted out that a child we nurtured and worshiped for decades had just died. It was that painful. Simultaneously, the heavy grief collapsed our backs, forced our knees to buckle, and only each other kept us from completely sinking into a quicksand of despair.

When we returned for the play, I could not stop crying. My students kept asking, "Are you OK?"

"It's beautiful," I replied. But I was focusing on the fact that somehow Dr. Diforno and I were the same as each other and that we would be together always. Andrew Lloyd Webber's words forecast our future.

No more talk of darkness
Forget these wide-eyed fears
I'm here, nothing can harm you
My words will warm and calm you
Let me be your freedom
Let daylight dry your tears
I'm here with you, beside you
To guard you and to guide you
Say you'll love me every winter morning
Turn my head with talk of summertime
Say you need me with you now and always
Promise me that all you say is true
That's all I ask of you
Let me be your shelter

Let me be your light
You're safe, no one will find you
Your fears are far behind you.

For the next couple of weeks, we met before school for breakfast and after school for pizza. We both even joined a racquetball league to meet at night and followed each session with a snack at a diner. All we did was eat and share so many funny stories related to our jobs at school. I told him about the time another English teacher walked up to me all in a huff with cheeks blushing in embarrassment. In her hand, she was shaking a Polaroid picture.

"Mrs. Stevens," she said, "one of your students left this in the library." She lifted her eyes as though to pull them over her bifocals to catch every moment of my reaction.

I sighed and looked down to see a Polaroid picture of a very long, thick, white penis with a shriveled pink head poking out and leaning to one side of a pair of blue jeans.

"What do you have to say to that?" the librarian asked.

I said, "If I had one like that, I'd take a picture of it, too," and walked away.

I found myself in the principal's office that afternoon being forced to apologize. "What was I supposed to do?" I asked. "Go around to each student in my class and try to ID it?"

As I relayed the story to the superintendent, I was amazed at the authentic love I saw on his face. I could feel him actually watching my eyes and lips as I talked and he laughed the way a proud parent enjoys the first words of his child. I had never felt this before and I was genuinely moved by it.

"You think that's bad," he added. "You should have been there for what I had to deal with today. Kevin, our janitor, went into the boy's locker room and found two girls having sex with one boy in the corner."

"What? What does that look like?"

He leaned closer to whisper, "They were both in front of him and were taking turns performing oral sex on him."

"Oh my God," I said, shocked.

"Wait," he laughed, "that's not even the best part." I leaned in to get the details. "The best part was that neither one of the girls performing the activity was his girlfriend. His girlfriend arranged this activity with these two girls, her friends, as a birthday present for the boyfriend."

"Are you kidding me?" I leaned back in shock.

"And guess what, my birthday's coming up!"

He and I both laughed, and our spirits were lifted so high. We really enjoyed each other's company and found ourselves in restaurants and bars across the county. One night, the blinking of the televisions in the sports bar, the inner warmth of the wine, or maybe the heat generated from sharing more intimate secrets made me feel so connected to him. We were both genuinely sharing our table together—happier than either had been in a long time. We ordered more wine and some chicken wings and continued laughing and sharing school war stories.

From out of nowhere, I finally said, "I want you tonight."

"Let's go," he said.

With that, he threw a $20 bill on the table and put his arm around my back and led me to his car.

We found ourselves at a cheesy Motel 6 far away from our home turf.

He went into the office and came out quickly with a room key. He said, "I'm going to drop you off and let you in the door, and then I'll find a safe place to park the car." It was a pretty iffy neighborhood. I could have been upset that he put the car's safety over mine, but I was too nervous. When I was alone in the room, I rushed to the bathroom and twisted the top off a small bottle of mouthwash I had in my purse. I poured the contents into my mouth and then swirled it around. Then I ripped off all of my clothes in a panic so that I could get under the blue/green tapestry bedspread before he got back.

Just as the doorknob turned, I placed my head on the pillow and folded the sheet and blanket neatly just over my bosom.

"Holy cow," he said, "I heard of easy, but this is ridiculous. I thought I was going to have to work hard to get your clothes off."

I covered my head with the blanket and laughed. "I didn't want you to see how fat I am."

During our cuddling, he told me that our next adventure was to attend a conference in Atlantic City together. He said, "I even want to drive with you, so I want you to meet me in the Park N Ride lot at 7:30 a.m. tomorrow morning so we can have the three-hour ride together." I was very excited, not only to be off of work for three days, but to be going to the Bally's Park Place Hotel for a little mini vacation.

"Do you like to gamble?" he asked.

"I play a little," I said.

He said, "Well, I'm going to teach you to play craps! It has the best odds in the casino."

I said, stealing one of his favorite expressions, "I forgot more about craps than you ever knew," then I added, "I'm only planning to bring $200 for gambling."

"Don't worry about money," he said. "You're with me."

We met that morning at 7:00 a.m. to head down to Atlantic City. We ordered two sausage, egg, and cheese sandwiches, two hash browns, and two apple pies for the ride. As we drove down the highway in the roomy Cadillac, I prepared his sandwich for him and continuously fed him pieces of hash brown potatoes dipped in ketchup.

After talking for a while, we decided to play "Name That Tune." I used the scan button on the radio to shuffle through oldies stations, R&B, country, and rock, and whoever yelled out the title of the song and the singer got a point.

He yelled, "My Prayer."

I yelled, "The Platters."

"I said it first," he said.

"Yeah, but you didn't know the artist."

"You didn't give me a chance."

"Hey, I said it first, that's all there is to it."

"Okay, 1 to 1."

Next it was "Only the Good Die Young," by Billy Joel.

I got both title and singer.

"That's not fair," he said. "I knew those."

"If you know it, show it, baby," I said, passing his coffee. I was careful to hold the cup steadily because the coffee was really hot and the car was jerking a bit. He put his lips to the cup three times before he drank it. While I was being careful not to burn him, he yelled out, "Have I Told You Lately that I Love You?"—Rod Stewart." His quick movement of his lip made the coffee spill out onto his white dress shirt.

I quickly dug in the bag for napkins and blotted it the best I could.

He asked, "This is a great song, isn't it?"

"Yeah," I said, but was more concerned about his shirt.

"I think of you every time I hear it. I brought the single for you."

"Really?" I thought that he was kidding, but his face seemed to change into a pensive look as he began singing with Rod.

"Fill my heart with gladness, take away all my sadness, ease my trouble, that's what you do."

I joined in: "Have I told you lately that I love you?"

He said, "Oh my God. You couldn't carry a tune in a handbag!"

I slapped his arm, spilling the coffee on my black skirt this time instead. I knew he was right, but the two of us continued to sing every song together after that, with me really singing loudly to exaggerate my lack of ability.

When Whitney Houston's "You Give Good Love to Me" started booming, he was singing, "You give good head to me, baby! It's so good," I changed the channel.

When "Bad Moon Rising" came on, he sang, "There's a bathroom on the right," for the chorus.

I said, "Those aren't the words."

"Are too."

Then we switched to what may have been a religious channel and began singing "Day by Day," from the play *Godspell*: "Day by day. Day by day. Oh dear Lord, three things I pray."

I asked, "Do you pray?"

"Sometimes," he answered.

"What do you pray for?"

He said, "To die."

"Shut up," I said. I added, "My sisters always used to sing 'Day by Day' in church on Sunday at the guitar mass."

He said, "Things really changed in the church, didn't they? Whatever happened to all the people that ate meat on Friday? That's not even a sin anymore. Are they still in hell?"

"No," I answered, "they're in limbo."

"Fucking limbo," he laughed. "What the hell was that?"

"I know. What bullshit! And how about confession in the first grade? I was so freaking scared that I didn't have any sins, so I went into the confessional and made up sins. I said, 'Bless me, Father, for I have sinned, it's been a week since my last confession and these are my sins. I lied or had impure thoughts,' when I really didn't. I didn't even know what an impure thought was back then."

"I am having impure thoughts right now," he said.

I was not distracted. "And how about those pagan babies we bought?"

"What do you mean?"

"When we were in Catholic school, we'd have to collect money to buy pagan babies in Africa because they were going to limbo because they weren't baptized."

"No, we didn't do that, but do you believe we had to say, 'Bless me, Father, for I have sinned, it's been a week since my last confession, and I accuse myself of the following'?"

"What?"

"That's right."

" 'I accuse myself of the following'?"

"Wow, what a guilt-driven religion."

"How about, did you have Yahweh?" I asked.

"What the hell is Yahweh?" he replied.

"When we were in Catholic grammar school, they used to call God Yahweh."

"No, we didn't have Yahweh. What is it?"

"I think it means 'to come into being' or 'He that is' or something philosophical."

"Is that like how many angels can you fit on the head of a pin?"

"Maybe. I don't know if Thomas Aquinas heard of Yahweh, but in a seventh-grade workbook, I had to draw a picture of Yahweh, so I drew Jesus as a hippie helping druggies in the park."

The superintendent said, "Hey, let's make up Yahweh songs."

I bent over laughing, causing all of the napkins to fall onto the crème colored plush carpet in the Cadillac as I listened to him doing an imitation of Frank Sinatra with his voice.

"I did it Y...A...H...W...A...Y."

We continued laughing as I sang, "It's Yahway or the highway."

We laughed and then stopped short as neither one of us could think of another song to use.

After an awkward moment passed, I said, "I wonder why I ever stopped going to church. It was really such an important part

of my life. We went every day for a while...in grammar school...
when the mass was still in Latin."

"I know when I stopped going," he said.

I turned my body in the car to face him as though giving him
the floor and my full attention. I brushed the remaining crumbs
from our breakfast off of my skirt.

"I was eleven when I stopped going."

"Why?" I asked.

He turned his eye from the road to fully face me for just a
second and said, "When Father Abbitino started sucking my best
friend's dick!"

I was so offended by the statement that I turned my head
quickly as if I were slapped.

"That's not even funny," I said and I turned away from him
again and stared out the window.

"No kidding," he said, grabbing my hand. "I'm serious."

I didn't say anything, but looked ahead in silence.

"How come you're mad at me?" he asked.

"Because that's not a joke. If it really happened, you would
know that."

"It did happen, but what do you want me to do now. Cry? It
was thirty years ago."

I couldn't respond before he switched to his gentle voice
and started the story. "When I was eleven and in the fifth or sixth
grade, my friend Anton and I went to the five-and-dime store
downtown and we stole GI Joe dolls and gear. The doll had this
button on his back that you could push and his arm would fly up
the air really fast like he was throwing a hand grenade."

I smiled because I could tell he really liked this doll.

"Anyway, every day, before my Mom came home, I hid the GI
Joe in my dad's old bowling bag in the hallway closet. He never
went bowling, so it was safe. One day, I was on the steps of our
fourth-floor apartment, and I had a string around GI Joe's waist
so he could rappel down to the hallway, and I turned around to

get my gun. When I turned back again, GI Joe was hitting my Mom in the head. She jerked it so hard it went flying at her and almost poked her eye out. When she came upstairs she wanted to know where I got GI Joe. I told her it was Anton's GI Joe. She immediately called Anton's mother, who said that he didn't have a GI Joe. So after smacking the hell out of me, I told the truth. Anton's mother made him go to the priest.

"He told me what happened and begged me never to tell anyone. He said that the priest asked, 'Do you know what happens to boys who steal?' The priest said, 'Their parents die.' Anton was so shocked. He thought that he was only going to have to say three Hail Marys or something. Then, the priest put his arm around Anton and said that he could be forgiven and could spare his parents a lot of pain.

"Anton asked how. The priest said that a priest can remove all of the evil and sin out of a little boy. Anton was relieved and prepared for the priest to bless him with holy water. Then, before he knew what even happened, the priest unzipped Anton's pants and began sucking his dick."

"Stop saying it like that," I said. "You're so crude."

"It was so terrible, and it scared me to death because it didn't stop there. Anton and I used to smoke in another friend's clubhouse. Then, when his father was taking down the clubhouse because it was falling apart, he saw all of the cigarette butts on the ground. He was furious. He pointed his finger at me and said, in an Italian accent, 'Make sure you tell the priest in confession that you were smoking, or I will tell your father.' I couldn't even imagine what the priest would do to me then.

"Anton's mother made him go back to priest and he said, 'You like GI Joe, don't you? Is that why you stole it?' Anton shook his head yes. The priest said, 'Well, do you like John Wayne and cowboys?' 'Sure,' Anton said. Then the priest said, 'Do you want to play cowboys?' Anton thought this was weird because he was a little old for cowboys, but he wanted his mother to get a good report. Then, I swear to God, Anton said that the priest turned away, pulled down his pants, got on his hands and knees, and said, 'Climb on. I'll be your pony.' "

Anton ran away. and he never went back to church again.

"Did you ever tell anybody?"

"Just you. Just now. How could I tell anyone? I promised Anton I wouldn't. Anton's parents blamed me for being a bad influence on him. The worst part was that I also, refused to go to church on Sunday, no matter how much my mother punished me, so my father stopped talking to me for one full year."

"Why?"

"Because he couldn't believe what I was putting my mother through. Still, he never laid a hand on me. His not talking to me was the worst beating I ever took. He never even looked in my direction at dinner."

"When did he start talking to you again?"

"When I joined the football team. He was so proud to be at the games that he just started talking again."

I was shocked into silence. I just stared ahead until I felt him shaking. I looked over to find him heaving and tears streaming down his face. "I loved Anton. He was like a brother to me."

"Pull over," I said. "Let me hold you."

"I'm fine," he said. "This is so stupid."

He composed himself and said that all through college he felt like he was having a heart attack. He was rushed to the hospital several times with chest pains and the doctors said he was suffering from panic attacks. He went to several psychiatrists, but it never helped. He thought that the stress was because of the Vietnam War, graduation, and his impending marriage, but he never really put it together that it could have been about Anton.

"The panic attacks were so real," he whispered.

"What do you think caused them?"

"Who knows?" he said. "I guess maybe I thought that every-thing I believed in was suddenly taken from me."

I said, "Jesus Christ! You can't have Communion in a Catholic church if you're divorced, but it's OK for priests to give naked pony rides. I was so fortunate that the nuns and priests I had in school were always so good to me. "

"What would Yahweh think?" he asked.

I put my head on his shoulder, and it remained there for the rest of the ride. I pressed my body against his so tightly that if I were any closer, I would be his soul. He bent down and kissed my head and sang along with the radio.

As we drove in silence, I nuzzled my head even deeper into his chest and listened as he changed the station back to oldies and sang with Elvis:

Wise men say only fools rush in.
But I can't help falling in love with you.

The superintendent and I saw each other and traveled back and forth to Atlantic City on a Friday night for years. Playing craps let me back to my religion, in a way. As he began to roll the dice, I whispered, "Hail Mary, up in heaven, please don't let this be a seven." Or "Holy Father, you are great, let the next roll be hard eight!" We had a great deal of fun, but I constantly asked myself: Does he really love me? How could he love me if he's married? Why can't I just accept that I'm just being used for sex? Certainly, there were far more attractive woman right in the school building that he could have. They all seemed to want him. I was filled with anger every time I heard Charleen, the principal's secretary, talk to him and touch him. He would be walking down the hall with a cupcake when Charleen would point to the cupcake and say, "Oh, I wish that was your cream. I would lick it all off."

He would just laugh and keep walking. But he didn't tell her to stop talking to him like that. He didn't say it was unprofessional.

He loved it. He also loved to tell me that when he was working late preparing for the monthly board meeting, Charleen often called over from the school building to say, "I see that your light is still on...is there anything I could do for you?"

I'd lash out, "Well, why don't you say yes? if you like it that much?"

"Are you going to hurt me now?" he'd ask.

"No, you're the one who will do the hurting."

"How can you say that when I love you so much?"

"How can you be in love with me when you're married?"

"Why do you have to bring that up again?" It has nothing to do with you."

"It has everything to do with me."

"Can't you tell how much I love you?"

"No, because maybe you just want sex."

He laughed and said, "Trust me. There is plenty of that around."

I slapped his arm.

I felt that there was so much more to it than he was saying. It was not all about sex, but then again, he was a man. Maybe it was just that simple. I reasoned that even if he was just using me, my life was much better with him than without him. That was enough for me.

Dr. Diforno and I shared many, many nights of joy and pleasure, mostly on Friday nights when my son, Aaron, was at his father's house. But then he started coming over to my house every day after school for a few hours before he went home.

One day, when we were embracing in my dining room, kissing and groping passionately, I was feeling free because I thought we were in the house alone. At first, I didn't realize that my son was in the living room playing his video game with the sound muted—which I frequently requested.

Then, as we tilted our heads from side to side, darting our tongues in and out of each other's mouths and allowing our hands to run up and down each other's bodies, I froze. In the glass of the dining room hutch, I suddenly caught the reflection of my sweet son's face looking back at me. He was seeing us in full view on an angle from where he was sitting on the living room couch.

Electric pulses suddenly jolted me like a Taser gun. Black-and-white flashbacks flipped through my mind like some psychotic slide presentation. Instantly, I could see my mother's ash blonde head rolling around her boyfriend Tony's face, with her serpent tongue darting in and out of his mouth. There, on our crumbling concrete front porch of our childhood house, she displayed her lust for all of the neighbors to see and with Nanny's eyes peering down from heaven. I felt her shame. The pit of my stomach, through body memory, recalled my sour disgust as I could see my mother squeezing her legs back and forth with her hands in her lap. My ears rang with the deafening tinnitus of her sing-songy, childlike voice saying, "My Tony, my Tony." Bile rose in my throat and scalded me as my mind instantly began assessing the most punishing questions of life: Had I become my mother? Should I be ashamed of myself?

Abruptly, I pulled away from the superintendent and stepped back.

"What's wrong?" he asked. He reached to hug me.

"Don't fucking touch me!" I screamed.

Shocked and rejected, he threw his hands up in the air. "What is it?"

"I don't feel well," I said. "You have to go."

"Why?"

"Just go!" I screeched. "Get out right now. You disgust me. You whoremaster!"

My son ran into the room and shouted, "What's wrong?" He had picked up a golf club in case he needed a weapon.

"Nothing is wrong," I said. "I don't feel well, that's all."

Looking from my son's face to mine, the superintendent said nothing else. He wouldn't do anything to upset a child. He put his head down and rushed out the back door. When he pulled away in his car, I was shaking uncontrollably and felt filled with grief. I walked to the kitchen sink and got a glass of water. I took a sip, dumped the rest, filled up the glass again, and did the same thing again. I did it one more time. Then, as I steadied myself by the sink with tears running down my face, my son came into the kitchen and opened the refrigerator and grabbed a Gatorade. He turned around and looked at me as though I were pathetic. I shrank with shame under his gaze.

He said, "Mom, you're so stupid to waste your time on a married man. I thought you were smarter than that." He put his blonde head down, shook it from side to side, and walked out.

I ran into my room and slammed the door. "Who are you to judge me?" Then words I hadn't thought of in a long time crossed my mind. "Burn in hell. I should burn in hell!" I remember the red lipstick on my mother's Bible on her bed.

CHAPTER 10

I began this exercise to offer one person's answers to prevalent questions asked by the media and peers—the various hows and whys of behavior that lead to judgment by our "moral" society. Perhaps I was also hoping to obtain some absolution for my own mortal sins. How sinful it was to have an affair with a married man, but what seems even worse now is how cruel it was to take away this one happiness from my own mother. As someone who finally understands the healing powers of the human touch, maybe I could have realized that Tony made my mother feel special. He was the one, singular, tiny crumb of happiness that fell from another woman's table to join the scraps that were her life. In a black hole of insatiable hunger, bottomless emptiness, and infinite despair, she found a tiny morsel to begin to fill her.

Perhaps I was the one person in our crazy world who knew exactly how she felt. Why was I willing to steal her happiness as casually as shoplifting a pack of gum? In her gloomy world, what I did was equivalent to the heist of her most precious, sacred commodity—all she held dear. Yet it was just a leftover Cracker Jack prize in an empty box of a life that had already been kicked down the street by a bum. What my mother had with Tony may not have been love, not that I could have even known, but it may have been the only isolated moments of joy she had in her adult life. All things are relative, and compared to harsh police restraints, the ardent touch of his olive skin pulsed through her body jolting her into some version of sanity. His broad arms wrapped her up even tighter than straightjacket buckles and kept her safe from a world who believed she should be isolated. His appreciation of her beauty glistening in his brown eyes; his joyous laughter at her jokes; his hunger to be filled by her and his strong desire to fill her emptiness; these were the effective tonics to soothe her nerves, tame her demons, and bring her some peace. Her mind told her she was being loved and that it was good. She knew joy. She had something weighty for once that held her in reality for a little while. Who gets to say this is wrong?

As a child, I couldn't have known any better. Every minute of every God-fearing day of Catholic school taught me that what she wanted was evil and that sex was sinful. "Don't ever let a man touch you." And even when I cast away the guilty shroud of the Catholic church, my own overpowering sense of injustice kept me from seeing my mother as a woman. How could my mother not love me? How could I be too ugly to kiss good night? How could it be my fault when everything went wrong? When Tony left, I thought, "Good, let her feel the hurt now. Let her know the pain and loneliness she caused me." Looking back now, I realize she had known it long before I ever did. Now, I forgive myself for failing to understand what Tony had to offer...I was doing the best I could with the information I had based on what I was taught. A child cannot know how a woman hungers for a human touch. But now I know not to judge.

I appreciate the effort and the time you dedicated to this exercise. This narrative is no longer an explanation or a confession. It is a celebration and a triumph! I only need to forgive myself for ever believing that any of it was my fault. I finally know now that I didn't make my mother crazy. Nor was I the sole cause of disharmony in my childhood home. I can place my hand on a bible of hospital records that confirms the facts. In my life, I did the best that I could at each step along the way. I also forgive my mother for being cruel. She, too, was doing the best she could and had no choice in the matter. I can touch proof of that every day, and I still do when it is necessary.

Unfortunately, I know firsthand that some people just will never know better. After we were so excited to meet my father, he never stepped up to the plate and met any responsibilities. We never received as much as a birthday card from him, although we saw him on family occasions every now and then. When he was fifty-nine, we got a call from my Uncle Mike who told us that our father had died of brain cancer. We felt like complete outsiders at his funeral because we didn't recognize anyone except our grandmother and Uncle Mike.

At the funeral home, I got the courage to go up to his stepdaughter, who lived with him and his girlfriend for most of his life. I expressed my sympathies and told her that I had been so jealous because she had my father and I didn't. She looked at me with moist hazel eyes and reached out her hand in a friendly gesture. She said, "Please don't ever waste one minute of your life being jealous of me. Your father came home drunk and beat the crap out of my mother and me for years. You were the lucky one all along." She gave me a robust hug and walked away.

He wasn't our savior. But I wasn't wrong about all men. My own married man was not just using me for sex. When my son graduated from college, I married my man in Las Vegas. Now I go to sleep every night on his shoulder and wake up every morning grateful that I didn't allow the guilt others tried to impose upon us to take him away from me. I thank God for shining his spotlight down upon a wonderful man so that I could see him and have him love me so thoroughly every day of my life. He still thinks I am beautiful, and for a girl who thought that she was okay with ugly, being loved by someone who sees me as beautiful is the jackpot of life that I never, ever expected.

Twelve years ago, my first husband, Stephen, suffered a severe stroke that left him paralyzed on one side of his body. He is bedridden in a nursing home. When I first visited him in the hospital, his doctor told me, "I know that you're divorced, but if the nursing home knows Steve has no family, they will warehouse him for the rest of his life." So I have been an advocate for Steve for years and have fought for him to receive treatment and proper care. It has been a terrible battle, but his impact on my life makes it worth the effort.

I have recently apologized to Steve for our divorce, because I realized that I had never lived with a man before and had no idea of their habits. It seems from talking to my female friends, Steve was pretty normal. I have learned that men often think they are Adonis and have a love affair with their penises. I was too young to know.

My second husband is retired now and we live on the beach in Florida, where I work from home as a grant writer for several school districts. I sprinkle a little bit of Newark Catholic into every grant proposal I write. In the past fourteen years, I have won millions of grant dollars that have helped schools to begin to offer the amazing programs that Newark Catholic offered thirty years ago. Grants that I won have funded after-school programs, technology integration, professional development, and more. Recently I won a grant to begin a summer golf program for teens with autism. As big as superintendents can dream, I can help their dreams come true by transforming words into funding.

The philosophy of education instilled in me by the wonderful Sisters of Charity, from Sister Rose to Sister Eileen, guides my work and my life on a daily basis. I am proud that I have had many opportunities to be a Sister Eileen in the lives of other girls and women that sought my assistance.

My son, Aaron, is twenty-seven now, and he loves me despite my shortcomings as a parent. He asks for no apologies from me for making him endure my failed relationships. I'm grateful to him for being much more forgiving than I was as a child. He graduated from Penn State University and has made me proud every single day of his life. Besides being brilliant, he is a truly decent young man who has tremendous empathy for those in need. He is building a wonderful life for himself and seems to have broken the cycle of failed relationships that kept me from happiness for years. He is in a committed relationship with a beautiful woman of substance, and I hope he has found other examples in life of how to be a good partner.

My sisters and brothers have all experienced tremendous success in life and have raised wonderful, healthy children. I have nine nieces and nephews in all; most have college degrees, one has a master's degree, and one is attending law school. They all have a great sense of humor from hanging out with their parents, aunts, and uncles over the years. Although they are well aware of our shortcomings, they appreciate all we have survived.

Now, each grateful morning, I walk on a beach speckled with both ragged seashells and smooth sand. Today, instead of incense, fear, and shame, my new kind of church is filled with pelicans, seagulls, and glistening waves touched by the same stream of heavenly light that led me to my husband. I turn my face towards the sky and feel grateful as I speak to the universe and to my handsome God who has secretly loved me through so many compassionate human faces throughout my life. At every stage, there has been someone who was able to look past my shabby exterior to see something special. Now, instead of saying, "Bless me, Father, for I have sinned," I say, "Thank you, Father, for I have lived and felt loved."

When I feel safe enough, inevitably some tears of sorrow fall from my face to the sand and then are quickly pulled away by the crashing waves of change and triumph. In the fleeting moments in between, I whisper an overdue prayer to my mother, to the prettiest girl in town, who never even made it past the age of fifty. My prayer goes something like this: "Thank you for giving me the experiences that have made me who I am today."

Then, with a hand raised to shield my eyes from the overpowering Florida sun, I steal a ray of warmth on my finger and bring it to my heart, where I finally light that special candle for my mother. I pray that her childlike spirit is eternally safe and surrounded by God's love. I no longer have to worry about not having a coin to put in the church box. In my new cathedral, money does not need to be exchanged for God's love.

This mass has ended. I go in peace.

ABOUT THE AUTHOR

Katie Roberta Stevens has worked as a professional grant writer for public school districts for the past fourteen years. Prior to that, she taught high school English for twelve years, during which she enjoyed serving as a basketball coach and advisor to various clubs. She considers herself a true "Jersey Girl," but now resides in Brevard County, Florida, with her husband of five years. She is currently working on her second book. You can visit her Web site at www.readkt.com.

Made in the USA
San Bernardino, CA
18 August 2014